Liver regulates urg

spaces /

(Citrus), esp. + melons, Clementine tangerines
+ DIGESTION

Kidneys regulate solid organs (muscles, brain, heart, tendons, ligaments) equilibrium + FLUIDS, all glands.

(grapes), tomatoes, leafy greens, citrus. (+ for (heart)

Endocrine system regulated by KID(S) + LIVER
↓ feel HOT or COLD

pg 42 Morning WATER intake is critical.
Also sips thru-out the day.

Acknowledgements

Those who need to be acknowledged: David Cintron, Carol Cintron, Sandy Sowards, Greg Barnett, Cindy Gray, Ken Wright, Rafael Tellez, David Buehrens, Karl Parker, Peter Gillham, Jim Kasmir, Katherine Kasmir, Stacy Plasch, Robert Harrison, Darryl Sanford, my best friend Ron, my brother, my mom and dad.

Unread books are glorified paperweights.
If you love this book, share your stories
and let those interested read directly from it.
It is very easy for me to look at someone and quickly detect
what is physically wrong with him or her. Some call me intuitive.
I have been told that I have the wisdom of an ancient sage,
and the formulation ability of a long dead Chinese herbal master.
In this book I am passing on those abilities in a form that can be duplicated.
If you intend to give this book away as a gift it is a good choice.
Our future is in our kids. Kids immediately get the gifts in this book.
Be sure to share this book with the under twenty crowd.

Neff/Harry Publishing ©2008 Design by Gregory Barnett | rocknmotion.com
First Printing November 2005 | Second Printing January 2006 Third Printing June 2006
Fourth Printing May 2007 | Fifth Printing March 2008

Roger Bezanis

Pure Body Institute.com, Ventura, CA 93001

230 S. Olive St

herbal remedies

305-653-5448

roger@pbiv.com

web pbiv.com

DIAGNOSTIC Face Reading and the Holistic You

by Roger Bezanis

82 mi fr Downey

101 N. Exit 70A go (R), follow signs for Calif. St (0.2 mi) (R) S. Calif St, immediate (L) E Thompson Blvd (0.5 mi) changes to W. Thomp. Bear (L) S. Garden (0.2 mi), (R) S. Olive

Table of Contents / Sections

There is much acrimony surrounding this book. Big Pharmaceuticals and the medical establishment as we know it are terrified that you will say "ENOUGH." That is why you are reading this book.

-Roger Bezanis

1 Starting Your Adventure

This is your book. You wanted to read it. In these pages you will find the jewels that will allow you to change your life. These same gifts are there for everyone you know. Unfortunately, some of your friends and family are not where you are in your life, health and consciousness. Of course, sharing this book and all of its gifts is just what you will want to do. When you do, please do not force it down anyone's throat. No one ever likes being force-fed. A rejected book is a useless book. If you badger people with the content of this book you will lose friends. Once the door is closed it tends to remain closed. Ergo, all those you could have helped are lost.

Individuals who read this manuscript need to discover it similar to the way you did. Let them. Share your excitement.

Set an example and live by this book. When those around you see you winning, they will naturally begin to ask what you are doing. Once this occurs, you have an ear and someone who wants to know how they too can heal. Correcting your health slows down your own aging process. Everyone you know will want to know what you did and how you did it.

RULE 1:
THERE ARE FOUR KINDS OF PEOPLE IN REGARDS TO THIS BOOK. THOSE WHO HAVE READ IT, NOT READ IT, BORROW IT AND THOSE WHO RECEIVE THIS BOOK AS A GIFT. THE ONLY VALUE THIS BOOK POSSESSES IS TO THE READER. IT MUST BE READ. FOR THE BORROWER, LET HIM OR HER KEEP THIS MANUSCRIPT FOR A DAY OR TWO OR WHEN THEY TRADE SOMETHING OF EQUAL VALUE. ONLY THEN DOES THE "BORROWER" HAVE AN INVESTMENT IN IT THIS MANUSCRIPT. GENERALLY PEOPLE VERY SELDOM PLACE MUCH VALUE IN WHAT IS BORROWED. LEARN BY HEART, UNTIL SOMEONE READS THIS BOOK (AS YOU HAVE) IT HAS NO VALUE WHATSOEVER.

RULE 2:
IF YOU ARE ASKED TO ANSWER QUESTIONS FROM THIS BOOK, DIRECT THEM TO THE PROPER PAGE TO READ. AGAIN, IF YOU WANT YOUR FRIENDS TO READ THIS BOOK, HAND IT TO THEM. OTHERWISE YOU WILL FOREVER BE ANSWERING QUESTIONS. YOU WILL EVERLASTINGLY BE THEIR CRUTCH. VERBAL ANSWERS DO NOT STICK. BUT THE WRITTEN WORD DOES. THAT IS WHY WE HAVE BOOKS. THE WRITTEN WORD IS YOUR ANSWER.

RULE 3:
YOU ARE RECEIVING INFORMATION THAT IS IN A DIFFERENT STRATUM THAN WHAT YOU ARE NORMALLY EXPOSED TO. THE DATA IN THESE PAGES IS NOT TAUGHT IN COLLEGES OR PART OF ANY MEDICAL CURRICULUM. THE ALTERNATIVE HEALTH COMMUNITY IS JUST NOW LEARNING THIS DATA. THEREFORE, DO NOT USE THIS BOOK TO MAKE SOMEONE WRONG. DO NOT MAKE WRONG THOSE WHO CANNOT SEE BEYOND WHAT THEY KNOW. DO NOT MAKE WRONG YOUR PARENTS, FRIENDS OR

ASSOCIATES. THEY ARE ALL DOING THE BEST THEY CAN WITH WHAT THEY HAVE AND KNOW. KINDNESS WILL WIN MORE BATTLES THAN ALL THE STEEL THAT YOU CAN MUSTER. WHEN SOMEONE ASKS TO SEE THIS BOOK, SHOW IT TO HIM OR HER. LIVE BY EXAMPLE AND YOU WILL WIN.

RULE 4:
DO NOT FORGET WHO HOLDS THE KEYS TO EARTH'S FUTURE. IT IS THE YOUNG. KIDS INSTANTLY KIDS INSTANTLY GET THIS BOOK. SHOW THIS BOOK TO THOSE WHO HAVE NOT BEEN FULLY BRAINWASHED BY OUR MEDIA. GET THIS BOOK INTO THE HANDS OF OUR KIDS. THEY AND THEIR CHILDREN WILL SAVE THIS PLANET.

"Diagnostic Face Reading and the Holistic You" is not like other books you have read. DFRHY is one of the more complicated books that most people will come across. The reason this book is such a challenging read is not because I wrote in language long dead and forgotten, but because I am saying things that are contradictory to what you have been taught. In this book I am giving you concepts that are foreign to what you currently know. This book will fly in the face of everything you have been told in a number of areas, that you think you know very well.

Therefore, considering the sheer "Oh come on", "What exactly did he say?" and the "Now hold on here a minute, that is impossible" factor of this book, it will need to be read multiple times. Test show that three reads per chapter is sufficient for people to really grasp what I am saying. The best way to read this book is one chapter a night and then sleep on it. Then reread the same chapter two more nights in a row. The first reading is for exposure to this new data, in the next nights reading you will start to grasp what I am saying. By the third reading you should be thinking with what I am saying. I want you to have the certainness that I do. That is the purpose of this book.

Realize that I made no mistakes in this book. Nowhere did I say something that I did not mean to say. Whenever I have included something in this book, it is because it works. These findings have been tested for years. Thousands of individuals have validated these results at a rate of better than 95%. Therefore it is very important for you to fully understand what I am saying.

Please understand that you should read this book with a dictionary at hand. When you do run into a word that you do not know the meaning of, you can look it up in your dictionary. If you do this, the book will make sense. To ignore this, I guarantee will leave you with blank spots (or sections) all over this book.

Again, when you find a word that you do not know the meaning of, look it up in a dictionary. If this book is not making sense, look for a word just before that section (that is confusing) that you do not comprehend. Do not read any further until you comprehend what that word means or the next few paragraphs will be a blank.

*****SPECIAL NOTE: Throughout this book I use the word poison. Because of that I am defining it here.***
***poi·son** (poi' zᵊn)*

n.
1. A substance taken internally or applied externally that is injurious to health or dangerous to life.
2. A chemical substance that inhibits another substance or a reaction.

Without understanding, this book is as good as a brick. Understand my words and capture understandings that you and less than 50,000 people on the planet recognize. If you fully appreciate what it is that I have written, you will be able to identify and repair any problem of the body.

2 Man's Responsibilities To Man

Like it or not, every one of us has a responsibility to OUR FELLOW MAN. Should man go extinct, it will be a cooperative failure. Collectively burying our heads in the sand while ignoring what is happening around us will make mankind a footnote in Earth's history. You have a huge accountability to your family, friends, you and all of mankind. Being productive and useful, you must survive and survive well.

Living to tell your tale and passing on what you have learned is vital to all of us. Isolation begets death. Every society in history that has isolated itself for an extended period of time has crumbled. A solitary man is no different.

If you are not surviving in good health, you are dying a little bit more every day.

The example you set does not go unnoticed by your peers. When you are spied eating a candy bar, you are communicating that candy bars are the things to eat. If you are seen eating a salad, salads are validated. The example you set could very well change someone's life. You never know who will be watching.

When you pull yourself out of the muck, your awareness improves. Imagine a man with a headache. Where is his awareness? On his head! If that same man feels good (no aches or pains) where is his awareness? Answer? Wherever, he chooses to put it. Sick people are of very little use to anyone as they are trapped being sick. Ailing individuals require vast amounts of attention and are draining on those around them.

Therefore, you have a responsibility, to yourself, and the planet to be in your best possible health. Excellent health is invaluable and needs to be sought after, respected and cherished.

Simply correcting your health allows you to be more responsible for the world you live in. Your new unfettered attention is then available for placement on problems of a global scale, rather than just on your woes. Good health is your responsibility to pursue, own, and nurture. Be healthy and you begin to take responsibility for all of us.

Your questions are always welcome. I am here for you.

Hippocrates said "Let food be your medicine and medicine be your food"

3 In the Beginning

The greatest single known source of information in the ancient world was the Great Library at Alexandria erected 283 B.C. and destroyed by fire in 47 B.C. The city of Alexandria lies along the coast of Egypt on the Mediterranean Sea. Alexandria was founded in Egypt by the greatest conqueror of the ancient world, Alexander the Great. His successor was Pharaoh Ptolomy II Soter, who founded the Museum or Royal Library of Alexandria in 283 B.C.

The Museum was a shrine of the Muses modeled after the Lyceum of Aristotle in Athens. The Museum or Library was a place of study, which included lecture areas, gardens, a zoo, and shrines for each of the nine muses as well as the Library itself. It has been calculated that between 400,000 and 700,000 scrolls (equal to our books of today) graced these halls at one time. The documents were a multinational mix from Assyria, Greece, Persia, Egypt, India and many other nations. More than 125 scholars lived at the Museum full time to perform research, write, lecture, translate and copy documents. The library was so large it actually had another branch or "daughter" library at the Temple of Serapis (also in Alexandria).

The library held scrolls containing data on the workings of the first mechanical clock, the first vending machine, surgical instruments (like the ones used today) and no doubt the blueprints and technology used to build the pyramids. Because it is gone and has been for centuries, man is still rediscovering lost technology. I am referencing it here, because the data that is contained in this manuscript has existed before. Perhaps it too was contained on a scroll or several. Much of the information on these pages has been hidden, much of it in plain view. But without the right key or context to put it in, the data would make little sense.

In the next two hundred plus pages what was a mystery will be explained. The mystery of you will unfold and for the first time make sense. Truth has a way of making sense. Imagine for yourself what would happen if civilization, as you knew it, suddenly disappeared. What would happen if all the people who knew how to fix our technology suddenly were taken from us? What if most of the world was destroyed except a few million individuals? How long might it take us to recover? Imagine further, that all of the plants and manufacturing facilities were gone. No books, no manuals.

What would become of us? When would the next inventor come along and reinvent the electric light bulb? This is the nightmare that would befall the inhabitants of the ancient world in Alexandria one night in 47 B.C. A majority of what was then known was swiftly gone as fire swept through the scrolls of knowledge housed at the Alexandria library.

If such a catastrophic event as mentioned above occurred today, at what future date would we replicate computers or re-harness the atom without someone or something to lead the way? We could dig ourselves out from such a morass, but it would take quite some time if not centuries.

Archeologists are just now discovering that not only was "our present day technology" known in antiquity it was widely used.

On these pages are the missing puzzle pieces collected and reset in proper order. The "experts" told you this knowledge DID NOT EXIST. They told you that you were stupid. They were wrong. Micro study of anything proves little. Examining an elephant's tail says little about the whole animal. The so-called best minds on the planet love to study the micro aspects of life. This proves nothing. If altering one atom for the better imbalanced the system in general, it is a bad correction. Microscope jockeys only seem to care about what they are myopically looking at. They pray for the day when they will witness matter & antimatter colliding.

This book is devoted to making life simple & livable for anyone. What matters is what the whole body is doing in relationship to the total body's functions.

What I have completed is revolutionary; I have combined seemingly incongruous modalities and practices into useable tested techniques and data so that you can experience what it is to be in charge of your body and life. I take all the puzzle pieces and lay them out exposing the full understandable big picture. You will not have to reinvent lost technology. I have spelled it out for you; your job is to test it and see if it is true for you.

I had no intentions of writing this or any book. I honestly had no idea I had anything to say. I had no idea that what I was teaching people was anything different than what others were already preaching. Yet, year after year as the looks of amazement kept swelling in number I realized that what I was saying was very unique. When other experts started cultivating my ideas and approaches, I began to get a glimpse that what I was doing was very special.

Teachers, professors and doctors started attending my lectures repeatedly. They all insisted that what I was teaching was quite unusual, so much so that it seemed otherworldly.

My work is your work; I am just presenting it to you in book form, as you must have forgotten it long ago. You the public demanded that this tome be written and advanced. This is your book.

Every technique in this book has been observed and then tested again and again. The empirical data is staggering. The human body <u>ALWAYS HEALS ITSELF</u>, unless its owner is actively poisoning it.

Do not lose sight of how simple fixing your health can be. I am not going to have you study your cells under a microscope. Nor will I have you subject yourself to x-rays or experimentation. I am not interested in micro-managing one aspect of health. We are all a collection of circuits and connections. It might be possible to learn something about an elephant by studying its tail, but it would be difficult and not something I am pursuing in this book. True natural medicine, or holistic medicine, treats the body as a whole.

If you cannot obtain 100 high-quality years out of your body, the question becomes, why? This is my total focus healthy-longevity.

It is because of this kind of work and my "no excuses" attitude that has made me a requested lecturer. I never intended to lecture. I constantly refused to lecture, regardless of how inspirational people told me I was. I refused to lecture until I was sure that I had incredible things to articulate.

Thanks to you, I lost the lecture battle almost 10 years ago.

Becoming one of Earth's leading formulators of herbal products was not on my list of things to achieve as a budding adult. Nevertheless, my lab tinkering caught the attention of many when I began sharing my formulas. Honestly, the vast swelling of medical community demand caught me off guard. Wasn't everyone making the same great products? Couldn't formulas similar to mine be gotten everywhere? No, as other formulators did not know how to think outside the box of tradition.

I had to produce my products 'en masse' or go broke being a charity worker. All of the observation that came from developing my products became the footnotes that eventually became this book. Testing again and again and noting what I was observing led to the most remarkable discoveries.

Because of my formulas, I was presented with a windfall of time, which has allowed me to give you this astonishing book.

I had to write this book or open up a practice. If I had a practice, I could only see 40 or so people a day. With this book millions can be helped every minute. This soft cover is not a fad or marketing tool. Without question, it is soon to be your best friend and confidant. I give you this book so that I can help you, even though I am not physically holding your hand.

Because of my integrity, nowhere in this book will I attempt to sell you something. This is not a sales pitch for a number of new improved (fill in the blank). Nowhere in this book is my herbal company listed. This book is self-contained. If you follow what is in this book, you will never need supplements, drugs and surgery.

You are on a collision course with discovery unlike anything that you believed possible. The public loves what is in this book because it all works.

To sum up, this book, like my formulas, is the result of curiosity; a burning drive to make a difference and a sudden avalanche of demand foisted on my shoulders. This book was never going to come out until I was forced to write it. Thank you for demanding it.

Feel free to attend my lectures and classes. There are those who have heard me speak dozens of times and are still getting new data. Use this book to save your life or the life of someone very dear to you.

Nothing for sale here! If you need to be sold the latest "health fad", turn on your T.V. some Sunday morning, or any late night, and watch away.

Here's to a new you!

If people want to read this book they will ask for it. You will not have to ask them. Let them ask you for it. If they do not ask for it you have not interested them in reading it. If you offer to let someone borrow this book without them asking you first, you have jumped the step of him or her reaching for the help this book offers.

4 The Door of Health Swings Both Ways

This book holds no allegiances or alliances with any group. I am not beholden to anything except results and your health. I am not on the payroll of a special interest conglomeration. I have no covert or nefarious agenda. I will not spew the brainwashing rhetoric of pharmaceutical scoundrels or lead you astray. I will never preach doctrine that could encumber your health or essence. The money I spend is not tainted by lies of blood-smeared principals.

I have one purpose, to teaching you:

- How to diagnose via reading the face
- How to diagnose via your fingernails
- How to diagnose via your tongue
- How to diagnose via your hands.
- How to diagnose via your eyebrows
- How to diagnose via your hair
- How to diagnose via symptoms
- How to heal yourself from any malady

- How to decode the world of medical speak
- How to take 100% responsibility for your health
- How to know if your supplements are working
- How to handle addictions
- How to awaken your latent powers of perception
- How to lose weight and keep it off

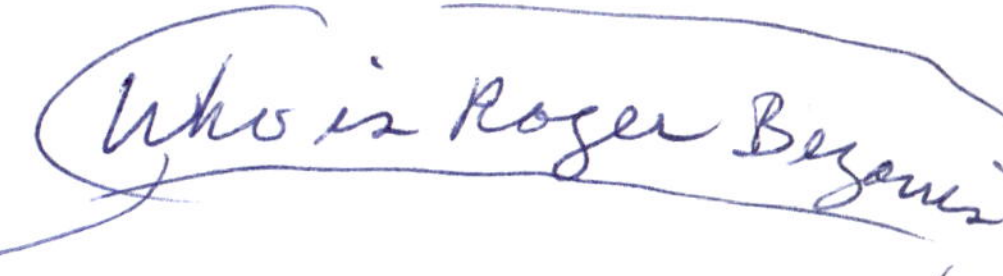

I do not trust teachers, writers, formulators or speakers that live their lives in ivory towers, never actually experiencing what they talk about. In my opinion, an educator to be legitimate had to have studied and worked in his field, to be sufficiently conversant, to pass it along. Not only have I walked in your shoes and had all of your problems, I have been worse than you in many ways.

Fortunately, I have lived through it all to tell you about it. Through these pages I am passing along experiences culled from my life that have shaped and saved the lives of many. I have not just lived my subject; I have exhaustively studied and experienced it. I have listened to the so-called experts and whenever I happened upon something promising, I tested it on myself, and then if successful on others.

When I could count on a 95% success rate or better, I passed it on. I have since formulated products to support these findings. Today I see my creations achieving a 98% success rate.

When I write about diet, I write from a position of having lived all the options. I know how to recover from knee surgery while walking without a limp or pain, 24 hours after the operation. I know what happens if you drink 240 ounces of water in one day. I have been down to 6% body fat. I know what happens if someone tries to live on B-Complex, etc.

In order to really know anything, you must get down and dirty in the stuff of life and envelop yourself in it, and I have. We have all been conditioned to believe that it takes time to correct longstanding conditions. The fact is, "The door to health swings both ways." Memorize that statement, say it again, and pronounce it out loud, "The door to health swings both ways"!

Whatever has gone wrong with the body can BE repaired if given a chance.

Grey hair has corrected itself if caught in the first stages of graying. I know this as I have changed my own hair color. You have heard about people going grey overnight? We all have. It is therefore more than possible to reverse it. What changed overnight can of course reverse.

Advancing this simple postulation to include the entire body, any condition can reverse! The door of health swings both ways!

The misguided world of diseases or chronic health issues would not only have you believe otherwise, they are counting on your confusion. The deception starts with the definition of disease.

Definition of Disease (circa 1850) - From Answers.Com

"A pathological condition of a part, organ, or system of an organism resulting from various causes, such as infection, genetic defect, or environmental stress, and characterized by an identifiable group of signs or symptoms"

TRANSLATION: ***Your condition (sickness) is not your responsibility. You had nothing to do with it.*** *To fully understand what was originally meant by the word disease you must understand the word history or derivation.*

WORD HISTORY: Disease; The condition of not being comfortable or not relieved or no freedom from pain. [Middle English disease, from Old French: des-, dis- + aise, ease; see ease] Prefix: dis- not or dissimilar PLUS no ease (experiencing pain). Simply, the word disease is supposed to convey IN THE PRESENCE OF PAIN.

Because the word DISEASE has been so altered and twisted by the medicos for the past 250+ years, I am redefining it and giving it the definition below.

DFRHY Disease definition: "A weakened condition of the body brought on by personal choices and ignorance of the natural laws that govern biology"

Additionally: You are 100% responsible for your condition. Your choices have brought about the condition you are in.

To further make it clear as to what the source of a problem of the body is, I am coining a new word. This word sparks a revolution in viewing sickness and now leads to correct handlings.

EXSURPO: Meaning EXACT-SOURCE-PAIN or exact source of the pain. Derivation: Ex: Latin, exactus = exact + Latin, surgere = source + Latin, poena = Pain.

Henceforth we will say the exsurpo of _______ (pain) is the kidney, liver etc.
Being sick requires a total and complete disconnection from you as source of you being sick. You must participate in ignoring what you did to cause or aid your illness. This ignorance is required for you to remain sick and thus REMAIN a victim of your acquired condition.

Sickness is the result of intelligent life granted freedom of choice, then brainwashed to believe there is no choice. If I did not have firsthand experience, I might agree with, "What is broken stays broken."

If you doubt the above paragraph, it is because the fear mongers have stolen your will to live!

Take your life back! The Powers That Be promise little while handing out candy-coated death. They want you ignorant to the fact that the human body is resilient and heals without drugs and surgery.

I will explain this in detail in the chapter "Disease Labels and Who Owns Them"

Your body is not only intelligent; it instantly reacts to stimulus. Do not remain blind to this fact or next you will accept the drug company's lies that your only hope comes in a bottle with a warning label.

You feel bad from a cocktail of chemicals, colorings, dyes and drugs. They affect you on contact and always have.

Big Pharma has invested billions to program you to believe that health improvement takes time: days, weeks, months or is impossible. Imagine what would happen if the current drug-company trained-doom speaking witch doctors started handing people hope rather than promising death within 30 days.

Families would sue!

Today's witch doctors don't dare breathe the possibility of hope and recovery. This is a fascinating dilemma. Doctors, who have no idea how the body heals, try to heal it. The public ignoring its own intuition, intention and determinism, sit idly by, waiting for the death wagon to arrive.

We are taught to worship our witch doctors in lab coats dispensing their drugs and surgery. Thanks to conditioning we glumly ask for a forecast of survival. If the doctor says anything other than "I don't know" or "Death in 30 days", he gets sued. Survival predictions not realized equal lawsuits. Let us all give a big "Thank you" to the American Bar Association.

You can see the problem: the blind are leading the brainwashed.

Promising death (or a bad outcome) protects the doctor and the drug companies. If you buy into the notion that it takes time to recover, then any therapy appears to work. Why? Because, the body is so resilient, even in the face of toxic drugs, it can and often does heal on its own, in spite of the doctor's efforts to kill it off.

My approach is completely different. I know that when the right item (or items) is given to the body, the body starts to correct itself immediately. Pain will dissipate; fever reduces, swelling releases, freedom of movement returns, sleep improves, high blood pressure lowers. The list goes on and on.

As far as supplements go, it is a fact that correctly made supplements point themselves at a target organ, and ALWAYS react on contact with the system. To understand more about this, read the chapter called "Your Body is Smarter than you." Pay special attention to the Energy Balancing Technique.

In a nutshell, your body feels sensation moment to moment as opposed to later. This is a survival mechanism. Imagine what would happen if your body took an hour or so to sense heat or taste.

You could singe your skin or exterminate yourself with spoiled food. The body reacts with everything it comes in contact with right now, not a week from now. When you smell cigarette smoke and sneeze, it is because your body is rejecting it now. Your body needs but a 100th of a second to process that information. You smelled it and then sneezed.

With that in mind, I have successfully tested these intimate universal phenomena hundreds of thousands of times. As a result, I question why supplement companies don't mention the 'instant response'. Supplements and all foods affect the body every time they are introduced. You are not told of this reaction because supplement and drug companies either have no awareness of the phenomena or are hiding what they know.

At least one pharmaceutical company does know this reaction. In their own commercials they warn woman not to touch or handle their product because of a specific birth defect. What about the rest of the drug companies, do they know too? Do they know or care that they are killing you?

You must demand that all supplement makers produce ingestibles that are so good, that they create a known instant, positive response on the body. Why won't all companies be doing this anytime soon?

Because it would require:

- Awareness of the phenomena
- Relearning all that they know
- Reformulating at least 50% of what they currently produce
- No longer copying other formulator's work
- Inventing products that actually do work
- Willingness to accept that 2% of the public will claim to not have a noticeable instant response

Money is the reason we will not see this change until you demand that it takes place. Cigarette sales are falling because you have said enough. One voice is the start of a chorus when another voice is added.

Big business does not like to take chances. Even though the supplement business is puny compared to the drug industry, they still follow the same path of least resistance. I, on the other hand, have no problem rocking the boat. I tell it like it actually is. Immediate results are something that supplement makers do not want to be involved in.

If we do not expect immediate results, we are not upset when they don't come.

Any company promoting this idea of immediate results is putting their hindquarters on the line with every bottle. I admire that.

Take a moment to realize, that if you sit and wait long enough, something will always happen. It may have nothing to do with your therapy or treatment, but something will happen. If you can't sleep, wait long enough and you will. Have a sore back, wait long enough, and it won't hurt.

In general when people feel physically or emotionally better they rightly or wrongly give credit to the product they have been taking. Conversely, when they feel worse, they again blame the product. You must be asking yourself why I am writing so many paragraphs to make this point.

This is why:

Feeling better or worse has practically nothing to do with the product you are taking, UNLESS FEELING BETTER OR WORSE OCCURED ON CONTACT WITH THAT PRODUCT. Contact = the moment you touched it. Yes, I said the moment you touched it.

The moment you touch anything, your body NOTICES and changes accordingly, even if only slightly.

If you think that I am saying that you can touch some food or supplement and pain will go away, THAT IS EXACTLY WHAT I AM SAYING.

When you take a supplement and hours go by before you feel better, it was because your body finally adjusted on its own. Perhaps a new substance that you just contacted did the trick. Should you feel worse, it was something you JUST ate, JUST drank, JUST inhaled or JUST splashed on your skin. Something you JUST contacted was the straw that broke the camel's back.

Therefore, if you eat a cookie and feel bad it was from the cookie not your job or the yard work. If you pick up a slice of pizza and notice that your low back suddenly hurts, it is your body saying HEY MISTER, PLEASE DON'T FEED ME PIZZA!

Every time you feel bad it is due to something that you just came in contact with that has pushed you over the edge.

But what if you took something and within a few seconds you felt better? That is to be expected. The only wild card in all of this is hormones from stress. Stress releases hormones and will stress the liver and give you a symptom. The treatment is the same, find the supplement or food that resets the liver and you will feel improved.

Instant body / condition / symptom improvement is an outrageous and foreign idea for most. There will be those who will read this entire chapter, and question what I am writing about. I assure you instant response is not only possible, it happens every day, and you never noticed it.

If all drug companies and supplement makers were held with their feet to the fire until they produced products that created a noticeable balance in the body, we would have a lot of burned feet.

We ignore the violent instant reaction from poison oak, poison ivy, pollen, peanut oil (causing, in some cases, anaphylactic shock and death), ragweed, dry cleaning solvents, the smell of tobacco, ammonia, industrial solvents, perfume, etc.

The poor allergist understands some of this yet even he is in the dark. He toils trying to cover or suppress symptoms. He is aware that some substances make his patients feel poorly, yet he has no idea that all substances have the ability to improve or worsen the system on contact.

When you use a supplement, you should feel improvement now, not later.

Below is how the body actually works

The Reactions

At the moment of contact with any substance the body will:

- Get hotter
- Get colder

- Contract / tighten
- Expand / loosen

- Feel more pain
- Feel less pain

- Accelerate or speed up
- Decelerates or slows down

- Age faster
- Age slower

- Release waste
- Retain waste

- Release water
- Retain water

- Relax
- Become tense

- Oxygenate
- Deoxygenate

- Awaken / more energy
- Sedate / less energy

- No reaction or neutral response

This occurs when the body is balanced and has the reserves to stay balanced.

In treating yourself you must remember the eleven categories above. If you find yourself taking a supplement that produces no perceivable benefit, ultimately it is a waste of money. You would probably not wash your car every hour. Taking supplements for no reason without defined benefit is akin to such an activity.

5 You and Your Doctor

Hippocrates studied patients over and over; he was fascinated in their stories but especially how they appeared. He trained himself to smell sickness as well as listen for it. He developed a sharpened eye and for him face reading became second nature. Thus he perfected an expert technique that has been lost. If you have ever wondered what "being in practice" meant, ask a doctor. He / she will tell you that what they learned in college, while valuable, was second to what they learned in the field or in practice.

Put yourself in the shoes of Aristotle; he too noticed the look of the ill. He saw dark, gaunt or swollen regions of the face and knew they meant something. He knew enough to ask. Eventually he knew it was a symptom of ill health.

Have you ever noticed what a stroke victim looks like? Aristotle, Hippocrates and I have. You will too. Good doctors care and ask questions.

Throughout history certain individuals have earned our respect and praise. They perform miracles every day and involve themselves in life and death.

They are called doctors.

Many feel their doctors walk on water. Even the worst practitioners of health receive praise and curiosity. Such was the fate of Nazi Doctor Josef Mengele a mad man and murderer. Hitler's personal doctor, Dr. Theodor Morell clearly a quack, who pumped Germany's WWII Fuhrer full of a cocktail of B-Vitamins and Amphetamines (speed a stimulant). Then there was the father of modern psychiatry, Wilhelm Wundt, another mad man. Finally, Atlanta dentist turned gunfighting, card shark, Tuberculosis sufferer and friend to Wyatt Earp, Doc Holiday. Not all doctors are serving up good health. It is their own ethic level that will determine their legacy. Witness the twisting road of Dr. Death, Jack Kevorkian, as he is both scorned and hailed.

The human race has placed this profession on a pedestal. When any individual can control the terms of life and death, reverence naturally follows. Is it deserved? You bet it is.

What makes a good doctor?

- Compassion
- Intelligence
- Knowledge of his field
- Ability to listen
- Ability to learn new things
- Little or no ego
- Good bedside manner
- Interested in you and your problems
- Knowledge of new advancements in medicine
- Intuition
- Willing to ask for help
- Understanding that they can always learn
- Willing to say "I don't know" and then find the answer
- Willing to hand off to a more qualified expert

The above description makes a good doctor. How does your doctor stack up? Is he listed above or more below?

What Makes a Bad Doctor?

If he is:

- Always right

- Argumentative
- Makes you wrong
- Won't listen to you
- Spends little time with you
- Dispenses drugs without an understanding of what he is dispensing
- Not willing to learn
- Not interested in what you have to say
- None or little compassion
- Poor bedside manner

If the list above describes your doctor, RUN!

Your doctor should be a partner in your health not the driver. When a doctor practically foaming at the mouth yells at you, it is often because you ventured into the sacred territory of diagnosis or self-diagnosis.

You need to be encouraged to participate in your own health care. You beyond all doubt have one true friend. This comrade knows everything about you. This companion goes everywhere you go, eats what you eat and has all of your habits. That friend is you.

Who is better qualified to give you a hand than you? You have personally observed yourself 24 hours a day for your entire life. You are over qualified to assist yourself with just a little training. Your doctor can help you get to this level or he can stop you.

Clearly, with a little work and some study, you could be your best ally in securing a healthier future. That is the purpose of this book. To teach you the basic principles of health that school, T.V., advertising, the AMA, FDA and God knows who else never taught you.

You can be healthy regardless of what your doctor, spouse, friend or confidant told you. When you show this book to your doctor, he or she should want to read it. He should be in favor of your reading it. If not, this is a bad sign.

When your health care practitioner is against you educating yourself and insists that his care is all that you need, get a new doctor. Should you be yelled at, belittled or made to doubt the validity of your decisions about your health, again this is red flag, find a new doctor.

You can be better, healthier and stronger and it starts now.

6 The History of Medicine

Much has been said about the rise of Traditional Medicine (also called Allopathic medicine) at the expense of Natural Medicine. This chapter brushes aside all the bias and rumor and just gives you the facts regarding who did what and when it occurred. Many of the players you will have heard of. You will probably be shocked to find out why your health care choices are so limited today. The demise of Natural Medicine was no accident. It was a well-crafted and devious plan.

As you read this chapter you will begin to understand how deep health care corruption really runs.

Why it is that natural medicine was assigned the new name of alternative medicine after 1900?

The history to be covered in this chapter includes:

7995-2995 BC, Ayurvedic Medicine appears in the mountains of Tibet

2630-2611 BC, Imhotep treats patients in the Third Dynasty of Egypt

Circa 2400 BC, Acupuncture and Chinese texts outline the use of herbs

1500 BC, Egyptian physicians write down techniques for the healing of the Pharaohs

1200 BC, soldiers are treated for wounds during the siege of Troy

400 BC, Hippocrates forms the first school of medicine; Naturopathic medicine is practiced

55 AD, Dioscorides documents herbal formulas for the Europeans

159, Galen invents new procedures and the instruments to perform surgical work

500-1400, the Dark Ages, no known advances in medicine survived this period

1200, Unani Medicine begins being practiced in the Middle East

1801, Homeopathic medicine is created

1810, with a mail order medical certificate, Jenner creates the Smallpox vaccine

1814, Germany starts issuing medical degrees

1841-1866, various forms of anesthesia started to be put in use

1847, the American Medical Association groundwork is put in place

1848, Samuel Weiss was fired for requiring surgeons to wash their hands

1867, Joseph Lister champions antiseptic surgical practices

1869, Pasteur creates Pasteurization and, with Koch, develops many vaccines

1880-1900, German psych-trained doctors begin taking positions of power in major American medical colleges

1906, the FDA is created with the Federal Food and Drug Act

1907, the AMA investigates medical colleges of the United States and Canada

1908, the AMA allows the Carnegie Foundation to investigate medical schools for them

1910, the Flexner Report on Medical Education in the United States and Canada is released

1910-1940, Carnegie, Rockefeller, Kellogg, Ford and others start paying off (bribing) medical schools that will implement new drug therapies (created by companies they support), while doing away with the current natural curriculums. Non-approved medical schools are forced to close at a mad rate due to a SUDDEN lack of funding and students. The country drops from 160 medical schools to 80 almost overnight. AMA membership soars, as all allopathic doctors must join to practice.

1915 to present day, Drug Company profits soar, as more drugs are created to combat the new diseases described and named by the AMA. All new drugs receive the blessings from the FDA and follow a diagnosis from the AMA. The world is starting to be drugged.

The Practice Of Medicine / An Unabridged Timeline

Ayurvedic Medicine 7995 to 2995 BC: This is considered the oldest form of healthcare in the world. It was born in the mountains of Tibet and in what is now known as present day India. Passed down verbally for generations, in approximately 2500 BC it was written down in Sanskrit (recognized as the world's oldest surviving language) on stone and clay tablets. These tablets are known as the Vedas; they are the oldest written knowledge found on Earth. Often called the "Mother of healing", Ayurveda spread to China and advanced through much of the then known world. It influenced Hippocrates in Greece and became known throughout the Middle East as Unani Medicine.

Current Ayurveda is drawn from three later sources, primarily the Caraka Samhita (approximately 1500 BC), the Ashtang Hrdyam (approximately 500 AD) and Sushrut Samhita (300 - 400 AD). These works are considered classics as they describe the basic principles and theories from which Ayurveda has evolved. They also contain large amounts of clinical data on the management of a multitude of diseases.

2630-2611 BC Imhotep: Egyptian physician to King Djoser (third dynasty) is believed to be the first physician in recorded history. He is credited with diagnosing & treating at least 100 diseases; many diseases of the abdomen and bladder, a dozen of the rectum, 30 of the eyes, and almost 20 skin, hair, nail and tongue problems. He's credited with treating tuberculosis, liver / gallstone problems, colon issues, appendicitis, kidney problems, diabetes, gout and arthritis problems. He performed surgery and even practiced some dentistry. Imhotep extracted herbal medicines from plants and knew the position and function of the vital organs as well as understanding the circulation of the blood system.

China circa 2400 BC: their first medical texts were laid down, documenting the use of herbs and diagramming the structure of the body, including meridians and organ function. Many believe that for thousands of years Ayurvedic and Chinese Medicine, which included acupuncture, were the only types of medicine being practiced on earth.

1500 BC: Ancient Egyptian physicians, in the court of the Pharaohs, understood the body and documented these findings in papyrus documents still being unearthed today. Machaon and his brother Polidarius treated soldiers at the battle of Troy, circa 1200 BC, for arrow wounds. Together they saved many lives on the battlefield.

460 - 377 BC: Hippocrates was born on the island of Cos, Greece. He laid down the 'Hippocratic Oath' (the pledge that doctors take today). He became known as the Father of medicine and was regarded as the greatest physician of his time. Hippocrates said "Let food be your medicine and medicine be your food."

Circa 400 BC: Naturopathic Medicine is first noted with the rise of the Hippocratic School of Medicine. Hippocrates preached "The healing power of nature" or "Vis Medicatrix Naturae" and the use of hydrotherapy and hygienics. The style of medicine being practiced was called "Eclectics", as were the doctors, since they used whatever means necessary to heal the patient.

Circa 55 AD: Dioscorides (Greek) compiled written formulas and herbs that were often direct forebears of what has been used for the last 1,000 years. His formulas and approach were largely unchanged in Western pharmacopeias until the twentieth century.

131 AD: Galen (Greek) studied at the historic medical school in Alexandria, Egypt. By the age of 28, he was saving the lives of gladiators. He was a pioneer in surgery and is credited with inventing most of the medical instruments used today. Galen favored the beliefs of Hippocrates and called on the healing power of nature to balance the body. He observed and noted symptoms and often treated with opposites, i.e. if a man appeared to have a fever, he treated it with something cold, if a man appeared to have a cold, he would be treated with heat. People who were weak were given hard physical exercise to build up their muscles. Those who had breathing problems due to bronchial issues were given singing exercises. He was a prolific writer and was still influencing doctors 1,000 years after his death.

1200: Unani Medicine, the framework of which is based on the teachings of Hippocrates. Unani was the culmination and the convergence of the works of Galen (131-210 AD), Islamic physicians Al-Razi, (Iran, 850-925 AD), Ibn Sina (Persia, 980-1037 AD), Al Zahravi (present day Spain) and the surgeon Ibn Nafis (Syria, 1210-1288 AD). Unani medicine has been practiced all over the Middle East and is considered the best of the medicines of Egypt, Syria, Iraq, Persia, India, China and other Middle East and far East countries.

500-1450 Middle Ages of Medicine: this period was basically a standstill. The use of bloodletting for curing illness was prominent. For lesser problems, leeches were used. Astrology started to influence medicine. No major advancements were made.

1801, Homeopathy appeared: In 1801 Samuel Hahnemann, a German physician, created Homeopathy (from Greek Homois=similar + Greek Pathos= suffering, Homeopathy = similar suffering). He codified the earlier suppositions of Hippocrates. After repeated direct success in applying his principals, he created Homeopathy. The label of Homeopathy would stick in 1902.

1810 Edward Jenner (1749-1823): in 1790 he purchased a medical certificate from St. Andrews University (a standard practice until 1814). After many troubling failures he finally developed a vaccine for Smallpox in 1810.

1814: Germany invents the "Degree" to show a level of proficiency and graduation from college.

1848 Samuel Weiss: A surgeon at the University of Vienna Medical School. Weiss noted that doctors routinely went directly from the morgue (handling the dead), to birthing wards delivering babies. When this practice was followed more than 50% of the infants died. He concluded that there was an element being carried from the dead to the infants that resulted in their premature deaths. He required surgeons to wash their hands before surgery. Due to the believed silliness of his supposition, he was fired.

1867 Joseph Lister (1827-1912): He literally cleans up surgery. He was the man who finally convinced the field of medicine that washing hands between surgeries is vital. Lister is known as the "Father of Antiseptic Surgery." "Ward fever deaths", caused by the un-cleanliness of surgeons and hospitals, fell from 12% to 1%. Lister insisted that all wounds had to be thoroughly cleaned and covered with a dressing soaked in Carbolic acid. As a result, his patient's mortality rate ran less than 2%.

Circa 1869 Louis Pasteur (1822 -1893) developed the "Germ Theory," that a weakened immune system can be attacked by germs that cause illness. He developed Pasteurization to kill bacteria. He collaborated with Dr. Robert Koch who had a detailed understanding of the human body (that Pasteur lacked) to develop numerous vaccines.

Due to the rapid expansion of the population across North America, good medicine had a very difficult time keeping up. Except on the settled east coast, standard or routine medicine was not being practiced in America. The new west was not a good place to be sick. Not that home remedies did not work, but it was the Snake Oil con man that was the problem. The lack of plentiful well educated Naturopaths and Homeopaths left America in the dire need of experts.

Early 1800s: powerful drugs came into recreational use all over the world. At this time in history Opium addiction was common in China, Europe, England and the United States. In these places more opium was consumed than beer.

1842 Dr. Crawford Williamson Long: On March 30, 1842 made the first use of ether to remove two tumors from a patient's neck. He used ether in minor surgery as early as 1841. Dr. Long eventually published his findings in The Southern Medical and Surgical Journal in 1848.

1843 Dr. Alexander Wood of Edinburgh: He loaded syringes with morphine and injected them in patients prior to surgery. This use gave far better results than oral administration. Wood found that injection was three times more effective than any other delivery method of killing pain.

1844 Dentist Horace Wells of Hartford, Connecticut: He promoted nitrous oxide anesthesia to the Boston medical community but there was little interest. Unfortunately in demonstration, after demonstration he received poor responses from colleagues and the public.

1846 Dr. Charles Jackson: He tutored Dr. William T.G. Morton in the use of nitrous oxide. During the next five years the American Dental Association adopted its use. Morton began secret experiments with ether. On September 30th, 1846, at his Boston office, he painlessly removed a tooth from a city worker.

1847: The future American Medical Association (AMA) was formed with one doctor as its sole member. The fledgling American Medical Association was incorporated in 1897.

1847: James Young Simpson first tested chloroform on himself on November 4, 1847. It created a very powerful narcotic effect and was known to cause death quickly when misused. The first fatality was a 15-year-old girl called Hannah Greener, who died on January 28, 1848.

1850 through 1899: Because the AMA was struggling to get members, there needed to be a way to drive up membership and thus drive up income.

1850-1866: the use of anesthesia started to become more common but the Civil War interrupted its progress and actually caused its use to slow until after the war. Nevertheless, those who did experience anesthesia appreciated the results.

1860-1865 American Civil War: doctors used unorthodox medicines and procedures often made up on the spot. For pain, they sparingly used medicines such as morphine, nitrous oxide, ether and chloroform. The normal treatment of a severe infected wound was amputation. As harsh as amputation was it saved more lives than it took. Due to lack of supplies, common surgery was still being performed on patients who were given only alcohol and opium.

1875-1930: German physicians and psychologist / psychiatrists start moving from German universities to positions of prestige within major universities in the United States. The leader of this movement was Wilhelm Wundt (1832-1920), German physiologist and psychologist, generally acknowledged as the founder of experimental psychology.

1875: Wilhelm Wundt takes a position at the University of Leipzig, and sets up the first German psychological lab. Simultaneously, William James, a student of Wundt, set up a similar lab in

America. Wundt's students found a pipeline directly into university positions in the United States. Most of these Wundt graduates went on to become eminent psychologists in the United States. It is widely accepted that the covert work of prestigious wealthy individuals living in America made all of this possible.

7 Crimes against the Soul of Man

In the last chapter we met Wilhelm Wundt. This one individual was responsible for the beginnings of the German / European attitude that man was an animal. A soulless being has no rights, can be owned and experimented on. Ask any lab rat how he feels about that. Without a soul a man and his brain can be (and has been) sliced up like a Christmas Turkey. Thinking begets consciousness and the presence of a soul was what Wundt wanted to separate from man. He knew there was no soul inherent or connected to man. His own writings and later actions prove it.

Wilhelm Wundt wrote the following in 'Lectures on Human and Animal Psychology'

"The old metaphysical prejudice that man "always thinks," has not yet entirely disappeared. I myself am inclined to hold that man really thinks very little and very seldom. Many an action, which looks like a manifestation of intelligence, most surely originates in association.

The Wundt Effect

Wundt was in the right place at the right time to change the course of psychological history and medical history. His students were plentiful and hungry for positions of power. The following is a list of Wundt's students who filled positions opened for them by very powerful and influential people. The wealthy industrialists that facilitated this drastic change are well known to you. A handful of men determined the way in which medicine would be practiced in the Americas. They attempted to predestine your medical future.

To overthrow any institution you must seize power at the top. The following list illustrates how a few of Wundt's students did just that.

James Mckeen Cattell was the first Professor of Psychology in the world (University of Pennsylvania, 1887). He studied in Leipzig under Wundt in 1882 and was appointed a fellow at John Hopkins University. He also lectured at Bryn Mawr, 1887; was the Professor of Psychology, University of Pennsylvania, 1888; head of the Department of Psychology and Philosophy at Columbia University from 1891-1905. He was the President of the American Psychological Association in 1895.

Edward Bradford Titchener, receiving his degree from Leipzig in 1892 was then appointed Assistant Professor of Psychology at Cornell University in the same year. He was made head of the psych laboratory that was founded the year before by Frank Angell, another Leipzig graduate. He went on to become the editor of studies from the Department of Psychology of Cornell University (1894-1927), American Editor, Mind (1894-1917) and Editor of the American Journal of Psychology (1895-1927).

Hugo Munsterberg moved from Germany to the United States to serve as the professor of psychology (1892-1916). He became the Director of the Harvard psychological laboratory in 1905.

G. Stanley Hall (1844-1924) pioneered American psychology in its early years. Hall taught briefly at Harvard before assuming a position at John Hopkins University in 1881. In 1887, Hall founded the American Journal of Psychology. He also served as the first President of the American Psychological Association in 1892 and was re-elected shortly before his death in 1924.

Lightner Witmer transferred to Leipzig University in Germany to study under Wilhelm Wundt. He obtained his Ph.D. in 1892, from Leipzig and then moved to Philadelphia to head an experimental laboratory at the University of Pennsylvania. Witmer established the world's first psychological clinic in 1896.

Charles Hubbard Judd completed his Ph.D. in 1896 under Wilhelm Wundt at Leipzig at only 23 years old. He later taught at the University of Cincinnati, Yale University, and finally the University of Chicago, where he was appointed as the Director of Education from 1909 until his retirement in 1938.

John D. Rockefeller, Andrew Carnegie, Will Keith Kellogg and Henry Ford became more and more interested in the German model of medicine. They independently decided to support the integration of German and American medicine. These multimillionaires and their vision would soon reshape the way medicine was practiced in America. Thanks to the efforts of the men listed above, foundations and groups like the FDA and AMA would flourish. I will be writing more on this topic of the FDA and AMA in later chapters.

Greed Takes Over

Prior to 1910, medicine in America was a melting pot of therapies. Doctors were good, but consistency was not the same when compared to the rigid doctors of Europe and Germany. The American doctor often had little training and used old time (yet effective) home remedies.

Homeopathy and Naturopathy were gaining more and more popularity. It worked and it was readily available in large cities. Yet, there was no formal medical degree as there was in Germany (first issued in 1814). Medical credentials could be purchased through the mail in America, while they were "earned" in Germany. It was clear that a large number of doctors received far less than adequate training.

Homeopathic doctors were flourishing in 1900. 100 homeopathic hospitals existed. Popularity of homeopathy in all classes of society soared. There were 22 homeopathic schools and over 1,000 homeopathic pharmacies.

But the AMA had no jurisdiction over homeopaths. Fighting for recognition and its very survival, in 1907, the AMA formed a committee to study American Medicine as it was being taught. The Council on Medical Education was formed with the intent to offer up reforms for medical education.

Surely a publicly made study would drive up membership and gain much needed repute for the organization. It was not to be as the committee ran out of money in 1908. This came to the attention of Andrew Carnegie, who created the Carnegie Foundation in 1905 to support such ventures. Realizing the benefits and buffers of an organization versus private donation, John D. Rockefeller started his foundation in 1911.

Independently they decided to alter the landscape of American medicine forever.

Understanding the woes of the AMA, the Carnegie Foundation dispatched Henry S. Pritchett, President of the Carnegie Foundation, and Abraham Flexner. Flexner was educated at the University of Berlin and at Johns Hopkins University. At the Carnegie Foundation he was a researcher. Flexner had a gift for assimilating large amounts of information and then forming it into an understandable format for readers. Via the Carnegie Foundation, Flexner spotted an opportunity to alter and thus control post-graduate education in the United States. Flexner and Pritchett were to meet with the AMA. Pritchett was instructed to make an offer of help that the AMA could not refuse.

The plan was to take complete control of the AMA study and thus control of their findings.

Pritchett was instructed to:

- Offer to absorb the previous cost of the AMA study
- Offer to take over the rest of the study for the AMA and therefore absorb any future costs. He had a directive from Carnegie to offer any amount of money it took to get the AMA to let Pritchett and Flexner finish off the study and compile the findings. Acceptance of this gift was the first step in a master plot to take over and change medicine in America. The cost of taking over the work was only $10,000!

The story goes, on a cold day, December 8, 1908, it took less than an hour and the deal was struck. Flexner would compile an exhaustive study of over 160 medical schools in America. Based on his findings he would recommend which schools should be shut down and which should be approached to improve their conditions.

This was the first nail in the coffin of natural medicine. The "Flexner Report" was a clever mix of truth and subtle deceptions. It painted a gloomy picture of natural medicine. Flexner's copious report 'Medical Education in the United States and Canada' (1910) was disseminated to the public in droves and did much to change public opinion. Soon pharmacology courses would be standard curriculum in new research departments at all qualified medical schools. Schools that gained the Flexner seal, of approval would receive huge amounts of grant money.

Ultimately, the decision as to who should and should not receive money went right to the top of the Rockefeller Foundation, Carnegie Foundation and others. These groups were anxiously signing grant checks. Homeopathy had been practiced in the United States since 1801, yet most Homeopathic schools were shut down. No chiropractic schools received any money. Osteopathic schools complied with Flexner's edicts and did get money. Soon thereafter, the Osteopathic Medical Doctor was created.

Expected AMA membership soared off the charts as doctors rushed in panic to protect their livelihood. In 1910, 1 billion dollars in grant checks found homes at favored universities. Those willing to play the new Flexner game were flourishing and paid very well.

Over the next 15 years, Flexner toured North America visiting, reforming and bestowing checks on schools that met his standards. In 1913 alone, the Rockefeller foundation gave away another 80 million dollars in grants. Not a small amount of money considering that the total gross budget for all US medical schools in 1920 was only $12 million.

It paid to be on the right side of the fence. Not all the money came from the R&C (Rockefeller and Carnegie) Foundations. The Henry Ford Foundation, Kellogg Foundation (Kellogg Cereal Fame) and the Macy Foundation contributed mightily as well. Nevertheless, R&C were the most prolific givers in this arena.

To be on the receiving end of this money a college had to affiliate itself with a "recognized" teaching hospital. All professors had to be full time instructors and not see patients to supplement their incomes. This was used against Homeopathy as the instructors at the smaller institutions with smaller enrollments had to practice to make ends meet. Not to mention that now finding a "recognized" hospital affiliation for a Homeopathic college would be impossible.

Agents friendly to the AMA and R&C now managed recognized hospitals. For a short while they were rewarded (with grants) for toeing the new line. This further closed the doors of "non-approved" colleges from surviving. Without the funds to attract faculty and pay for new equipment, Chiropractic, Naturopathic, Homeopathic and Osteopathic colleges were nearly dead.

The schools that survived were those who would accept the yoke of the Rockefeller-Carnegie and their new Allopathic (drug based) curriculum. If it were not for newly formed and aggressive alumni organizations with private investments we would no longer have natural medicine.

The term allopathy was coined in 1842 by Hahnemann to designate the usual practice of medicine (allo = other + pathy = therapy, or use of drugs) as opposed to homeopathy (use of like substances).

In 1906 the FDA came into existence with the passage of the Federal Food and Drug Act. This act / law made it a crime for a processed consumable to be sold without an FDA approval. The FDA later partnered with the AMA to control the flow of drugs. Today, drugs approved by the FDA are those that can be isolated through chemical reaction (laboratory process). This of course excludes all natural substances such as herbs and herbal formulas as they do not go through lab processing. The chemical process renders drugs patentable as they are created in a laboratory and not in nature. The FDA does recognize Homeopathy due to its limited laboratory processing.

The only processing that herbal formulas receive is via cold pressing into capsules or tablets, hardly a dense chemical- laden laboratory process. Because of that, the dried leaves, roots, twigs, flowers and barks used in these mixtures are still viable and healing to the body. Therefore, the FDA does not recognize herbals as their lack of processing precludes them. The FDA is only interested in chemicals, drugs and big money. Herbal formulas are small potatoes compared to the remarkably lucrative drug industry.
In essence, this aspect of the FDA charter forever closes the door on herbal formulas being recognized by our Food and Drug Administration. Unless the FDA changes its charter, no one will ever see an herbal formula receive FDA approval.

Connecting the Dots!

Those of you who love a good conspiracy theory will love this. This is not a theory. The Rockefeller's, Carnegie's, Ford's, Kellogg's and Macy have conspired to run an influential agency (the AMA) from 1908 until circa 1920. This is due to the Flexner report 'Medical Education in the United States and Canada' (1910). With that report, sweeping policies were affected that changed the practice of medicine.

Is there any reason to believe that these 'moguls' ever relinquished control?
Is there a direct link from the FDA to the AMA?

It is well known that the AMA names the problem (disease). The FDA approves the drug for the disease and takes an 800 million payoff from the lucky pharmaceutical company who will make the drug. Who controls the FDA? We know who controls the AMA.

Are trillion dollar families such as the aforementioned and the Rothschild's (bankers in France and England) still calling the shots for health care worldwide? Can it be possible that they are acting as puppeteers over world governments?

If you were handed pseudo government power and could manage the flow of trillions of dollars in drug sales a year, would you relinquish control?

There are many who believe that the FDA is a government agency under private control.

Using the Rockefeller Effect to Beat Them Back

The reason the tactics of this chapter were so effective in changing medicine was due to the strategy of "Getting them while they're young." Doctors had to be educated at the foundation root student level if they were going to be of any use. The brainwashing rhetoric had to be beaten in hard with no other option given. This profound incessant indoctrination led us to the insanity of what is called "modern medicine."

If you want to change this planet, get this book into the hands of kids. Yes, I have explained face reading to 10-17 year olds and they instantly get the simplicity and ease of the technique. Since face reading is so simple, anyone can do it.

Yet the other gifts of this book are even deeper and again our future is riding on us doing something about it.

Kids instantly get what I write and say. Why? Because their un-brainwashed minds instantly recognize truth. This book is bursting at the seams with easily understood and tested truths.

Get this book to your nieces and nephews. I have often said that giving this book away is a bad idea. When it comes to kids, give it away. Give lots of them away. Purchase dozens of them for donation to elementary and high schools. Find out where I am lecturing next and bring your sons, daughters and their friends.

For you under 20 year olds reading this book, you can change the world. Yes, all of you young / pre adults can transform the humankind. Like it or not, you and your friends are going to run this planet. I am appealing to you to do something about the creeping crud that is overwhelming society today. Get all of your friends to read every page of this book. Have your high schools invite me to spend three hours presenting all of the truth contained herein. Do a book report and present it to your class. Use your high school budget to purchase this book for your school library. On these pages are the kinds of Earth shaking truths that can change mega-business and man's future forever.

If you don't do it, you are condoning the poisoning of your friends. They will become sick.

It all starts with you! I cannot do it alone. I need your help, as I cannot be everywhere. We have to do this together. The world needs you and me standing together shoulder-to-shoulder marching forward. I am counting on you.

8 Behind the Medicine Cabinet

Transgressions and crimes from WW I have been buried for almost 100 years. Surprisingly, details from this long dead conflict are still influencing our lives today. One very well known company was a huge player in both world wars. It is still a huge player today. This mystery company is not one you would associate with death, yet it has had a direct hand in the deaths of millions.

- The company that invented Aspirin in 1899
- Produced Mustard gas for Germany in WW I
- Developed Heroin in 1898, used as a pain killer
- Developed Tabum, a nerve gas used in WWI
- Developed Chlorine gas, used in WWI

The company was Bayer and Co.

With war looming in the future, a decision was made in 1925 to consolidate Germany's industrial might 'under-one' banner. Brokered by Hermann Schmitz (who would 20 years later be convicted of war crimes at Nuremberg) a mega merger was about to take place. Hermann married the following companies: Bayer (the Aspirin folks), Badische, Anilin, Hoechst, Agfa, BASF, Hoechst, Griesheim-Elektron and Weiler-Ter-Meer. These chemical / drug companies would form one of the largest drug dye and chemical conglomerates known to man. The new company was christened I.G. Farben (full name, Interessen Gemeinschaft Farenindustrie Aktiengesellschaft).

I.G. Farben's purpose was to make war possible for the Nazis and Hitler. In 1948 Schmitz was convicted of war crimes and sentenced to two (2) years in prison. It has been suggested that if Standard Oil, Ford Motor Company and Dow Chemical had not sold to I.G. Farben and the Nazis, WWII could never have been launched. Since Hermann Schmitz was a convenient fall guy, Ford Motor, Standard Oil and Dow Chemical were never brought up on charges.

I.G. Farben supplied the following to the Nazis:

- 100% of the Zyklon B gas chamber gas
- 95% of all poison gases used in gas chambers
- 84% of the explosives used by all German armed forces
- 100% of the synthetic rubber used by the German armed forces
- 70% of the gunpowder used by all German armed forces
- 46% of the German aviation fuel

- 90% of the plastics used by the German armed forces
- 95% of the nickel used to make weapons
- 100% of the lubricating oil used by the German armed forces

Farben also operated Auschwitz, labor camps, used slave labor and conducted human experiments with Joseph Mengele. The list of atrocities committed by Farben is long and gruesome. The 1945 Potsdam Agreement called for the breakup of I.G Farben. It wasn't until 1951 that it changed its name and resumed business as Farbenfabriken Bay AG. In 1972 the name was again shortened to Bay AG. The post World War II Bayer is built on the ashes of millions of Jews, gypsies, dissidents, the racially impure and Russians. Bayer's roots are forever firmly planted in the manufacture of death from two world wars.

There have been more recent transgressions in the drug world but to list them here just becomes redundant. Do more investigative reading by looking up the history of Prozac and Ritalin on the Internet. These stories are tragic. Please note that the practice of Allopathy, the use of drugs to treat illness, supports drug companies who make and sell drugs, which in turn directly supports the FDA.

How does the FDA operate? They take payments from drug companies who want to introduce new drugs to market. The payment for the FDA to rubberstamp a new drug is 100 million dollars. The check should hopefully include any applicable lab testing guaranteeing the drug's safety. Often this step is brushed aside: witness the unexplained "new drug deaths" every year. The cost to bring drugs to market in the United States is astronomically high. This is where the patent process comes into play. Patents ensure seven (7) years of product copy protection before generics can be introduced. Example, first there was Viagra, now there is Levitra, Cialis etc. All exist for erectile dysfunction (ED). The first drug to market for ED was Viagra.

After the FDA signs off on your product, you are free to advertise and sell your new drug for the full 7 years without competition. A new drug, if marginally successful will pull in over 1 billion dollars a year.

Hippocrates said "Let food be your medicine and medicine be your food."

Hippocrates did not say, "Swallow dangerous chemical poisons and hope for the best."

WHAT IS IN YOUR MEDICINE CABINET?

9 Genesis of the Liver and Kidneys

Seconds after the moment of our conception, the first systems to go on line are our waste retrieval and removal systems. Call it a full-blown 24 hour a day / emergency filtering and processing system. All life, no matter how big or small is dependent on this exchange. No advanced organism can exist in a filthy environment of its own making.

Some organisms live on the waste of other organisms. But waste deriving from the same organism is dangerous to that organism.

This is not limited to life inside the body. These rules extend to every aspect of life on planet earth.

If you have ever found yourself standing in front of a construction site, watching as a building was being built or razed, there was the obligatory dumpster waiting to be filled. Sure this big long metal thing may have been an eye sore, but it had a very important purpose. What is the job of a dumpster? Its sole purpose is to collect waste for removal from the site. Waste of any size impedes production at every level of existence.
Garbage tends to be acidic and erodes the healthy tissue or organic life. There is a poem that many learned in grammar school that has also been performed in song. It was burned into my memory in my teens. It makes an indelible point about garbage, clearly illustrating the dangers of garbage and why our personal waste removal system is so important.

Circa 1970, Shel Silverstein penned this immortal poem:

Sarah Cynthia Sylvia Stout

Oh Sarah Cynthia Sylvia Stout
Would not take the garbage out!
She'd scrub the dishes and scrape the pans,
Cook the yams and spice the hams,
And though her parents would scream and shout,
She simply would not take the garbage out.

And so it piled up to the ceilings:
Coffee grounds, potato peelings,
Brown bananas, rotten peas,
Chunks of sour cottage cheese.

It filled the can it covered the floor,
It cracked the window and blocked the door
With bacon rinds and chicken bones,

Drippy ends of ice cream cones,
Prune pits, peach pits, orange peel,

Goopy clumps of cold oatmeal,
Pizza crust and withered greens,
Soggy beans and tangerines,

Crusts of black burned buttered toast,
Gristly bits of beefy roasts...

The garbage rolled on down the hall,
It raised the roof it broke the walls...

Greasy napkins, cookie crumbs,
Globs of gooey bubble gum,
Cellophane from green baloney,
Rubbery blubbery macaroni

Peanut butter, caked and dry,
Curdled milk and crusts of pie,
Moldy melons, dried-up mustard,
Eggshells mixed with lemon custard,
Cold French fries and rancid meat,
Yellow lumps of cream of wheat.
At last the garbage reached so high
That finally it touched the sky.

And all the neighbors moved away,
And none of her friends would come to play.

And finally said Sarah Cynthia Sylvia Stout,
"Ok, I'll take the garbage out!"

But then, of course, it was too late...
The garbage reached across the state,
It slithered from New York to the golden gate.

And there, in the garbage she did hate,
Poor Sarah met an awful fate,
That I cannot right now relate,
Because, the hour is much too late.

But children, remember Sarah Cynthia Sylvia Stout
And always take the garbage out!

As painful as the above poem may have been, you now hopefully have a much better appreciation for dumpsters and those who fill them. Imagine that there were no garbage men.

The Black Plague of the middle ages was made worse by the unclean conditions of Europe at the time. It was common to defecate in the streets and wade through ankle deep household waste dumped from the windows above. These conditions contributed to the unbelievable survival rate of the plague-carrying flea-ridden rats. At the same time, as you know, the rats carried the fleas that passed the plague via bites to humans.

How does this relate to our body?

You would not want garbage collecting in your house; the human body (and all organisms) is no different.

The first systems to go on line at conception follow the sequence below.

Conception

Blood or energy flow is established.

Simultaneously the liver and kidneys go on line.

Blastula / First - Second - Third Cell Divisions

Zygote

Embryo

Fetus

Birth

As the body develops, two organs (liver / kidneys) process our waste and safely excrete it. When you consider that all food before it can be used is also passed to the liver for processing, you get the full picture.

Without these two vital organs on line quickly, the human body (like any organism) would perish. The result is that, either the liver or kidneys regulate every function of our bodies. It is therefore imperative to keep these two filters up / running and happy.

Even today all life in the human body is dependent on the liver and kidneys.

NOW HOLD ONTO YOUR SEAT... ARE YOU HOLDING? HOLD TIGHTER!

Every malady of the body can be traced back to one of these two major organs.

How to think with what the Liver regulates

The liver regulates the skin of every organ of our body (including the skin itself). To your liver there is no difference between the skin of your pancreas or leg. To the body, anything that coats anything is skin and is under the watchful eye of the liver. The liver also regulates ALL hollow organs.

Therefore your lungs, sinuses, nasal cavities, colon, intestines, uterus and mouth are under the domain of the liver. Your liver regulates the skin of your mouth, tongue and gums. This also extends down to the hollow of your ears, throat (or esophagus), into your stomach. Yet your kidneys regulate your equilibrium.

Your kidneys regulate all organs NOT hollow. This list includes all muscles, the brain, tendons, ligaments, cartilage and the heart (to name a few), all regulated by your kidneys.

This means that a cancer (just an evil word for toxic mass) that shows up on the outside (or inside) of any organ (this includes melanoma) is at its source, a liver problem. Treating any problem such as "surface cancer" as a liver problem solves the problem.

On the other hand "deep tissue cancer" is at its source a kidney problem. If you address each problem correctly, your results will be excellent every time.

You might ask, "Should I work on both the kidneys and liver at the same time"? The answer is of course, yes. You can never make a mistake doing liver support and kidney support at the same time.

To capsulate, the liver and kidney dominate the function of the entire body head to toe. As a result, if you made it your job to help turn on your liver and kidneys and then keep them running, you would be very wise.

With the above data really understood, all of your health choices / health repair choices become uncomplicated. All you have to do is understand your symptoms and they will dictate your actions. With a little practice and attention, this does become trouble-free.

How to think with what the Kidneys regulate

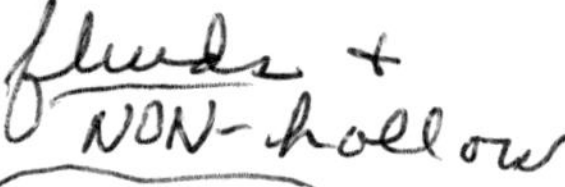

The kidneys are solely responsible for all fluids of your body. They regulate blood pressure, the fluid of the eye, blood, saliva, your sweat, your tears and urine. They also regulate all the fluids made by the other organs and their movements in the body, including bile.

The fluid in your system transports waste from its current location to the processing point for its final handling. Your kidneys must process lactic acid (the result of physical exertion or muscle stress) that is found in the muscle. When it is present to any degree the muscle affected will feel tired, sore and stiff. Muscle cannot fully repair until this fluid is removed after you work out.

If you have ever worked out and felt the "burn", what has taken place was a slight tearing of the muscle. Lactic acid produced by muscle activity is present at the point of the torn muscle. The muscle, if this activity is repeated over a period of days or weeks, grows back larger. Thus we have bodybuilding.

Uric Acid can be found all over the body, as it is a byproduct of destroyed cells. Uric acid is like spent uranium from nuclear fission in the body. Anywhere uric acid is lying stagnant; there will be irritation and some swelling. When allopathic medicine notices sore joints, they call it arthritis. It is just unmoving uric acid creating the pain and swelling. Gout is a severe form of the same phenomena.

These symptoms are the telling signs of weak kidneys. The medical profession does not understand this relationship at all. They want you to purchase drugs to suppress your systems. If you also listen to the ads for drugs, they warn of kidney problems associated with their use. Amazing!

Two Rules/Facts

1) The kidneys process Uric Acid. This acid can be found anywhere in the body but it harbors in the joints. Once there it causes irritation and pain. A large percentage of diagnosed arthritis is actually due to kidney overload, as weak kidneys will have trouble sweeping the joints free of uric acid.

2) The kidneys process Lactic Acid. This acid can be found in the muscle after physical activity of any kind. Once generated, uric acid causes irritation and pain. Sore aching muscles are actually due to kidney overload and lack of processing power. Weak kidneys will have trouble sweeping the body free of lactic acid and uric acid.

The moment you are labeled with "has arthritis" and you agree with it, finding the true answer becomes an unlikely prospect. Your medical doctor is unaware of this data. Later in this book you will learn how to test the origins of your arthritis-like symptoms.

Remember, unless your doctor is your partner in your health, he is your advisory. Doctors who insist what is right regardless of what is right must be let go. If your doctor insists that you have arthritis and he will not consider other possibilities (such as he is wrong), get a new doctor.

Arthritis is just a symptom of weak kidneys. I have corrected thousands with extreme symptoms; yours should be no more challenging. Turn on your kidneys and turn off your pain.

It was these kinds of observations that led the Chinese to call the kidneys, "The Master Organ", in large part because of the massive job they undertake. The heart has a job this large and the kidneys too regulate it. The heart may pump the blood but the kidneys monitor it and then keep us healthy moment to moment.

Remember, your kidneys need you to understand them to best survive.

10 Understanding Your Body Clock

Many modalities and traditions recognize the function of the human internal body clock. The existence of this invisible apparatus is not argued by anyone except the uniformed. Yet not everyone knows when and what the body is repairing throughout the day. Few people realize that every organ of the body has a repair or maintenance period. Think of it like the days before cable TV when TV signed off at 1:00 am. Suddenly, all programming would cease (except on the local station which might be playing an old black and white). First, you would see a waving American Flag (in the U.S.) and listen to an instrumental of the Star Spangled Banner. Then you would get a second or two of snow. Finally, the "Test Pattern Indian Chief" would then dominate your TV screen until morning, when programming would resume. You would also be serenaded with a continuous tone (like a hearing test tone). For all those in the dark about what a test pattern Indian is, go to Google and type in 'test patterns' and look at the images.

The purpose of this time period was to do technical adjustments for the next day's broadcasts. In the dark days when there were only 13 local channels, life was rough.

Likewise, each day, whether you like it or not, your body will try to repair the damage done to it from the previous days, weeks, months, years and tens of years. During these cycles you may feel tired, worn out, sluggish, irritable, foggy, etc. If you do, your body is trying to repair major damage and the feelings you have are caused by the energy expended in the repair process.

These are all classic liver symptoms, which I will cover later in this book

You are about to read the body clock table that has been foreshadowed in the previous paragraphs. More than likely you have never been exposed to this before. It involves the times of the day that your internal organs repair themselves. It is a common question to ask what influences these times. Is it the sun, moon, stars, habits?

All biological organisms are subject to the same natural phenomena from one species to another, from the largest to the smallest. There are no exceptions.

For example, Idaho farmers know that if potatoes are planted in a waxing (lighted area increasing) moon they will take root and grow. This has been verified by science when they took potatoes indoors to the labs. They discovered it did not matter if the potatoes were exposed to the moon or kept in a dark room, they would only grow correctly when they were planted during a waxing moon. In the early Chinese texts, it is said that we should rise with the sun and sleep when the sun sets. Another example of this is in the aquatic world where there is a changing of the guard at sunset as nocturnal animals take over the great reefs as day turns to night.

Man has been trying to beat this natural law and reshape his life. He has attempted to manipulate nature by ignoring it. It is a very unsuccessful thing to do, trying to fool Mother Nature. A single man can get used to a reverse schedule of sleeping in the daytime. It will play havoc on the body for weeks or months if it is adhered to. The worst possible schedule is the one that is constantly in flux (day sleeping, night sleeping, day sleeping, etc.). Third shift can be difficult to adjust to as well. While your body clock will continue to run the same program, it may slowly alter.

Mankind is not immune or above mutation. In just two generations we have seen the usual robust head of hair replaced by the shaved head. What is driving these phenomena? Is it cool to be bald or is there something else at work? Just as girls are experiencing adolescence at an earlier and earlier age, humans are going bald as a group. The same force that is making young girls full figured and busty at an earlier and earlier age is mutating all of mankind. I will cover this later in these pages. Mutation is a result of powerful forces pushing life to adapt or succumb. These forces can occur due to climatory change (ice age, etc) or directly due to man's changing habits. As a result, if all males suddenly became solely nocturnal it might only be two or three generations before males would have better night vision than females.

Burning the candle at both ends and "second shift work" will take its toll on the individual attempting to live such a lifestyle. Like it or not nature is inflicting forces on all of us that we are only partially aware of. The tides that crash on our shores drive nature and the planet, and will continue to affect us regardless of how we fight it. When we sleep as nature does at sunset and then rise with the sun, we will be healthier and survive better. Nature does not care about our schedules but it will influence us whether we like it or not. The spud and plankton cannot fight with universal forces they can only react to them.

"If man is not affected in-some-way by the Moon he is the only thing on Earth that isn't", (Robert Millikan, 1868-1953, U.S. physicist and 1923 Nobel Prize winner). This, of course, explains why you feel so badly when you are off your schedule, are up all night or pull a shift 48 hours long. To make this chart work for you, apply it exactly by the clock as your body is going to follow the tides as all life has for millions of years.

"Every Cause has its Effect; every Effect has its Cause; everything happens according to Law; Chance is but a name for Law not recognized; there are many planes of causation, but nothing escapes the Law."
– *The Kybalion, 4th Principal of the Hermetic Principles*

"Everything flows, out and in; everything has its tides; all things rise and fall; the pendulum-swing manifests in everything; the measure of the swing to the right is the measure of the swing to the left; rhythm compensates."
– *The Kybalion, 5th Principal of the Hermetic Principles*

The following table is a hybrid of my earlier works. It is now possible to chart what your body will be experiencing at anytime of the day. If more data is uncovered, this chart will morph again.

The repair times of your body:

a) Lungs / Eyes / Liver / Large Intestines — 3 am - 5 am

b) Large Intestine / Lungs / Eyes / Liver — 5 am - 7 am

c) Stomach / Lungs / Respiratory System / Liver — 7 am - 9 am

d) Spleen / Heart / Kidneys / Liver 9 am - 11 am
e) Heart / Kidneys / Liver 11 am - 1 pm
f) Intestines / Heart / Adrenal Glands / Liver / Kidneys 1 pm - 3 pm
g) Bladder / Reproductive System / Kidneys/ Liver 3 pm - 5 pm
h) Kidneys / Joints / Muscle / Reproductive System / Liver 5 pm - 7 pm
I) Pancreas / Circulatory & Endocrine System / Kidneys / Liver 7 pm - 9 pm
j) Circulatory System / Endocrine System / Kidneys/ Liver 9 pm - 11 pm
k) Gallbladder / Liver / Kidneys / Transverse colon 11 pm - 1 am
l) Liver / Kidneys / Transverse colon 1 am - 3 am

This list is the result of years of research and is complete. You will notice that the liver and kidneys play a role in every function of the body. Consequently all repair of the body can be modified by this knowledge. With this table you can forecast what issues you will have at various times of the day. How you use this data will dictate how good you feel. You will also know what organs and systems have been causing your health issues

There are exact phenomena that take place when the body is in the repair mode. I will address each of these points one at a time.

Morning symptoms 3-9 AM

Coughing
Sneezing
Runny nose
Itching skin
Itching scalp
Itching throat
Itching inner ear
Watery eyes / burning eyes / itchy eyes
Need to evacuate your colon (bowel movement)
Crabby / moody / irritable

****Support your morning by supporting your liver and digestive tract*

Mid morning symptoms 9 AM - 1 PM

Tight chest
Heart double beating
Heart skipping a beat
Heart triple beating
Low back pain
Left shoulder pain
Left side of the neck pain
Joint pain
Ringing in the ears
High blood pressure
Slight fever (1 degree or less)

****Support your kidneys and heart via your kidneys.*

Mid afternoon - Mid evening symptoms 1 - 11 PM

- Bloating / gas
- Blood pressure fluctuations
- Low back pain
- Bladder discomfort
- Energy low or drifting / Lethargy
- Moody / Irritable
- Reproductive performance issues
- Cold hands, feet or feeling cold
- Feeling hot
- Itching inner ear

******Support your digestive tract, kidneys and liver***

Late night - Early morning symptoms 11 PM - 3 AM

- Right side rib pain
- Moody / Irritable
- Eye irritation or blurring
- Itchy skin
- Insomnia
- Restless sleep / Tossing and turning
- Frequent urination
- Right shoulder pain and stiffness
- Left shoulder pain and stiffness
- Leg cramps
- Bloated or irritated abdomen
- Pressure in the abdomen

11 Inner Anatomy Keys

As explained in the previous chapter, the body is executing exact processes at precise times of our 24-hour day. Early in the morning your body is going through a variety of processes that all involve starting the day. To rise with the sun we need oxygen, energy, less internal waste and finally vision to see the world. All of these systems are dependent on the liver for support. You may be one of the many people who wake up coughing or sneezing as if every day starts with an allergy. Your scalp or skin may itch as if you have fleas. You might be moody or tight lipped in the morning. You may struggle with mucus-filled eyes.

Your internal systems are just resetting themselves. A completely healthy system will not experience these issues. But once you and your energy are balanced, symptoms subside or never occur in the first place. Your symptoms directly correlate to your diet and lifestyle. The better you are the better you can be.

The 3 parts or your colon are; the ascending colon, starting just above your right hip and stretching up to the bottom of your rib cage on your right side; the transverse colon, starting just below the right side of your rib cage and crawling across your abdomen to the bottom of your left rib cage, and the descending colon starting just below the left side of your rib cage and drops down to the rectum, where evacuation takes place.

The colon needs to be lubricated for evacuation to take place. It must flush and process waste matter around the clock. Dedicated and routine morning intake of water / fresh juice is vital for proper colon / intestinal function. Again, the most important time to give your colon fluid is in the morning. Fluids need to be ingested little by little around the clock, but morning intake is critical.

Without question caffeine is one of the worst substances you can ever put in your body. Why? Because caffeine is a diuretic, a diuretic diverts water away from your colon causing your colon to paralyze. With caffeine present, your entire system crashes to rock solid standstill. Do not ever consume caffeine-bearing drinks. You cannot be at your healthiest with caffeine as health and caffeine are incongruous. The body must have plentiful amounts of water and fresh juices, period.

The results of a body deprived of water are obvious as the body will be or experience; weakness, constipation, sluggish, fatigue, weight gain, increased blood pressure, heart attacks, immune system dysfunction, kidney disorders including diabetes, aches /pains, bad moods, poor skin, poor sleep, insomnia, allergies and more.

By irrigating your system every morning with fluid (12 to 20 ounces or up to ? a liter of water or fresh juice), you give yourself the best chance to be healthy. Some people wait until their first elimination of the day before they eat anything solid. This does work, as it is a signal that your digestive tract has caught up on its work. Ideally you should never use something to cause the elimination, as you are only masking the problem, but not solving it. This does not mean that there is no application for a good colon formula or herb, but chronic use is never recommended. Recapping, the colon knows when it is ready to start the day and will signal you via elimination. A healthy colon runs itself.

The Stomach: In the morning, it is vital to give the stomach as little stress as possible. The wrong thing to do is eat a big meal in the morning. This does not negate the old standard that "Breakfast is the most important meal of the day." In reality, it is true, yet eating anything that needs any digestion in the morning is a mistake. Oatmeal, cereal, toast, eggs, all meat, pancakes, scrambled eggs, protein bars, protein drinks all need digestion, as does so much more.

The morning meal should consist of fresh: fruit, juices and vegetables. You can also include freshly made smoothies from your favorite juice bar. For those who need more protein, include a raw egg or two in your smoothie. The reason for eating this way is to make the morning digestive process distress free. All of the above items digest themselves, and therefore require the body to do very little. Another great item in the morning is green salad (with no meat or cheese), which I eat every day. Salad is another item that due to its plentiful live enzymes allows the body to heal itself. Whenever you eat a meal that digests itself, the body uses its energy to correct its problems.

Recap: Eating easily digested fresh fruit; fresh juice, salads or water is necessary if you are to start your day successfully.

The Spleen: Sits behind the stomach and above the diaphragm. It is a somewhat misunderstood organ. It works hand in glove with the liver and kidneys to form the hub of our immune system. It produces antibodies whenever there is an infection. It is constantly monitoring the blood for such invaders. Without a healthy spleen even a common cold could be fatal. If you thought of the spleen as a pre-liver you would basically be right. Should your spleen be stressed with work during its repair cycle, you may feel weak experience allergies or mild cold-like symptoms. The same successful treatments for the liver are also good for the spleen. Again, think of your spleen as a pre-liver, which is an accurate description.

The Heart: When it is healthy is about the size of your fist. It should beat 60 to 70 beats a minute for the average healthy person at rest. An athlete can have a resting pulse in the 40s. The only rest the heart gets is between beats. The fewer beats your heart executes per minute the less wear and tear it will experience. Amazingly, as the heart enters its repair cycle (as seen in the chart in the last chapter), 70% of all heart attacks occur (as per the Framingham study).

The Small Intestines: Your small intestines coils like a snake through 20 feet of your abdominal cavity. Its mass dominates your belly and is the culprit as soon as you are bloated. When you feel any discomfort in your abdomen, your small intestine is in some degree distressed. You may feel indigestion, bloating, pain, intense pressure or spasms. When the Ileoceco Valve (the connection between the small intestines and the ascending colon, just above the right hip) is blocked, you will feel pain or blockage in that region. Many people think this is a bladder issue or appendicitis. Some women who experience this believe it is a uterine issue when in actual fact it is just an Ileoceco valve blockage issue.

When the small intestine is running slow you may very well feel and look a bit fat. Either way, a proper diet is needed or the intestines will bloat and your midsection will become distended (you will look fat).

The Kidneys, Bladder, Pancreas, For thousands of years the Chinese have said that the kidneys are the master organs of the human body. Later, when you read all the function that they perform, you will wholeheartedly agree. Your kidneys filter all of the fluid of your body; regulate protein synthesis, spent protein removal, and collect lactic acid, uric acid and much more. Think of your kidneys as the water filter and pumping company for the body. If your joints or muscles need to be flushed, it is the kidneys that direct the clean up. As the body is 70% water, you can appreciate the importance of your kidneys. When the kidneys are going through their repair cycle, various symptoms may occur, such as, fatigue (needing a nap), sore muscles, left shoulder pain, ankle pain, intense craving for sweets, intense carving for meat, frequent urination, sore joints, reproductive failure or issues, ringing in the ears, vertigo (dizziness) and more. During these times, eat grapes, tomatoes and citrus, as these help to reset the kidneys and all that they regulate.

They regulate all mucus production and its pickup and disposal.

The Liver / Gallbladder / Endocrine System / Circulatory System: The liver sits just under and a little below the right side of the ribcage. It is a warehouse of chemicals and vitamins used to break down matter into usable food. It also works to dilute poisons and then excrete them from the body. It does not actually absorb or hold toxins; it is strictly a processing plant similar to a sewage facility. Along with the kidneys it regulates energy, clarity of thought, emotions, brightness of vision, right shoulder pain, skin, lungs, and the digestive tract. It also regulates the lungs, sinuses and sleep. The liver and kidneys modify the endocrine system. Yet the kidneys primarily regulate all glands including the Pituitary, Hypothalamus, Pineal, Thyroid and Parathyroid, Adrenals, Ovaries and Testes. All of these glands produce hormones that adjust temperature, blood flow, energy, muscle function and more. When these systems are off you may feel weaker, tired, exhausted, stressed, sleepless, task obsessed, restless, moody, hot or cold and off sexually. If you understand that all non-optimum functions of the body, are caused by continual contact with toxins, then you are on your way to correcting your body and your life. These systems respond to citrus, i.e. oranges, grapefruit, tangerines, lemons, limes and fruit in general including grapes and tomatoes.

12 Herbs by Their Action

I am forever being asked to explain the proper herb for the proper problem. Years of work, and hands on experience have revealed the following. A word of note, never use any herb or formula that forces the body to do something against its will. Example: using Uva Ursa Root to cleanse the kidneys is a bad idea as is an astringent and will cause the kidneys to spasm and release fluid.

To heal the body you must introduce substances to aid the body in naturally resetting itself, not forcing it off its schedule. I have attached some asterisks (*) to herbs that overpower the body. To be sure of their actions, look them up. There is no reason why you should not be an expert in healing yourself.

The only organs that can be safely flushed out are the colon, sinuses, lungs and skin. The liver regulates all of these organs.

LIVER

- Dandelion
- Gentian
- Bupleurum
- Beet Root
- False Unicorn
- Tribulus Terrestris
- Dong Quai Root
- Peony Root
- Hyssop Root
- Chinese Mint Leaf
- Phyllanthus
- Artichoke
- Schizandra
- Chinese Skull Cap
- Reishi Mushroom
- Hyssop
- Wasabi Japonica

KIDNEY

Gravel Root**
Uva Ursa Root**
False Unicorn
Tribulus Terrestris
Corn Silk**
Cinnamon Bark
Borage
Cedar
Red Raspberry
Pygeum Bark
Holy Basil
Beet Root
Lycci Fructus
Agrimony
Aspen
Astragalus
Black haw
Buchu
Bugleweed
Burdock
Bush clover
California poppy
Canadian fleabane
Cattail
Cedar
Celery seed**
Chickweed
Chlorophyll
Cleavers
Cramp bark
Horsetail - Equisetum spp.
Irish moss
Juniper
Kava-kava**
Mallow
Marshmallow**
Mullein root
Nettles
Oatstraw
Parsley
Plantain
Poke Root
Prickly Ash
St. Johns Wort
Saw palmetto
Shepherd's purse
Silk Tassel
Skullcap
Stoneroot**
Sweet sumac
Wild hydrangea**
Wild yam**
Yarrow
Yellow Jessamine
Yellow pond lily
Yerba Santa
Squawvine leaves
Damiana Leaves
Corydalis

Many of these herbs for kidneys are diuretics that force the kidneys to expel fluid. This is not recommended. Your kidneys can and should run themselves. If they are not constantly poisoned with sugars, sodium and junk food, they will heal. Please use herbs and formulas for the kidneys that support their function rather than forcing them "off line" by either retaining fluid or expelling fluid. If allowed to be healthy, the kidneys keep you healthy.

INTESTINES AND COLON

Cascara Sagrada
Psyllium Husk
Burdock Root
Buckthorn Bark
Black Walnut Hulls
Wormwood
Senna
Fedegosso
Black Sesame Seeds
Flax Seed
Rhubarb Root
Aloe
African Bird Peppers
Habanero Pepper
Boldo Leaves
Buchu Leaves
Slippery Elm Bark
Fenugreek

Our immune system is supposed to recognize anything that is foreign and destroy it. But, depending on diet, it could be running at 30% of capacity, or worse. Cells in the circulatory and the lym-

phatic systems perform this recognition and destruction on an hourly basis. These cells are produced in the bone marrow and lymphatic tissue (thymus, lymph nodes, spleen and tonsils).

Whenever we take a part of the lymphatic system out, it is weakened. Prior to 1975, it was common to have the tonsils taken out. In recent years, the procedure is not nearly as common. These fearless cells are called "stem cells." Now that you know a little more about Stem Cells, forget what you know. Stem Cells without a body to work in are useless. A parachute is no good to a skydiver unless he is wearing it.

A healthy body produces all the stem cells it needs. The harvesting of Stem Cells for experimentation takes us down the road to Frankenstein's Castle. There is no point to goofing around with our chemistry if we understand the basics of life.

Focus on the bigger picture of your WHOLE BODY. Remember, you can't see much of the elephant by studying its tail. When I speak of the immune system, I mean the whole body fighting a whole problem, not some fragmentation.

When we look at the body as a whole, and not as independent separate parts, as modern allopathic medicine does, we can solve issues in a sane manner. Holistic means whole, and the body is a whole organ with circuits and meridians that connect as a whole. If one part of the body is affected, every cell of the body is affected. In other words, what you do to your toe affects your hair as well. Our immune system is composed of the liver, kidneys, lungs, spleen, lymphatic system and more. When experts talk about organ detoxification or similar compartmentalization, they are making a fundamental error. The error is in breaking down bodily functions into segments rather than addressing the totality of the body.

GENERAL IMMUNE SYSTEM

- Golden Seal Root
- Echinacea Root
- Astragalus Root
- Lime Flower
- Schizandra
- Lavender Flower
- Cats Claw
- Suma
- Anise Seed
- Una De Gato
- Ashwagandha
- Olive Leaf
- Hyssop
- Royal Jelly
- White Peony Root
- Corydalis
- Panax Ginseng
- Figwort
- Poke Root
- Juniper Berries
- Red Clover

13 Body / Health Indicators

Healing requires not book sense but human sense. One must use all of their faculties to understand the indicators or the body. Relying on idiot gauges (x-ray, MRI, microscopes, stethoscopes etc,) today's practitioners have gotten lazy and are not taught to observe. They are taught to study readouts but not their own patients. Today's doctors are educated in the theory of sickness and the administering of drugs but not how to restore health. To heal anyone, you must look, smell, touch and listen.

Step one: look at the color of the individual. What is his color? Is he pasty white? Grey? Is he ruddy? Is the skin almost transparent where veins are very clear and vivid? The more extreme the skin tone is from its ideal, the more unbalanced the individual is.

Step two: How long has this condition been present?

Step three: What has the person been eating? What we eat will affect us immediately. When bad eating habits are continually practiced, the body will break down faster. Often the current body complaints are directly tied to what we had in the last 24 hours or less.

Step four: Notice the smell of the body. Sickness does not smell healthy. It is pungent and stale. Does the body smell or is it just the breath? The less foul odor emanating from the body, the better indicator it is for a quick recovery.

Step five: Evaluate the posture. The more erect the stance, the stronger the will, and stronger the life energy of the body.

Step six: Eye color, are they grey or bright? The more grey and dull they are, the more the immune system is compromised.

Step seven: Back of hand skin elasticity. Hand should be flat / straight, not in a fist. Is the skin tension loose or taught? Does the skin immediately snap back to the hand or is it slow? The better the skin tension on the back of the hands the better. The right hand indicates the state of the liver and its corresponding organs and the left hand indicates the same data for the kidneys. The better the body is hydrated, the quicker the body will recover.

Step eight: Is the person hot (running a fever)? Fever is an obvious indicator of an infection being fought.

Step nine: Are there parts of the body that are cold? These areas are not receiving energy flow. If you understand what organ (liver or kidney) dominates this area of the body, you will further know what to correct.

Old time Osteopaths, Naturopaths and any good practitioner knew the value of these points and always used them. These simple observations are senior to x-rays, MRI's, Stethoscopes and other device dependent tests.

Doctors and healers from pre-history to 1940's often gave prescriptions that included rest, sun, water, fresh food, fresh juices and various herbs. They used nature to heal the body as the body was derived from nature and needed nature to heal.

Quant as this happens to sound; the above paragraph gives the key to understanding and healing the body. Allopathic doctors do not care about quaint or effective. They are focused on not being wrong based on insurance, laws suits and AMA membership and guidelines.

Armed with what you learn in this book, if you stay focused on face reading for diagnostic purposes and employ all the gifts that I give you, you cannot fail.

You will be amazed at what you can do and achieve.

When will you know that you are successful with these techniques and face reading? When what you observe leads to long-range, positive and accurate applications and gains. You can do this, and you can be expert in it.

Remember the last time you or a friend / loved one was sick? What did they look like? What was the color of their skin? What did their eyes look like? Did they look older? Did they look tired? We always look different when we are "off." Use these tools. Use these tools. Use these tools.

If you have noticed, the face always looks different depending on the following factors:

A. How much sleep we have gotten.
B. How much water we have consumed
C. The use of caffeine
D. Use of drugs
E. Consumption of salt or sodium.
F. What kind of diet we have had over a period of hours or years
G. Heredity
H. Environmental factors
I. Habits and routines
J. Use of tobacco
K. Use of alcohol

When toxins physically tax us, we demonstrate the fact like a neon sign. Your internal organs are working overtime. From the early physicians such as Hippocrates, and the Shaman and Indian medicine men before him, healers used observation to diagnose.

These early practitioners were good because they practiced and honed their skills.

This book is dedicated to the precise time-proven, ancient technique of diagnostic analysis, via empirical observation. You can know what Hippocrates knew and of course what I know, as I am going to teach you through this book.

14 The History of Face Reading

Man has always tried to predict the future and control his environment. Lacking a deep perception of human motives and fear of the unknown, EARLY MAN was grasping at straws. How can anyone protect their family, personal interests and trust friends without a system of detection?

This was the plight of man. Create a system to identify who were friend or foe or risk danger and perhaps even death.

Some of the greatest minds in the ancient world took on these challenges. Since the face was how man was identified, it was logical to study the face and head for clues. Greek philosophers, Socrates (469-399 BC), Plato (427-347 BC), and Aristotle (384-322 BC) all speculated on the nature of man.

Aristotle appears to be the source of an early form of face reading called Physiognomy. It tried to predict actions and personality. For the first 1500 years or so man took many wayward attempts at prediction that led directly into fantasy.

The stirrings brought on by Socrates and passed down to Plato, who then instilled them in Aristotle, led him to speculate that a chart on face reading of a different sort was possible. His attempts compared man to beast and healthy to unhealthy.

Aristotle said that:

> *"Thick, bulbous noses belong to persons who are insensitive and swinish."*
>
> *"Sharp-lipped noses belong to persons who are irritable and easily provoked, like dogs."*
>
> *"Rounded noses belong to generous, lion-like individuals."*

He was credited with the following formula:

Round foreheads add x 1% to honesty and x 2% to intellect

Large noses add x Y1% to will power.

Clearly, an esoteric formula, Aristotle's scribing proved basically nothing but did not tarnish his reputation. Nevertheless, even with the bizarre postulations in Aristotle's early work, his empirical study led to much advancement in the field of healing. The world of healing did not start with Aristotle and the Greeks, far from it. Man wanted to know about man long before this.

The concept of face reading is as old as man himself. Prior to man building monoliths and monuments, pyramids and palaces, there were caves and cave walls for painting. His own reflection in stream water was captivating, but his fellow man was fascinating. He had to understand. He also thirsted to know who he was and what made him tick. Early medicine was not enough. Even the casual observer could see that a sick man not only smelled different, he looked different. What was really at work? What did it all mean?

To appreciate DIAGNOSTIC FACE READING, you have to know what it is and what it is not.

BELOW IS WHAT DIAGNOSTIC FACE READING IS NOT.

PHYSIOGNOMY

From Webster's 1913 Dictionary:
Physiognomy, Phys`i*og"no*my\, n.; pl. {Physiognomies}. Etymology: OE.fisonomie, phisonomie, fisnamie, OF. phisonomie, F. physiognomie, physiognomonie, from Gr. ?; fy`sis nature + ? one who knows or examines, a judge, fr. ?, ?, to know.

1. The art and science of discovering the predominant temper, and other characteristic qualities of the mind, by the outward appearance, especially by the features of the face.

PHRENOLOGY

From Webster's 1913 Dictionary:
Phrenology: \Phre*nol"o*gy\, n.
Etymology: Gr. ?, ?, the mind + -logy: cf. F. phr['e]nologie.

1. In popular usage, the physiological hypothesis of Gall that the mental faculties, and traits of character, are shown on the surface of the head or skull; craniology.

PERSONOLOGY

The Skeptics Dictionary
Personology is a recent "New Age" variant of the ancient pseudoscience of Physiognomy, which is closely related to the disproved study of Phrenology. It is a system of face reading that purports to show a correlation between a person's physical features and appearance, and the person's behavior, personality and character. Mainstream science considers Personology to be a wholly false pseudoscience.

The dirt on Personology: Edward Jones, who developed Personology in the 1930s, was a Los Angeles judge. According to Naomi Tickle, author of "It's all in the Face -The Key to Finding

Your Life Purpose" (1997), "Jones became fascinated by those who appeared before him in court. He felt there was a relationship between facial features and behavior patterns" Jones believed there was a direct and undeniable correlation between what people looked like, and what they did in life. He was certain he knew who the criminals were on sight. His theories / musings became well known in the early 1930s.

When his practices were put to the test in a controlled trial, he failed miserably. Personology was dead by the end of 1935 and Jones, a laughing stock.

The true history of the above three attempts at "mankind prediction" are fascinating reading and important to understand as you again must know what DIAGNOSTIC FACE READING is to really understand what it is not.

The first book on record concerning face reading which devoted itself to the study and comparison of humans was Giovanni Battista Della Porta's De Humana Physiognomonia 1586. In this book, he made comparisons of humans to animals and attempted to predict aggressive behavior. This study of internal character from external appearances - most notably the face - was a partly aesthetic and partly philosophical practice, which preceded phrenology. Its main advocate in the late eighteenth century was the Swiss clergyman J. G. Lavater (1741-1801) in his Physiognomical Fragments (1775-1778). Thanks to his labors, he and his themes started to become popular. Much of the work in these early practices have been lost, some of the more recent advancements are still with us. Even though this book is not based or devoted to these earlier works, it is important to note them and understand something of them.

Battista Della Porta's vast work led to lectures and many later books by Charles Le Brun circa 1698 (the head of the French Academy). Physiognomy became popular thanks to the frenetic work of Le Brun and several other late 18th and 19th century French doctors who specialized and reveled in the subject.

It wasn't long until the new term Phrenology was coined. It is derived from the Greek roots: phren: 'mind' and logos: 'study/discourse'. *"[Before phrenology] all we knew about the brain was how to slice it..."*
- R. Chenevix (phrenologist), 1828.

Phrenology was a forerunner to present day psychology and psychiatry. The term came into general use around 1819/1820 in Britain. The physician T.I.M. Forster coined phrenology, as a term. In fact if you take a look at the placement of this often sneered at pseudoscience, you will see its rise led directly to experiments on the brain including the lobotomy*, shock treatment and the frontal orbital leucotomy* (a procedure of shoving an ice pick up through the top of both eye sockets, then thrusting it into the frontal lobe of the brain using an arc motion, thus destroying vital nerve centers, leaving the patient dormant, intensely angry and often suicidal).

** I go into depth on both of these subjects in the chapter, YOUR LIVER AND MOODS.*

Phrenology's brain studies eventually led to skull study. This because, as per phrenology, the indentations and bumps in the skull were studied in order to establish personality. These studies led to the disparaging term Bumpology. Ridicule was often levied at phrenology for two reasons,

1) It was a fairly ridiculous notion to read the ridges and low points of the skull to establish behavior.

2) Due to a relative lack of training needed to perform Phrenology, it attracted various rogue elements, which sought only to increase their reputation. With everybody from psychics to pub owners attempting to pick up the "skill", it lowered the perceived value of the entire movement. Misguided as they were, many of the 19th-century phrenologists called it "the only true science of mind." And now Phrenology had reached the Americas thanks to Viennese physician Franz

Joseph Gall (1758-1828) From 1913 Encyclopedia Britannica, "Note: Gall marked out on his model of the head the places of twenty-six organs, as round enclosures with vacant interspaces. Spurzheim and Combe divided the whole scalp into oblong and conterminous patches."

Gall laid down the basic tenets of Phrenology, which were:

1. The brain is the organ of the mind.
2. The mind is composed of multiple distinct, innate faculties.
3. Because they are distinct, each faculty must have a separate seat or "organ" in the brain.
4. The size of an organ, other things being equal, is a measure of its power.
5. The shape of the brain is determined by the development of the various organs.
6. As the skull takes its shape from the brain, the surface of the skull can be read as an accurate index of psychological aptitudes and tendencies.

Number 1-5 above are clearly off in left field, ignoring the presence of a soul or life force that is free of the body, but most will agree that number 6 is not only off in left field, it is in left field in another state.

Remember "Bumpology"?

Physiognomy led to Phrenology, which led to the short-lived Personology.

But there were satellite studies that accidentally / intentionally linked previous work to anthropology which would later enhance Phrenology. Personology was coming next and, with a little imagination, you will be able to see the connection.

Simultaneously various European scientists studying anthropology such as Petrus Camper (1722 - 1789) started to blend with Physiognomy.

A Dutch naturalist, Camper, developed a similar physiognomical theory based on facial angle, which was a great influence on contemporary and nineteenth-century aesthetics and anthropology. Camper's facial angle was based on comparative anatomy and prescribed that the more vertical the angle of a straight line drawn from the chin to forehead, the closer to the ideal head, the classical head being assumed as the epitome of aesthetic and anatomical perfection.

Camper provided diagrams in his posthumous Über den natürlichen Unterschied der Gesichtszüge (1792) showing a scale of perfection from monkeys at the bottom of the scale, to an Apollo at the termination. Camper's facial angle would later be joined with phrenology in nineteenth-century racial anthropology.

Johann Friedrich Blumenbach (1752 - 1840), a German naturalist and anthropologist, introduced and developed the science of comparative anatomy in Germany. His De Generis Humani Varietate Nativa (1775; tr. "On the Natural Varieties of Mankind", 1865, repr. 1969) marked the beginnings of physical anthropology and described the five divisions of mankind that have been the basis of all subsequent racial classifications. Via his foundation of his craniometrical research (analysis of human skulls, published as Collectio Craniorum Diversarum Gentium), he divided the human species into five races: the Caucasian or white race, the Mongolian or yellow, the Malayan or brown race, the Negro or black race, and the American or red race. Apart from physical characteristics, he assigned psychological characteristics.

In Blumenbach's day, physical characteristics like skin color, cranial profile, etc., went hand in hand with declarations of group character and aptitude. The "fairness" and relatively high brows of "Caucasians" were held to be apt physical expressions of a loftier mentality and a more generous spirit.

The epicanthic folds around the eyes of "Mongolians" and their slightly sallow outer epidermal layer bespoke their supposedly crafty, literal-minded nature. The dark skin and relatively sloping craniums of "Ethiopians" were taken as wholesale proof of a closer genetic proximity to the primates, despite the fact that the skin of chimpanzees and gorillas beneath the hair is whiter than the average "Caucasian" skin and that orangutans and some monkey species have foreheads fully as vertical as any human of any race

The work was mysterious and fostered much curiosity. This calls to mind what the great Greek philosopher Plato said, "Everything that deceives may be said to enchant." Due to this mystery, it became the temporary rage of Europe and the Americas. The aforementioned researchers arduously labored to establish "Body types" for predicting personality, character traits, honesty, capacity to rear children and more.

In the early 1900s, the work of Orson Squire Fowler (1809 - 1887) was used as the new Personology / Phrenology springboard. Criminologists often attempted to use facial analysis for spotting criminals, with faulty results.

This brings us full circle back to our laughable 1930s judge, Edward Jones. People's criminal motives while at times being sensed, do not show up on the face. With his public failures and embarrassment, it is a wonder that face reading, even on a diagnostic health front, didn't die altogether.

Some of the old terminology found in Phrenology is still in use today. At present, there are still Phrenology terms found in our language such as, "High / Low Brow", "Bull Headed" etc. Now these phrases have a completely different meaning and have no application here. For the purposes of this book, we are going to ignore most, if not all, of those earlier quaint and flawed works.

When you discuss Diagnostic Face Reading with others, if they try to bring up Physiognomy / Phrenology / Personology, you are now armed. If someone should challenge you in any way, you know the history of what really happened.

15 What Your Face Really Says

You have now learned the bombastic and even dangerous beginnings of this thing called face reading. The earlier works on the subject, while not being complete hoaxes, were fraught with folly. Time has an interesting way of sifting to the bottom of truth.

The face and the eyes, through thousands of years of literature, poetry and music, are clearly the center of our emotional universe. Look at Shakespeare, or consider the volumes of love songs, the popularity of plastic surgery and the amount of beauty creams sold every day. The face really is the center of our universe. Thousands of years of woman have been sold the notion that facial youth and beauty is what it takes to be alluring and sexy. That statement is very interesting when you consider when I was first exposed to face reading.

I ran across my first face reading chart at health care conference in 1991. I was at the San Jose Skin Care convention where Estiticians (skin care experts) came to learn new techniques and examine new products. While there I noticed a Homeopathic Medicine doctor was exhibiting. Looking at his promotional pieces, I spotted a very colorful yet very confusing face reading chart. I was drawn to it.

Immediately understanding what he was doing, I knew it could be done better. He was trying to convey that the face reflected the state of the internal organs. And that through internal work the face will change (which is true).

His presentation though was very confusing. Yet I was intrigued. I went home and started researching the subject. Every original (not melting pot) culture on the planet had its own chart for the purpose of predicting health. Every Asian country had a chart and sometimes two or three. I collected all of these charts and realized that they often argued on the exact same points. One would say this area is the liver while another chart said it was the kidneys and so on.

I had to develop a way to be sure what part of the face represented what organ. The question was how to do it! I realized that I had to do as scientific a study as possible. Choosing one organ (the kidneys), I collected two hundred people with known kidney issues and studied their faces. This revealed absolutely nothing. I could not honestly detect anything from just this observation. Examining two hundred people without kidney issues revealed zero as well.

The only way to establish where the kidneys were was to treat them and look for changes. It was not until I gave the whole group herbs and herbal combinations for the kidneys (one at a time over days) that I saw anything of significance.

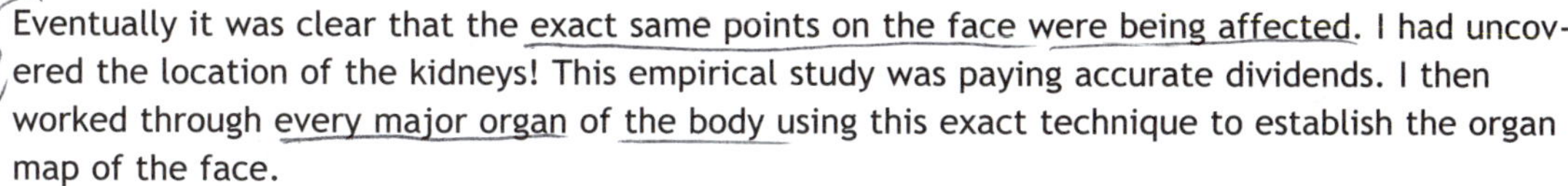

Eventually it was clear that the exact same points on the face were being affected. I had uncovered the location of the kidneys! This empirical study was paying accurate dividends. I then worked through every major organ of the body using this exact technique to establish the organ map of the face.

Anyone could have conducted this empirical study; I was just the one who did it. These results have been verified thousands of times over the last eight years. They are routinely validated on a daily basis.

To be very clear, this is my personal face reading technique. It is not drawn from any of the known works. This book is a laser precise unveiling of the truth regarding all aspects of your health. This has been a work in progress since I was a teenager. No group owns this work or me. My allegiance is to you the reader and to what works to make you healthy.

I take my hat off to all the thinkers and sages that have came before me. I applaud them. My work may have never taken place unless someone developed them first thousands of years ago. I have no illusions as regards discovering these amazing techniques or analysis. I am sure that I have rediscovered data lost long ago. If we dig deep enough maybe one day we will find the authors of my work. In the mean time I present it to you here.

The face reveals three very distinct pieces of data:

- The predisposition to organ weakness.
- A current weakened organ or system that is inflamed or troublesome right now.
- An area of weakness that has strengthened yet is still a weak link and may be a problem in the future.

Summation: Your face tells you moment to moment just how healthy you are and how healthy you are going to be. It is that simple.

16 Laws of Face Reading

LAW 1 - Aging and looking older are not synonymous. One has nothing to do with the other. You have seen people who are in their '70s, '80s and '90s with snow white hair and yet smooth wrinkle free skin. How is that possible if "WE MUST LOOK OLDER AS WE AGE"? It is not possible as it is a lie.

We look older for a variety of factors but age is not one of them.

LAW 2 - When you look at someone you are seeing the whole of their ancestry and habits represented from ear to ear and chin to scalp. The face does not lie.

LAW 3 - All wrinkles, blemishes, pimples, moles, bumps, red spots, brown spots, age spots, flaking, dry areas, peeling areas, scars, pockmarks, growths and discoloration are realized in areas of the face that are connected to irritated organs or organs that have an inherent weakness.

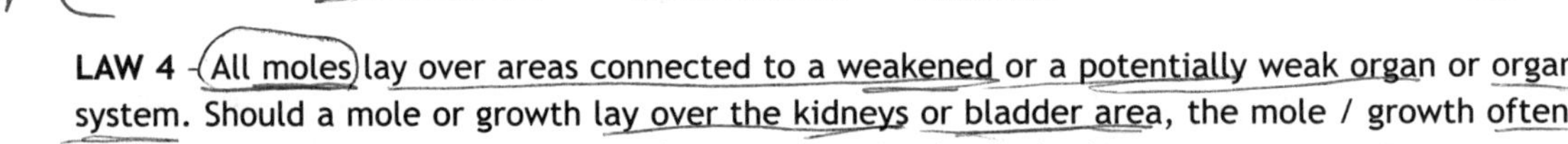

LAW 4 - All moles lay over areas connected to a weakened or a potentially weak organ or organ system. Should a mole or growth lay over the kidneys or bladder area, the mole / growth often represents a growth on the organ in the same location in the body.

LAW 5 - All redness, flaking and irritation, including dry skin, indicate that the organ is irritated and not getting proper circulation and water.

LAW 6 - All scars on the face should heal. When they do not, it is an indicator that the corresponding organ to that part of the face is weak. To validate this point, why have some of your pockmarks healed and others did not? Scars are a road map to organ weakness.

LAW 7 - Acne always represents temporary irritations of corresponding organs to the part of the face affected.

LAW 8 - The human face is not set; it constantly changes from moment to moment and hour to hour. Remember the last time you woke and looked terrible? It was just a few minutes after your shower that you looked rested and felt rejuvenated. Your body balances and reflects changes rapidly.

LAW 9 - The only reason the skin of our face is not smooth, supple and perfect, is due to drugs, chemicals, excess hormones, a poor diet or heredity. Sun also damages the skin of the face and the body. Anything in excess can cause damage to the human body.

LAW 10 - Piercings on the face, including the ears, create weakness in the organs where the piercing took place.

LAW 11 - All swelling or puffy regions of the face represent a swollen, irritated or enlarged region of the body associated with the face.

LAW 12 - Discolorations of the skin represent damage or potential damage in the associated organ for that region of the face.

LAW 13 - All damage to the body (unless surgery or accident has removed an organ, etc) can be repaired. The only caveat being the length of time it will take to do it. The same is true for the face.

LAW 14 - Face reading gives you notice of problems months and years in advance of the events manifesting themselves. If you apply what is in this book you can spot and handle these tribulations before they slow you down.

Heredity: We have all been handed our genetic makeup from our parents and their parents. There is nothing you can do to change that. Therefore, how you look has been influenced by their habits. What happens after that is entirely your choice. If you learn to listen to your body, you will look and feel AS FIRST-RATE AS POSSIBLE. Should your organs start giving you problems, it is incumbent upon you to get to the bottom of the difficulty and correct it.

Rule 1 - If the face has wrinkles, blemishes, pimples, moles, bumps, red spots, brown spots, age spots, flaking, dry areas, peeling areas, scars, pockmarks, growths or discoloration, it is solely due to drugs, chemicals, excess hormones, sun, poor diet or heredity.

Rule 2- If the face does not improve when you treat it, you are not treating the correct organ, what you are using is faulty or you are trying to treat a hereditary state that has not manifested itself yet.

Rule 3 - In treating any condition always consult the symptoms of the body. Symptoms indicate the presence and severity of the issue being addressed

Rule 4 - Anyone who is treated will feel better and look improved when the correct food or herbal is applied to the organ in question.

17 Parts of the Face

NOTE: *Many of the internal organs have the same shape as the areas of the face that represent them.*

NOTE: *Face reading extends from the jawbone to the ears and includes the scalp. It does not include anything below the jaw line (such as the neck).*

NOTE: You will be looking for wrinkles, blemishes, pimples, moles, bumps, red spots, brown spots, age spots, flaking, dry areas, peeling areas, scars, pockmarks, growths or discoloration.

NOTE: The ileocecal valve is located just above the right hip and is a valve that connects the small intestines to the ascending colon.

Two major organs govern not only the body but also the look of the face. These two organs, the liver and kidneys (as you read in the History of the Kidneys and Liver) regulate every function of the human body. If the parent organ is running well, the system will function at its optimum level.

VITAL NOTE OF COMPLIANCE: *The descriptions of the face that you are about to read are somewhat esoteric (understood by few). READ THIS SECTION WHILE REFERRING to a mirror. If you hope to fully grasp each part of the face, do not just read these explanations. Study them again and again. Do not go on to the next description until you fully understand the last one. You are building your future success in face reading. Take your time.*

Starting at the top and working our way down the face, we find:

THE SCALP

The scalp is a representation of the **BLADDER & REPRODUCTIVE SYSTEM**. The Kidneys regulate the entire area.

MIDDLE OF THE FOREHEAD

The middle of the forehead represents the **SMALL INTESTINES**. Have you ever noticed the creases of the forehead that snake across its surface? Your intestinal tract looks similar in its construction. The LIVER regulates the entire area.

RIGHT & LEFT CORNERS OF YOUR FOREHEAD

The right and left corners of your forehead represent the right and left side of your **BLADDER.** Imagine a line stretching from the innermost point of your eyebrow (nearest your nose) that backtracks across your eyebrow to your hairline. Now imagine another line stretching from the same inside point of your eyebrow (nearest your nose) and stretching diagonally back over the brow to the corner of your hairline (where the hair on the side of your head meets the hair on the top). These two triangle-shaped areas are the right and left side of the bladder. The kidneys, via the bladder, supervise these two areas. The Kidneys regulate the entire area.

THE ENTIRE OUTER RIM OF THE RIGHT AND LEFT EARS

The entire outer rim of the right and left ears represents the **KIDNEYS.**

THE ENTIRE EARLOBE OF THE RIGHT AND LEFT EAR

The entire earlobe of the right and left ears represents your **HEART.** The Kidneys regulate the entire area.

THE ENTIRE RIGHT AND LEFT EYE (EYE BALL ONLY)
The entire right and left eyeball represents the state of the **LIVER.**

BRIDGE OF THE NOSE BETWEEN THE EYEBROWS
The center space at the bridge of the nose between the eyebrows represents the **LIVER**.

THE CROW'S-FEET AREA TO THE LEFT AND RIGHT OF EACH EYE
The crow's-feet area to the left and right of each eye represent the **LIVER**.

THE HALF MOON UNDER THE RIGHT AND LEFT EYE
The half moon under the right eye and left eye represents the **RIGHT AND LEFT KIDNEY.** The outer most area (near the crows feet portion of the face) is the **ADRENAL GLAND** on the right and left kidney. When irritated, this area can appear swollen like a black-eyed pea. The Kidneys regulate the entire area.

THE ENTIRE NOSE AND UPPER LIP FROM SMILE LINE TO SMILE LINE
The entire nose and upper lip area from smile line to smile line is a representation of the **HEART.** The Kidneys regulate the entire area.

THE RIGHT AND LEFT CHEEKBONES
The right and left cheekbones are a representation of the **STOMACH.** The LIVER regulates the entire area.

RIGHT AND LEFT SMILE LINES
The right and left smile lines represent the **ASSENDING COLON / ILEOCECAL VALVE** (nearest the nose), the **TRANSVERSE COLON**, in the middle of the smile line and the **DECENDING COLON** closest to the top of the upper lip. The LIVER regulates the entire area.

RIGHT AND LEFT HOLLOW OF THE CHEEK
The right and left hollow of the cheek represents the **RIGHT AND LEFT LUNG.** The LIVER regulates this entire area.

THE ENDOCRINE STRIP
The Endocrine Strip starts at the innermost bottom corner of the right and left eye and stretches down next to the half moons under each eye, along the nose, outer smile lines, next the stomach (cheekbones), and lungs (hallows of the cheeks) down to the jaw line. This area is a representation of the ENDOCRINE SYSTEM. The KIDNEYS and LIVER regulate the endocrine system.

THE CHIN AND LOWER LIP
The entire chin and lower lip, stretching across the chin, from Endocrine Strip to Endocrine Strip, Represents the **MALE AND FEMALE REPRODUCTIVE SYSTEM.** The Kidneys regulate the entire area.

18 How to Read the Face

You are assessing the person's wrinkles, blemishes, pimples, moles, bumps, red spots, brown spots, age spots, flaking, dry areas, peeling areas, scars, pockmarks, growths or discolorations, against perfection. Perfection equals none of the above and is practically impossible to find.

The reason you are learning face reading is either for your own personal needs, your family or in your business (practitioner of some sort). Understanding that, it is very important to recognize the power that you are wielding. What you say will be very personal to the individual you are working with. You are predicting the person's future and reading secrets that they did not know they were revealing. Face reading is very powerful. Do not misuse it.

Guideline 1: Be gentle; do not crush someone with your investigation or observations. Some people are very sensitive. All you are trying to do is bring about an understanding that how a person feels directly corresponds to how they look.

Guideline 2: Unless you are doing a full assessment from ear to ear and chin to scalp, stop when you have interested the person in changing something about them. When you have accomplished this, the person will want to get better. After you have discovered the core issue for the person, direct them to a solution.

Step 1 - Have the person stand in good lighting.

Step 2 - He or she should remain still as you observe them.

Step 3 - Be sure the individual being observed is not smiling or frowning. Nothing can be seen unless the face is calm and relaxed.

Step 4 - Briefly enlighten the person being observed about what you are about to do.

Step 5 - Hand the individual being observed a hand mirror so that he or she can follow what you are pointing out.

Step 6 - Quickly look over the face and observe what jumps out at you. The worst area is always the lynch pin of their problems.

Step 7 - A—Start at the hairline and cover the entire face one area at a time. Picking one area at a time fully investigates it. Your job is to be a good detective.

Step 7 - B— Zero in on the top 4 (or 4 worst) areas of the face and indicate them to the individual in ascending order (smallest problem to the largest). Remember, you are looking for wrinkles, blemishes, pimples, red spots, brown spots, age spots, flaking, dry areas, peeling, moles, scars, growths, swelling and discolorations. You will almost always see puffiness, bagging and or dark circles under the eyes.

Step 8 - With this book as a reference, let them use the hand mirror and compare their face to the face-reading gallery in the book and see if their assessment agrees with yours.

Based on your findings, use the questions that follow later to find out just what are the person's problems based on what you are observing. Do not make the person wrong; gently probe to get to the bottom of what you are looking at. It is always good to make note of what you have spotted and the answers they have given you. Probe gently; the answers are always there.

Offer them a solution based on diet or supplements or both.

19 Accessing What You Are Looking At

When you find wrinkles, blemishes, pimples, moles, bumps, red spots, brown spots, age spots, flaking, dry areas, peeling areas, scars, pockmarks, growths or discolorations on the face, compare these areas to each other to determine the severity of the condition or potential condition.

Areas of comparison will tell you how severe the problem or potential problem is.

BLADDER ISSUES / REPRODUCTIVE ISSUES
Scalp
Bladder areas above each eye
Chin and lower lip area

DIGESTIVE DISTURBANCE
Intestines (center forehead)
Stomach (cheekbones)
Colon (smile lines left and right)

STOMACH ISSUES
Cheekbones

COLON ISSUES
Entire smile line, both sides (these lines break down into three parts, see below)

ASSENDING COLON / ILEOCECAL VALVE
Portion of the smile line connecting at the nostrils of the nose

TRANSVERSE COLON
The middle of the smile line

DESCENDING COLON
The lowest part of the smile line nearest the mouth

LUNG ISSUES
Hollow of each left and right cheek

LIVER ISSUES
Area between the eyebrows at the bridge of the nose
Eyes themselves
Crow's feet area to the outer left and right eye

HEART ISSUES
The entire nose
The left and right earlobe
The entire upper lip area, from smile line to smile line is the heart

***** % Percentage rate for each affected area toward a heart condition:***

20% Affected nose

20% Affected upper lip region

30% Right earlobe

30% Left earlobe

Therefore if a person has an affected nose and right earlobe, their chances of having a heart condition are 50% (nose = 20% + earlobe = 30% = 50%)

ENDOCRINE SYSTEM
Endocrine Strip (see last chapter)

REPRODUCTIVE ISSUES
Entire chin (reproductive system)
Scalp (reproductive system and bladder)
Half Moons under the eyes (kidneys)

KIDNEY ISSUES
Kidney issues are represented in the half moon area under the left and right eyes as well as the upper rim of the left and right ear.

20 Notes on Face Reading

Face reading cures nothing and is solely a diagnostic tool for detecting areas of inner body stress. The liver and kidneys dominate the body and therefore the face.

When examining any one part of the face or organ system, always look to compare organ systems on the face that are in the same bracket. Regularly, multiple areas in the bracket are affected at the same time.

LIVER BRACKETS

<u>*Liver issues also look at:</u>

Small Intestines
Eyes
Stomach
Colon
Lungs

<u>*Small intestine issues also look at:</u>

Liver
Eyes
Stomach
Colon
Lungs

<u>*Eye issues also look at:</u>

Small intestines
Liver
Stomach
Colon
Lungs

<u>*Stomach issues also look at:</u>

Small intestines
Liver
Eyes
Colon
Lungs

<u>*Colon issues also look at:</u>

Small intestines
Liver
Eyes
Stomach
Lungs

<u>*Lung issues also look at:</u>

Small intestines
Liver
Eyes
Stomach
Colon

KIDNEY BRACKET

<u>*Bladder issues also check:</u>

All areas related to the bladder
Kidneys

Adrenal glands
Endocrine system
Heart (all areas related to the heart)
Reproductive system (all areas related to the Reproductive system)

***Kidney issues also check:**

Bladder (all areas related to the bladder)
Adrenal glands
Endocrine system
Heart (all areas related to the heart)
Reproductive system (all areas related to the Reproductive system)

***Adrenal Gland issues also check:**

Bladder (all areas related to the bladder)
Kidneys
Endocrine system
Heart (all areas related to the heart)
Reproductive system (all areas related to the Reproductive system)

***Endocrine System issues also check:**

Bladder (all areas related to the bladder)
Kidneys
Adrenal glands
Heart (all areas related to the heart)
Reproductive system (all areas related to the Reproductive system)

***Heart issues also check:**

Bladder (all areas related to the bladder)
Kidneys
Adrenal glands
Endocrine system
All areas related to the heart
Reproductive system (all areas related to the Reproductive system)

***Reproductive System also check:**

Bladder (all areas related to the bladder)
Kidneys
Adrenal glands
Endocrine system
All areas related to the heart
All areas related to the Reproductive system

When looking at the face "think" in groups. When one area is affected, it is normal to find one or more of the "other" areas affected under the same control (i.e. kidney / liver).

The next step is to compare what you see on the face to the symptoms on the energy-balancing chart. These symptoms will tell you whether you are looking at a weakness or full-blown irritation.

Remember, no matter what technique you use to get to the source of a problem, the symptom analysis from the Energy Balancing Technique will always guide you correctly. Never neglect the fact that symptoms are always immediate and 100% accurate. The body never imagines pain. Never discount the power of the body's symptoms, as they are how the body speaks to you. To ignore a symptom is tantamount to turning your back on helping someone in need.

21 Face Reading Interview Questions

This section is devoted to teaching you what questions to ask to reveal the severity of any condition you are assessing. These questions probe deeply but are of little use if they are not employed. Before you start questioning your patient, be very sure your patient is willing to speak to you honestly. If your patient is trying to convince you that everything is fantastic, you will not get very far. This is normally not an issue but can surprise you when you least expect it. Speaking to a patient who is interested in your help is rejuvenating. The opposite is worse than pulling teeth.

The symptoms / questions on this list have been developed over the last 10 years. Every one of these questions is valid in uncovering an actual problem in the affected organ.

Conducting Your Interview for Anything Kidney Related

Trust these questions; they UNCOVER THE SYMPTOMS RELATED TO THE EXACT QUESTION UNDER THE HEADING OFFERED. Once a person is interested in their personal condition they will allow you to help them. This is the complete purpose of face reading.

Regulated by the kidneys are: the bladder, blood pressure, ovaries, ovum production, estrogen, period cramps, testicles, testosterone, sperm production, uterus, prostate, sex drive, pancreas, spleen, lymphatic system, heart, left elbow, all ligaments*, all tendons*, all joints*, ears, scalp, left side of your neck, right and left low back, mid back, left upper back, left shoulder, left deltoid, left trapezoid, left pectoral muscle, left scapula, left latissimus dorsi muscle (lat for short), both forearms, both biceps, both wrists, both hands, both thumbs, both sets of fingers, both hips, both thighs, both hamstrings, both knees, both calves, both ankles, both feet, both sets of toes and soles of both feet. The right shoulder, which includes the right trapezoid, right side of your neck, right deltoid muscle, right pectoral muscle, right scapula and the right lat are all regulated by the liver and will be discussed later.

* *Except the right elbow, the stomach regulates this point only.*
The upcoming section can be used verbatim. It is written the same way that I have done this testing for the past 10 years. Once you have one or several yes answers, you can move on to the ENERGY BALANCING TECHNIQUE (coming up in a later chapter).

NOTE TO DOCTORS: *If you are taking a patient history, note all of your patients symptoms and file them along with a picture taken of them today (digital or Polaroid) with whatever therapy you are going to give them (adjustment, herbal supplements, vitamins, exercise, diet, etc.). Thirty days later bring your patient back in to be looked at again. Take a new history and take a new picture and compare the two. The results can be staggering.*

At this point you have already performed a full-face reading.

*Have your patient rate each area of irritation on a 1-10 scale, 10 being worst and 0 being the best or most desirable. If kidney issues show up on the face that you are looking at, you would ask:

Questions to ask to establish KIDNEY weakness

WHAT YOU MIGHT SEE WITH A PERSON LIKE THIS - Darkness or puffiness under or around the eyes. You may also see growths, wrinkles or discolorations in the right or left eye bag region under each eye.

Do you feel pain or stiffness or soreness in the left side of your neck?
Have you been told you have Tempro-Mandibular Joint (TMJ) issues?
Do you feel pain or stiffness or soreness in the left trapezoid muscle?
Do you feel pain or stiffness or soreness in the left pectoral?
Do you feel pain or stiffness or soreness in the left scapula?
Do you feel pain or stiffness or soreness in the left bicep?
Do you feel pain or stiffness or soreness in the left triceps?
Do you feel pain or stiffness or soreness in the left elbow?
Do you feel pain or stiffness or soreness in the left upper forearm?
Do you feel pain or stiffness or soreness in the RIGHT lower forearm?
Do you feel pain or stiffness or soreness in the left lower forearm?
Do you feel pain or stiffness or soreness in the left wrist?
Do you feel pain or stiffness or soreness in the RIGHT wrist?
Have you been told that you have carpel tunnel syndrome in either wrist?
Do you feel pain or stiffness or soreness in the left hand?
Do you feel pain or stiffness or soreness in the RIGHT hand?
Do you feel pain or stiffness or soreness in the left fingers or thumb?
Do you feel pain or stiffness or soreness in the RIGHT fingers or thumb?

Do you feel pain or stiffness or soreness in the upper left back area?
Do you feel pain or stiffness or soreness in the center mid back area?
Do you feel pain or stiffness or soreness in the left center back area?
Do you feel pain or stiffness or soreness in the RIGHT lower back area?
Do you feel pain or stiffness or soreness in the left lower back area?
Do you feel pain or stiffness or soreness in the RIGHT hip area?
Do you feel pain or stiffness or soreness in the left hip area?
Do you feel pain or stiffness or soreness in the left hamstring area?
Do you feel pain or stiffness or soreness in the RIGHT hamstring area?
Do you feel pain or stiffness or soreness in the left front thigh area?
Do you feel pain or stiffness or soreness in the RIGHT thigh area?
Do you feel pain or stiffness or soreness in the left knee area?
Do you feel pain or stiffness or soreness in the RIGHT knee area?
Do you feel pain or stiffness or soreness in the left calf area?
Do you feel pain or stiffness or soreness in the RIGHT calf area?
Do you feel pain or stiffness or soreness in the left ankle area?
Do you feel pain or stiffness or soreness in the RIGHT ankle area?
Do you feel pain or stiffness or soreness in the left foot area?
Do you feel pain or stiffness or soreness in the Right foot area?
Do you feel pain or stiffness or soreness in the left foot toes?
Do you feel pain or stiffness or soreness in the Right foot toes?
Do you have dizziness / vertigo in the left ear?
Do you have dizziness / vertigo in the right ear?
Do you have ringing / tinnitus in the left ear?
Do you have ringing / tinnitus in the right ear?
Have you ever had kidney stones?
Are you prone to kidney stones?
Do you frequently urinate during the night (more than once)?
Do you experience arthritis- like symptoms in your joints?
Have you had any swollen joints (with or without pain)?
Do you have floaters (clear shapes) cross your field of vision?
Do you have or have you had weak nails that chip or break?
Do you have high blood pressure?
Have you had gout?
Have you been told you have diabetes?
Are you aware of having any "diabetic" symptoms?
Are any of your muscles ever numb or tingly?
Do you eat a diet high in meat protein?
Do you eat a diet high in peanuts, walnuts, almonds, cashews, pistachios or other nuts?
Are you exhausted a short time after eating?
Are you exhausted from 3 pm till 11 pm daily?
Do you find that your energy is often depleted throughout the day?
Do you need a nap before bedtime?

Do you need a nap before dinner?
Have you been told that you have weak adrenal glands?
Do you consume caffeine?
Do you consume sodium?
Do you consume salt?
Are you retaining water?
Is there a history of kidney problems in your family?
**Have you taken or used Ephedra (Ma Wang)?
**Have you taken or used cocaine?
**Have you taken stimulants?
**Do you take stimulants?
**Have you taken Cialis, Levitra, Viagra or like substances?
**Have you taken any other cocaine like substances?

** *These substances are damaging to the kidneys, as they are heavy stimulants.*

NOTE: *Kidney issues often present themselves as pain, weakness or stiffness of the left side of the body first.*

The above are the questions you would ask to establish **kidney weakness.**

Questions to ask to establish a BLADDER (run by the kidneys) problem:

WHAT YOU MIGHT SEE WITH A PERSON LIKE THIS Corners of the forehead broken out or creased, puffy or discolored. You may also notice a receding hairline or little or no hair on the head.

Do you have pain or discomfort in the bladder?
Do you have trouble urinating?
Do you feel intense pressure when urinating?
Do you frequently have to urinate?
Have you ever had a bladder infection?
Do you have a history of bladder infections?
Has urination caused pain, burning or itching?
Does your bladder swell?
Is your bladder swollen?
Do you have trouble with the leaking of urine (incontinence)?
Is your scalp frequently itchy?
Is your scalp frequently broken out?
Is your scalp dry?
Have you suddenly started to lose your hair?

Do you consume caffeine?
Do you consume sodium?
Do you consume salt?
Are you retaining water?
Is there a history of bladder problems in your family?
**Have you taken or used Ephedra (Ma Wang)?
**Have you taken or used cocaine?
**Have you taken stimulants?
**Do you take stimulants?
**Have you taken Cialis, Levitra, Viagra or like substances?
**Have you taken any other cocaine like substances?

** *These substances are damaging to the bladder, as they are heavy stimulants.*

The above are the questions you would ask to establish a **bladder weakness**.

Questions to ask to establish a HEART weakness (run by the kidneys):

WHAT YOU MIGHT SEE WITH A PERSON LIKE THIS - Deep furrows or creases on the earlobes, a red or irritated nose, scars, blemishes or moles on the nose, redness, blemishes or wrinkling on the upper lip.

Does your heart double beat?
Does your heart skip a beat?
Does your heart flutter?
Have you had any discomfort in the chest?
Do you feel faint from time to time?
Do you feel severe pounding in your chest during some light activities?
Have you had heart surgery?
Do you have congestive heart failure?
Are you taking heart medications?
Have you had a heart attack?
Have you had a stroke?
Does your heart pound late at night for no apparent reason?
Is there a history of heart problems in your family?
Do you consume caffeine?
Do you consume sodium?
Do you consume salt?
Are you retaining water?
**Have you taken or used Ephedra (Ma Wang)?
**Have you taken or used cocaine?

**Have you taken stimulants?
**Do you take stimulants?
**Have you taken Cialis, Levitra, Viagra or like substances?
**Have you taken any other cocaine like substances?

** *These substances are damaging to the heart, as they are heavy stimulants.*

The above are the questions you would ask to establish a **heart weakness**.

Questions to ask to establish a REPRODUCTIVE SYSTEM weakness (run by the kidneys)

WHAT YOU MIGHT SEE WITH A PERSON LIKE THIS - The chin may be heavily creased, red, irritated with acne, scars, swelling or moles.

Have you experienced sexual performance issues?
Do you have a difficult time staying aroused?
Do you suffer with a lack of interest in sex?
Do you suffer with a lack of lubrication during sex?
Do you suffer from a lack of orgasm during sex?
Do you experience unexpected pain during sex?
Do you have a low sperm count?
Do you have trouble getting pregnant?
Have you had an abortion?
Have you taken fertility drugs?
Do you have heavy bleeding during your period?
Do you have ovarian cysts?
Do you have uterine cysts?
Do you experience unusual vaginal discharge?
Have you had issues related to the uterus?
Do you experience heavy cramps during your period?
Is your scrotum overly sensitive to the touch?
Do you experience a lack of sensation in the penis?
Do you often have low back pain?
Do you have dull or sharp pain in the groin area?
**Have you taken or used Ephedra (Ma Wang)?
**Have you taken or used cocaine?
**Have you taken stimulants?
**Do you take stimulants?
**Have you taken Cialis, Levitra, Viagra or like substances?
**Have you taken any other cocaine like substances?
The above covers the questions you would ask to establish a r**eproductive system weakness.**

Questions to ask to establish a LIVER WEAKNESS

WHAT YOU MIGHT SEE WITH A PERSON LIKE THIS - Deep furrow or blemishes between the eyebrows, deep crow's feet, blemishes on the left or right outside of either eye, red, burning, watery or irritated eyes.

Do you feel pain stiffness or soreness in the RIGHT side of your neck?
Do you feel pain stiffness or soreness in the RIGHT base of your skull?
Do you feel pain stiffness or soreness in the RIGHT trapezoid muscle?
Do you feel pain stiffness or soreness in the RIGHT rotator cuff region of your shoulder?
Do you feel pain stiffness or soreness in the RIGHT deltoid region of your shoulder?
Do you feel pain stiffness or soreness in the RIGHT scapula area?
Do you feel pain stiffness or soreness in the RIGHT pectoral muscle?
Do you feel pain stiffness or soreness in the RIGHT Latissimus Dorsi muscle?
Do you feel pain stiffness or soreness in the RIGHT area just under the RIGHT rib cage?
Do you feel pain stiffness or soreness in the RIGHT rib cage area?
Do you feel pain stiffness or soreness in the RIGHT bicep?
Do you feel pain stiffness or soreness in the RIGHT Triceps?
Do you have a hard time sleeping between 11pm and 5 am?
Do you get unexpectedly depressed or does your depression linger?
Do you get angry at times?
Are you moody?
Do you get irritable?
Does your energy fluctuate off and on all daylong?
Do you need a nap during the day?
Do you get fearful or paranoid?
Are you obsessive or compulsive about situations in life?
Do you find it hard to stay in a good mood?
Do you have brief outbursts?
Do you have long outbursts?
Do you stay angry longer than you should?
Does it take a superhuman effort to control your anger?
When you get upset do your ears get hot?
Do you warm all over when you are upset?
Do you have a hard time concentrating?
Do you have a poor memory?
Do you feel drugged at times?
Do you feel dull at times?
Do you have fuzzy vision at times?
Do your eyes itch or burn during the day?
Do your eyes water?
Does the room seem dimly lit at times?
Do you wake up sneezing?

Does your nose frequently run?
Does your nose get stuffy?
Do your sinuses get full or stuffy?
Do you get sinus headaches?
Do your lungs get congested?
Do you wake up coughing?
Do your eyes burn or itch on waking?
Do you always want to rub your eyes?
Do you have sneezing fits without warning?
Do you have random headaches that quickly disappear?
Does your skin burn anywhere?
Are you prone to rashes?
Is your skin sensitive?
Does cologne make you sneeze?
Does perfume make you sneeze?
Does cigarette smoke make you sneeze?
Are there other substances that make you sneeze?
Do certain scents make you groggy?
Does your tongue burn?
Does the inside of your mouth burn?
Does your throat burn?
Do you have skin that is numb anywhere?
Do you have skin that tingles anywhere?
Do you have skin that itches or is routinely itchy in a certain place?
Have you been told that you have high cholesterol?
Have you been told that you have high liver enzymes?
Have you been told that you have gallstones?
Do you have liver spots?
Do you have age spots?
Do you have skin tags?
Do you have strawberry marks?
Do you have acne?
Do you have boils?
Do you have allergies?

The above covers the questions you would ask to establish a **liver weakness.**

Questions to ask to establish a LUNG WEAKNESS

WHAT YOU MIGHT SEE WITH A PERSON LIKE THIS - Deep furrow, blemishes, creasing, age spots, sun spots, liver spots, growths, acne, boils, redness flaking or irritation in on the hollow of either cheek.

Do you experience pain in the right side of your chest?
Do you experience pain in the left side of your chest?
Do you get short of breath?
Does it hurt to take a deep breath?
Is something restricting your breathing?
Do you cough in the morning?
Do you cough during the day?
Do you wake up coughing at night?
Do you cough up discharge from your lungs?
Have you been diagnosed with emphysema?
Have you had pneumonia?
Have you been told that you have tuberculosis?
Have you been told that you have lung cancer?
Do you have bronchitis?
Have you been told that you have pulmonary fibrosis?
Have you been told that you have Sarcoidosis?
Have you been diagnosed with respiratory failure?
Do you have asthma?
Are you out of breath easily?
Do you smoke?
Are you around air borne toxins?
Do you use an inhaler?

The above covers the questions you would ask to establish a **lung weakness.**

Questions to ask to establish a STOMACH WEAKNESS

Do you have a stiff right elbow?
Do you have right forearm pain?
Do you have right forearm soreness?
Do you have ulcers?
Do you have gas?
Do you experience heartburn?
Do you experience acid reflux?
Do you experience GERD (Gastroesophgeal Reflux Disease)?
Do you experience indigestion?
Do you use antacids?
Do certain foods set you off?
Do you often have an upset stomach?
Do you get bloated?
Do get abdominal distention?
Do you belch more than a little after you eat?

Do you feel tired after you eat?
Do you have a Hiatal hernia?

The above covers the questions you would ask to establish a **stomach weakness.**

Questions to ask to establish an INTESTINAL WEAKNESS (small intestines)

Do you have a stiff right elbow?
Do you experience pain / cramping just above the right hip?
Do you experience abdominal pain or soreness?
Do you experience abdominal spasms?
Is your abdomen sensitive to direct pressure?
Do you have gas?
Is your abdomen distended (bloated)?
Do you carry your weight in your abdominal area?
Are you overweight?
Are you constipated less-than-one-elimination-per-meal-eaten?
Do you experience indigestion?
Do certain foods set you off?

The above covers the questions you would ask to establish an **intestinal weakness.**

Questions to ask to establish a COLON WEAKNESS

Do you have a stiff right elbow?
Do you experience pain / cramping just above the right hip (ileocecal valve)?
Do you experience abdominal pain or soreness?
Do you experience abdominal spasms?
Have you been told that you have leaky gut syndrome?
Have you been told that you have polyps?
Have you been told that you have ulcerative colitis?
Have you been told that you have diverticulitis?
Have you been told that you have diverticulosis?
Have you been told that you have IBS (irritable bowel syndrome)?
Have you been told that you have Crohn's disease?
Have you been told that you have chronic fatigue syndrome?
Have you been told that you have Epstein-Barr?
Have you been told that you have Sprue?
Have you been told that you have H. pylori (Heliobacter pylori)?
Do you suffer with hemorrhoids?

Do you have candida?
Do you have bloody stools?
Do you have painful stools?
Do you have foul smelling stools?
Do you have foul gas?
Do you have to use laxatives to eliminate?
Is your abdomen sensitive to direct pressure?
Is your abdomen distended (bloated)?
Do you carry your weight in your abdominal area?
Are you constipated less-than-one-elimination-per-meal-eaten?

The above covers the questions you would ask to establish a **colon weakness.**

Questions to ask to establish an ENDOCRINE SYSTEM challenge

Do you often feel extremely hot?
Do you often feel extremely cold?
Do you often feel dizzy?
Do you often lose your balance?
Do you often feel faint at times?
Do you sometimes faint?
If you do not eat right away do you feel faint?
Do you sometimes feel light headed?
Do you often feel overwhelmingly exhausted?
Do you often feel overwhelmingly hyper energized?
Do you often feel wired or jumpy?
Do you have low blood pressure?
Does your heart suddenly race for no reason?
Do you suddenly start sweating for no reason?
Can you not put on weight?
Do you never feel hungry?
When hungry, is your vision dark or cloudy?
Is your thinking often cloudy?
Do you suddenly have poor concentration?
Do you become forgetful?
Are you always forgetful?
Can you suddenly get very moody?
Are your armpits often sore or swollen?
Is either side of your groin area often sore or swollen?
Do you often see clear shapes (floaters) in your vision?

Do your breasts produce milk long after pregnancy?
Do you have a persistent infection?
Do you have a persistent allergy?
Do you have a persistent cold symptom?

SPECIAL NOTE: *It is not unusual to find the Endocrine Strip red and irritated when a person has a history of drinking alcohol or has a diet high in oils or protein derived from nuts. These oils coat not only the liver (see chapter Oil a Life Obsession) but block all major glands of the body.*

The above covers the questions you would ask to establish an **endocrine system weakness.**

22 Face Reading Gallery

The following photos are examples of what can be seen and diagnosed with the use of Face Reading. Utilize this section of my book to interest your patients in face reading. Hand them this book opened to the gallery section and tell them to look at the pictures and descriptions. Direct them to a mirror so that they can compare their face to the photos.

With these photos you have the tools and the power to understand and change your own personal conditions. These photos are a gift that you can use or ignore. But once you read this book, to turn your back on what you have learned is tantamount to committing treason against yourself.

Since you are your own best friend, I hope that is not the case.

ORIGIN
The origin of face reading is unknown.

DEFINITIONS

FACE: Etymology: Middle English, from Old French, from (assumed) Vulgar Latin facia, from Latin facies make, form, face, from facere to make, do — more at DO.
1 a: the front part of the human head including the chin, mouth, nose, cheeks, eyes, and usually the forehead.
b: the face as a means of identification: COUNTENANCE <would know that face anywhere>

READING
Etymology: Middle English redden; to advise interpret, read, from Old English raedan; akin to Old High German; Atan to advise form Sanskrit Adhnoti he achieves, prepares.
1 a (1): to receive or take in the sense of (as letters or symbols) especially by sight or touch (2):

to study the movements of (as lips) with mental formulation of the communication expressed:

UNDERSTAND, COMPREHEND

2 a: to interpret the meaning or significance of <read palms> b: FORETELL, PREDICT <able to read his fortune>

FACE READING

The study or observation of the face used to detect the state of a current health or a predisposition of future health of the organs of the body.

DIAGNOSTIC FACE READING CHART

Roger Bezanis' FACE READING TECHNIQUE

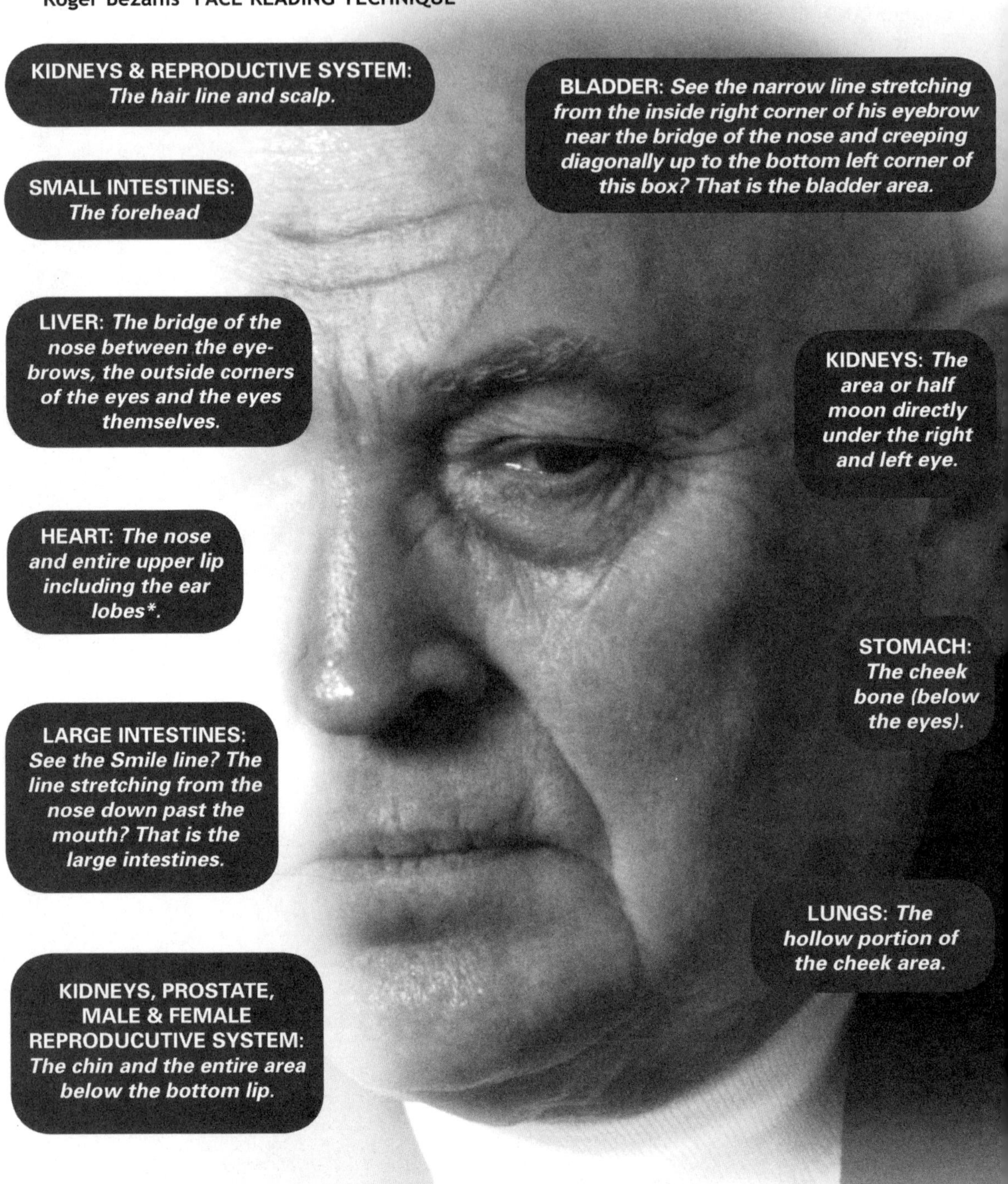

KIDNEYS & REPRODUCTIVE SYSTEM: *The hair line and scalp.*

BLADDER: *See the narrow line stretching from the inside right corner of his eyebrow near the bridge of the nose and creeping diagonally up to the bottom left corner of this box? That is the bladder area.*

SMALL INTESTINES: *The forehead*

LIVER: *The bridge of the nose between the eye-brows, the outside corners of the eyes and the eyes themselves.*

KIDNEYS: *The area or half moon directly under the right and left eye.*

HEART: *The nose and entire upper lip including the ear lobes*.*

STOMACH: *The cheek bone (below the eyes).*

LARGE INTESTINES: *See the Smile line? The line stretching from the nose down past the mouth? That is the large intestines.*

LUNGS: *The hollow portion of the cheek area.*

KIDNEYS, PROSTATE, MALE & FEMALE REPRODUCUTIVE SYSTEM: *The chin and the entire area below the bottom lip.*

"The face is not set; it constantly changes based on the health of our organs".

THE OBSERVABLE MAN

This fellow looks TERRIBLE. That is why I chose him. He has ALMOST every problem one can have.

1) The horizontal lines on his forehead say WEAK SMALL INTESTINES.
2) The diagonal line above his right eyebrow says WEAK BLADDER.
3) The upper lip, vertical line on his earlobe and the slight bump on his nose all say WEAK HEART.
4) His puffy eyes (bags) say WEAK RIGHT and LEFT KIDNEY.
5) The right outside corner (bean-shaped) of his right eye bag is raised. It represents his swollen / irritated right WEAK ADRENAL GLAND.
6) The furrows at the bridge of his nose & his glassy eyes say WEAK LIVER.
7) His smile lines indicate a WEAK COLON. The uppermost smile line attached at the nostril indicates a WEAK ILEOCECAL VALVE. The ASSENDING COLON follows next. Then comes the TRANSVERSE COLON in the middle of the smile line. The last section nearest the mouth is the DESENDING COLON.
7) His chin wrinkles say BLADDER / REPRODUCTIVE SYSTEM / PROSTATE.
8) His cheekbones are not bad but if they were they would say STOMACH.
9) The hollows of his cheeks are not bad either but if they were they would say LUNGS.

In doing face reading, always NOTICE the worst or most dominant area FIRST and work backward. The worst item is often the key to solving the health puzzle. Most problems start with poor digestion due to a bad diet.

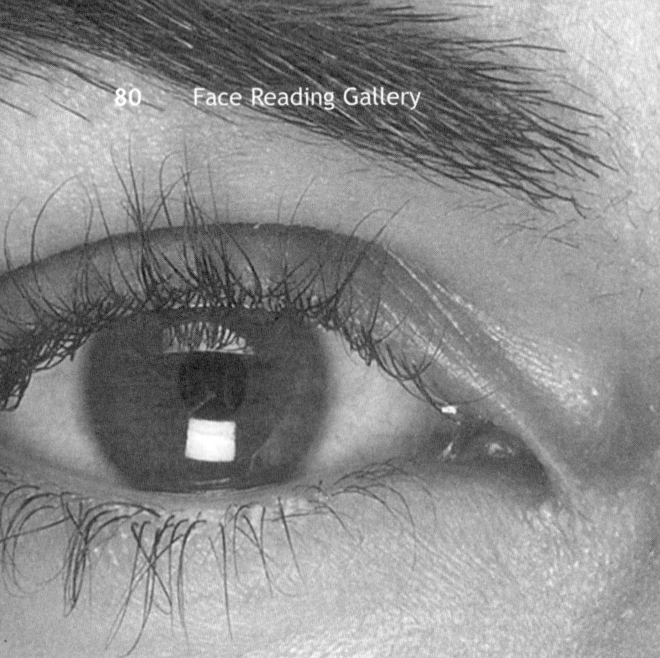

Face: Scars / pockmarks on the nose (heart). Very irritated endocrine strip (immune system / virus issues) on the right and left side. Defined smile lines near the mouth (descending colon).

Problem: His heart double beats and has a "Heart Murmur." It is made worse by the ingestion of coffee drinks and sugary sodas. His endocrine strip is made worse and irritated by recreational use of drugs and male virility tonics. Because of this, he is constantly fighting a cold.

Solution: Eliminate use of all drugs including caffeine and sugary drinks. Correct diet with cinnamon supplements, immune system boosting herbs with apples, garlic, citrus and grape juice as needed.

Face: Scar at hairline or upper forehead (intestines), left under eye swelling (kidney), right endocrine strip (immune system / virus issues), and slight indentations at the lower smile line (descending colon).

Problem: Built in weakness in the intestines not yet realized. There is also left kidney and adrenal gland weakness. Hemorrhoids are present and causing routine irritation.

Solution: Protect intestines via a diet rich in whole foods. Whole foods such as grapes, tomatoes, leafy green vegetables and citrus heal the kidneys and will correct her hemorrhoids.

Face: Crease above right eye (bladder). Furrow at the bridge of the nose (liver). See the puffiness under both eyes (right and left kidneys). Notice the swelling in the endocrine strip near the nose (Immune system / virus issues). Defined smile lines (colon). Crease on the chin (reproductive).

Problem: The colon is blocked and irritating the entire system. Uses of prostate “healing” drugs and male virility tonics have made his condition worse.

Solution: Eliminate all breads, candy, energy drinks, alcohol, tobacco and cut down on processed meats. Do an entire body detox (a deep systemic cleanse). Eat fresh fruit, especially melons, apples, pears, plums and pineapple.

THIRTEEN AND ALREADY IN TROUBLE!

Face: Upper middle forehead blemishes (intestines). Slight wrinkling above left eye (bladder). Eyebrow ring in left brow (bladder / kidneys). There are blemishes and discoloring at bridge of the nose. She is dark under each eye (adrenal glands / kidneys). She has blemishes in the right endocrine strip (immune system). There are blemishes and discolorations on her nose (heart). She has deep smile lines (all three parts of the colon). There is a deep furrow and blemish on her chin (reproductive system / uterine / ovary irritation).

Problem: Popular caffeine loaded drinks have greatly affected her kidney function. Since she is hyper from the caffeine, her parents put her on RITALIN (which is destroying her liver, kidneys, emotions and digestive tract). Processed foods have further blocked her colon and affected her reproductive system (she is now prone to ovarian cysts). Her sleep problems are due to the caffeine; Ritalin and sugar in her diet, thus causing adrenal gland burnout.

Solution: Immediately cease Ritalin use. Cut out all caffeine and processed sugar intake including breads and pasta. Eliminate breads, pasta, rice cakes and crackers (all convert to sugar). Add fresh fruit, vegetables and juices (not juice drinks). Use liver, kidney and circulation herbs frequently 4-5 times a day as needed.

Face: Perfect no issues.

Problem: Occasional eye irritation brought on by eyeliner.

Solution: Change eyeliner and protect the liver as needed.

Face: Furrow on forehead (intestines), puffy under each eye (kidney), furrow at bridge of nose (liver), crow's feet (liver), deep smile lines (all three parts of the colon, deep philtrum (heart), swelling on chin (reproductive system).

Problem: Bloating, indigestion, kidney stones (right kidney) and weak prostate.

Solution: Total body cleanse, give up caffeine, smoking, dairy products and cocktails (alcohol) before bedtime.

Face: Slight growths and furrows at the bridge of the nose (liver).

Problem: Poor moods brought on by use of Tylenol and other liver irritants. There is also soreness under the right ribcage.

Solution: Use of bupleurum, gentian and other beneficial liver strengthening herbs, citrus, increased water consumption, skin brushing, hot showers and elimination of all processed oils.

Face: Furrow at bridge of the nose (liver), puffy right and left eye bags (kidneys) deep smile lines (all three parts of the colon).

Problem: Swollen liver, constipation and severe kidney weakness.

Solution: Eliminate alcohol, caffeine and fried foods. Also reduce stress and use a liver support formula.

Face: Eyebrow piercing (bladder), nose piercing (heart), endocrine strip irritation (immune system / virus issues) and smile lines (colon).

Problem: At 17 he has a body that is breaking down quickly due to his piercings and tattoos. His diet is terrible and full of sugar and caffeine.

Solution: Take out all piercings, do a full liver support program, use herbs to support his immune system and completely upgrade his diet. He needs to flush and rebuild with fresh fruit and veggies.

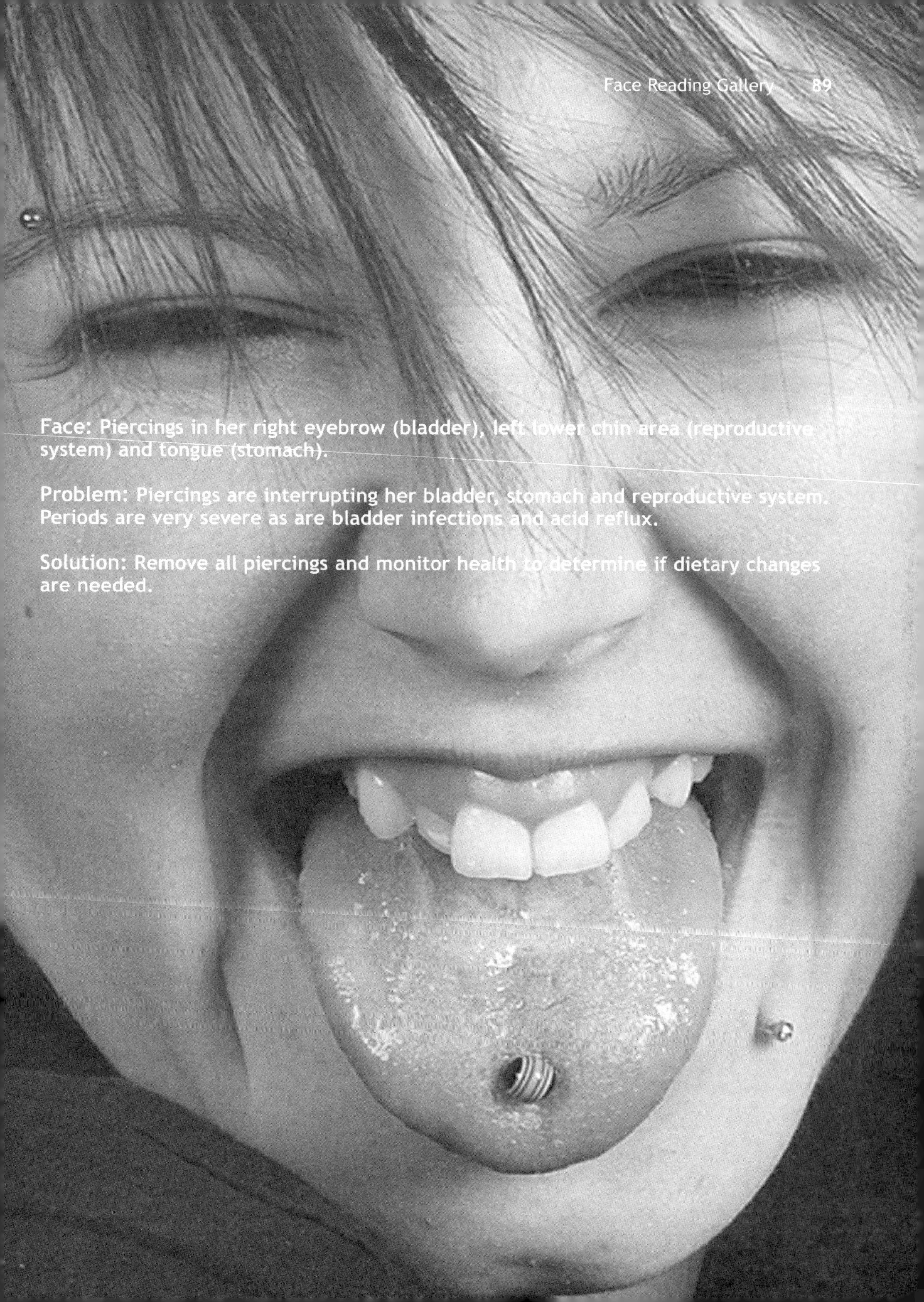

Face: Piercings in her right eyebrow (bladder), left lower chin area (reproductive system) and tongue (stomach).

Problem: Piercings are interrupting her bladder, stomach and reproductive system. Periods are very severe as are bladder infections and acid reflux.

Solution: Remove all piercings and monitor health to determine if dietary changes are needed.

Face: Horizontal and diagonal creases on the left and right corner of the forehead (bladder right and left side). Deep furrows across the middle of the forehead (intestines). Deep furrows at the bridge of the nose (liver). Notice the crow's feet at the outside of each eye (liver). Very puffy eye bags (right and left kidney). Dimple in the chin (reproductive system).

Problem: His bladder and kidneys are very weak and he is susceptible to kidney stones. The kidneys are very swollen which gives him 'arthritis-like' symptoms all over his body. His prostate is swollen as his kidneys regulate it.

Solution: Lose forty pounds via diet and exercise (after a physical). Eliminate caffeine, salt, white sugar and all artificial sweeteners. No more alcoholic 'nightcaps' before bedtime. No eating six hours before bedtime unless it is fresh fruit or juice.

Face: Very dark circles under the eyes (adrenal gland). Also notice the dark spots to the outside of her eyes at the corners (adrenal glands). She has slight swelling below her lower lip (reproductive) and slight smile lines near her mouth (descending colon).

Problem: Caffeine and a lack of sleep are burning out her adrenal glands causing low back pain and left shoulder pain. Her diet is full of rice and grains and they are congesting her colon and irritating her reproductive system.

Solution: Get off coffee and all sweetened drinks. Consume grapes, tomatoes, citrus and fruit juices. Use herbs to support her kidneys.

Face: Scar on the tip of the nose (heart), middle and low smile lines (transverse and descending colon).

Problem: Slight weakness in the heart (double beating and skipping a beat), slight constipation.

Solution: Cayenne, Hawthorne Berry, Wasabi Japonica and various heart and circulation aiding herbs. Constipation aided by increased water consumption and fewer processed foods (bread, cookies, rice, pasta and cereals).

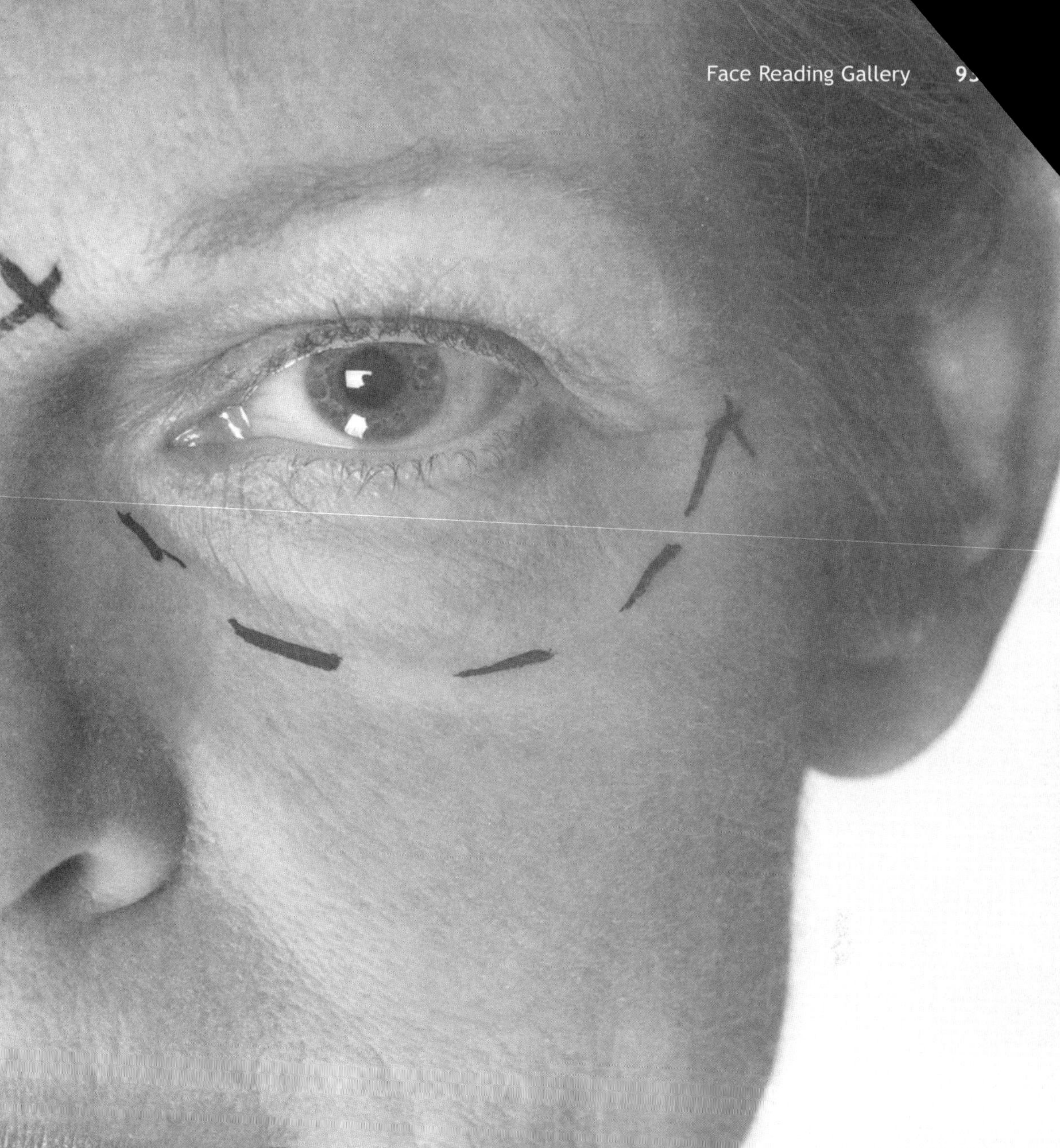

No amount of plastic surgery will correct a problem that is caused by what you are doing to the body. What you eat and have exposed yourself brought you here. Surgery will only hide the issue. Surgery is not a solution.

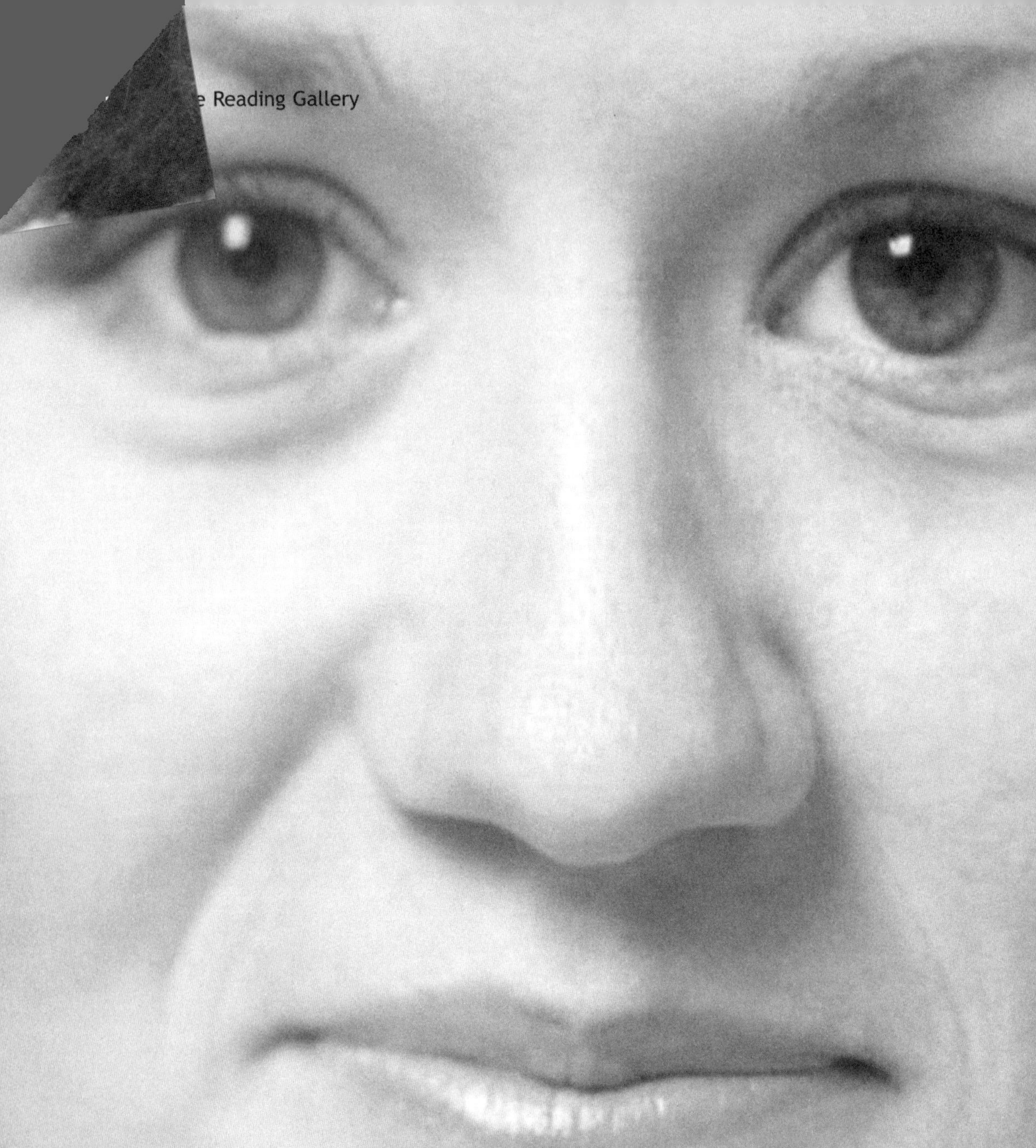

Face: Right eye bag swelling including slight left eye bag swelling (kidneys). Smile line indentations on the right and left side (colon).

Problem: Medium right kidney swelling and slight left kidney swelling. Colon congestion is present and frequent constipation including hemorrhoids.

Solution: Cut out use of ephedra for weight control and eliminate green tea (full of caffeine). Start using grape juice to help purge the colon. Also reduce salt intake.

Face: Slight creasing above the left eyebrow (left side of the bladder). Notice the small growth at the left nostril of her nose (heart = 20% chance of trouble). She has a deep or defined philtrum (indentation on the upper lip below her nose - heart = 20% chance of trouble) Near the mouth, notice the deep crease (descending colon and hemorrhoids). Notice the irritation on her chin (reproductive system).

Problem: A poor diet and energy drinks are causing constipation (less than 1 elimination per meal eaten) resulting in hemorrhoids. Her backed up colon is also affecting her bladder and heart adversely. Her define philtrum guarantees a 20% chance of a heart issues, as does the growth on her left nostril. Both added together give her a 40% chance of a heart Murmur (which she has).

Solution: Cut out use of all energy drinks and caffeine. Immediately eliminate fried and processed foods. Use a good multivitamin while supporting the kidneys, digestion and heart.

Heart Murmur = Double beating and or skipping a beat to varying degrees.

Face: Line or scar across the nose (heart). Darkness is present under both eyes (kidneys). Notice the slight puffiness on the chin (reproductive system).

Problem: He has a slight weakness in his heart that was inherited. His kidneys are also a bit weak as is his reproductive system.

Solution: Cut out all caffeinated beverages, fried foods, fast foods and white sugar.

Face: Crease at bridge of nose (liver), puffy eye bag under both eyes (kidneys), scar on nose (heart), deep smile lines (all parts of the colon) and small moles and creasing on his chin (reproductive system).

Problem: Drinking has caused severe liver and kidney issues; his poor diet full of meat protein has clogged his colon and his reproductive system is in near shut down for the same reasons. His heart is moderately weak as well.

Solution: Cut out all alcohol; switch over to a raw food diet and use a colon formula to open up his congested colon. His heart will respond to cinnamon and grapes, as will his kidneys.

Face: Blemish at bridge of nose (liver), growth and darkness under left eye (kidney), small growths in the endocrine strip (immune issues / virus issues).

Problem: Poor moods, insomnia, irritated eyes, left shoulder pain. Left low back pain, routine lumbar and low thoracic subluxations. There are also immune system and glandular issues (i.e. hypoglycemia) present.

Solution: Stop drinking beer and smoking marijuana; drink more water, employ citrus, cut out white sugar, added salt and get more sleep. Use herbs to repair circulation, oxygen and energy movement in the body. Use them further to repair kidney function.

Face: Notice the slightly swollen or raised areas just below the inside corner of her eyebrows (right and left kidney). Also notice the mole on left and right endocrine strip (immune system). Notice the mole on the right side of her chin (ovaries and uterus). There is also slight creasing just below the corners of her lower lip (hemorrhoids). Notice the slight growths or pimples on her chin (reproductive issues).

Problem: Her colon is clogged due to too much cooked animal protein. This is directly affecting her kidneys and her weak endocrine system. All of this is contributing to her multiple uterine cysts, painful periods and hemorrhoids.

Solution: Eliminate cooked animal protein and watch the cysts to detect if there are other factors (birth control pills, caffeine, etc.) irritating these conditions. Use various herbs for the kidneys as they regulate the reproductive system of both sexes. Eliminate caffeine; drink juices and plentiful amounts of water (dependant on activity level and climate).

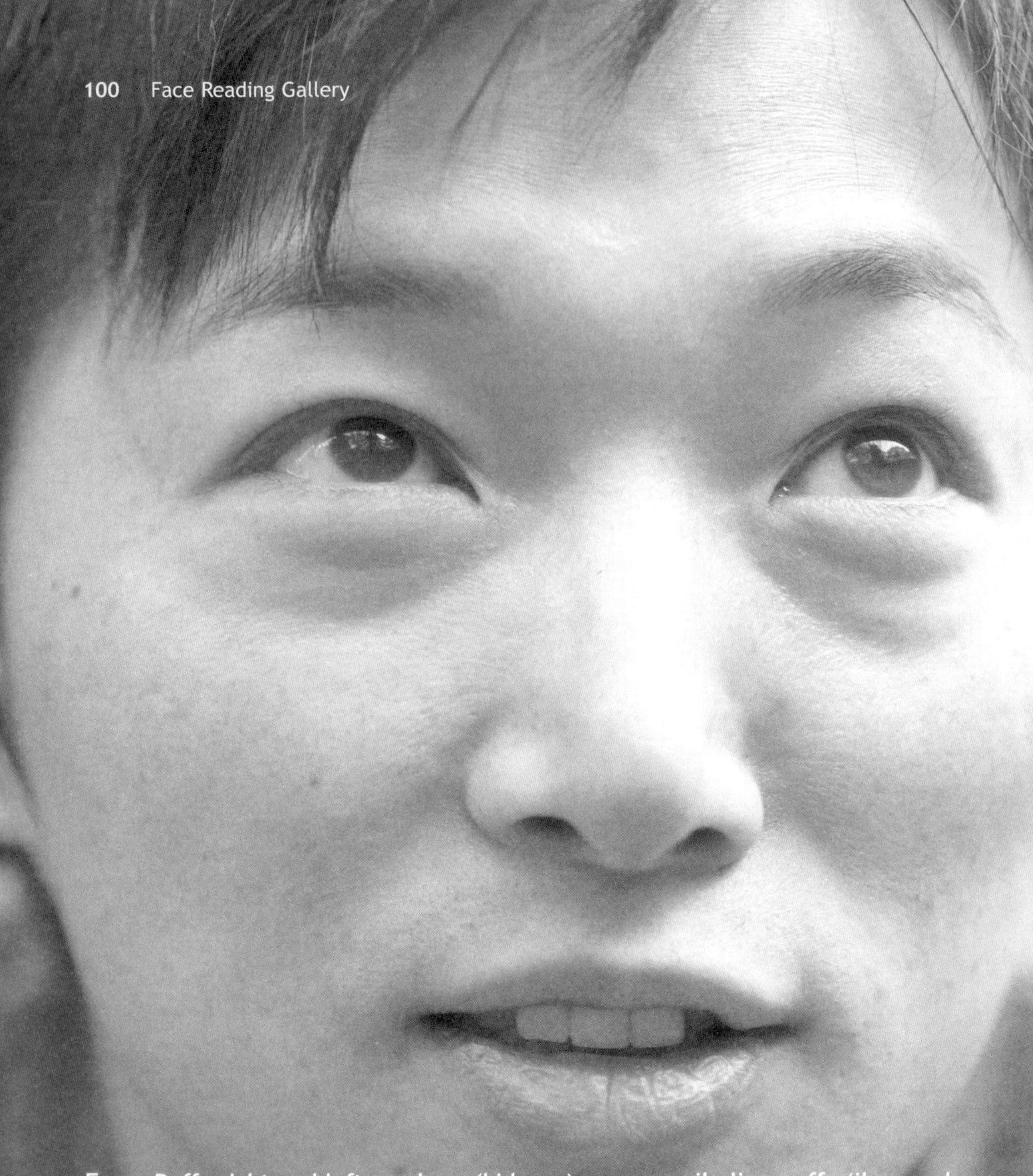

Face: Puffy right and left eye bags (kidneys), upper smile line puffy (ileocecal valve)

Problem: Right and left kidney swollen, blocked ileocecal valve (causing spasms above right hip).

Solution: Eliminate sugar, caffeine and excess salt. Eat citrus 4-5 times a day and after meals. Use a colon cleanser as needed.

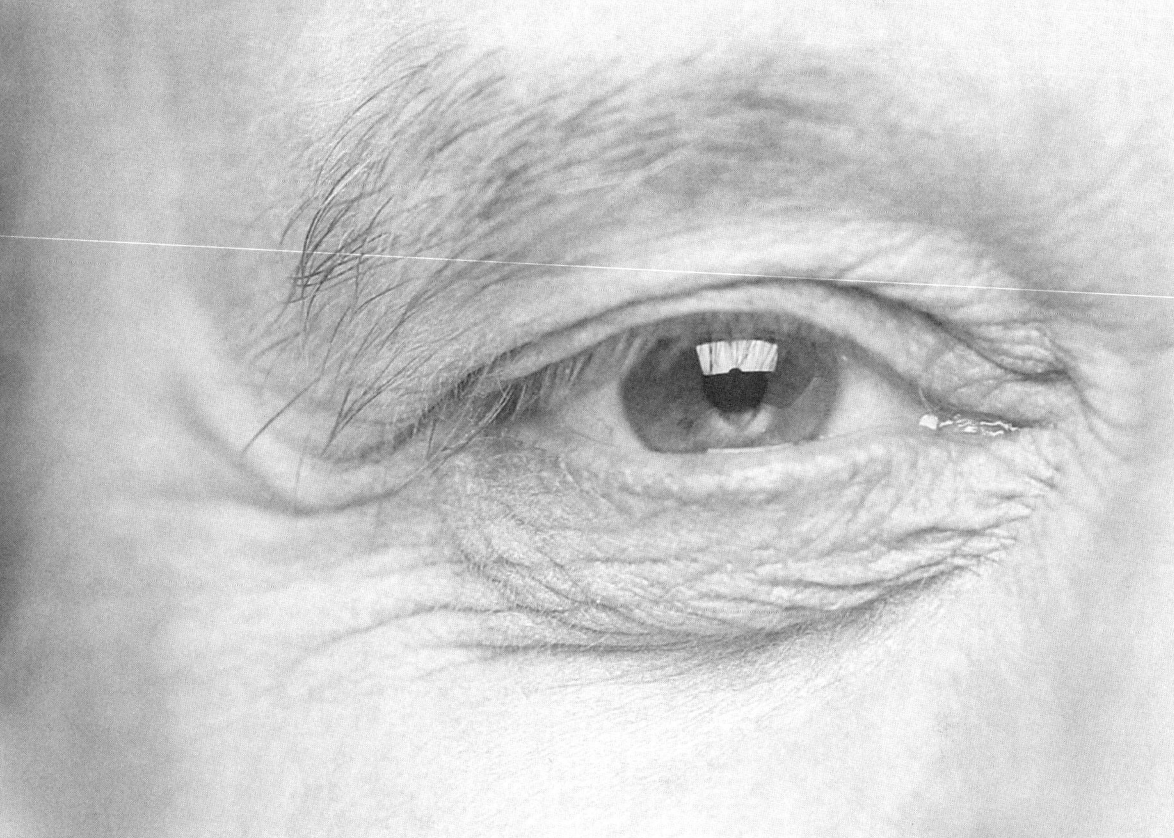

Face: Crows feet (liver), puffy under eye (kidney), deep smile line (colon).

Problem: Severe colon overloads leading to liver and kidney congestion.

Solution: Eliminate sugar, coffee, breads and dairy products. Increase water consumption and do a good colon cleansing.

Face: Deep furrow between eyes at bridge of nose (liver), smile lines (colon).

Problem: Liver overwhelm, ascending colon and descending colon blockages.

Solution: Liver support, fresh fruit especially citrus, melons and a good cellular detox. She must also stop taking over the counter sleep aids and diet aids.

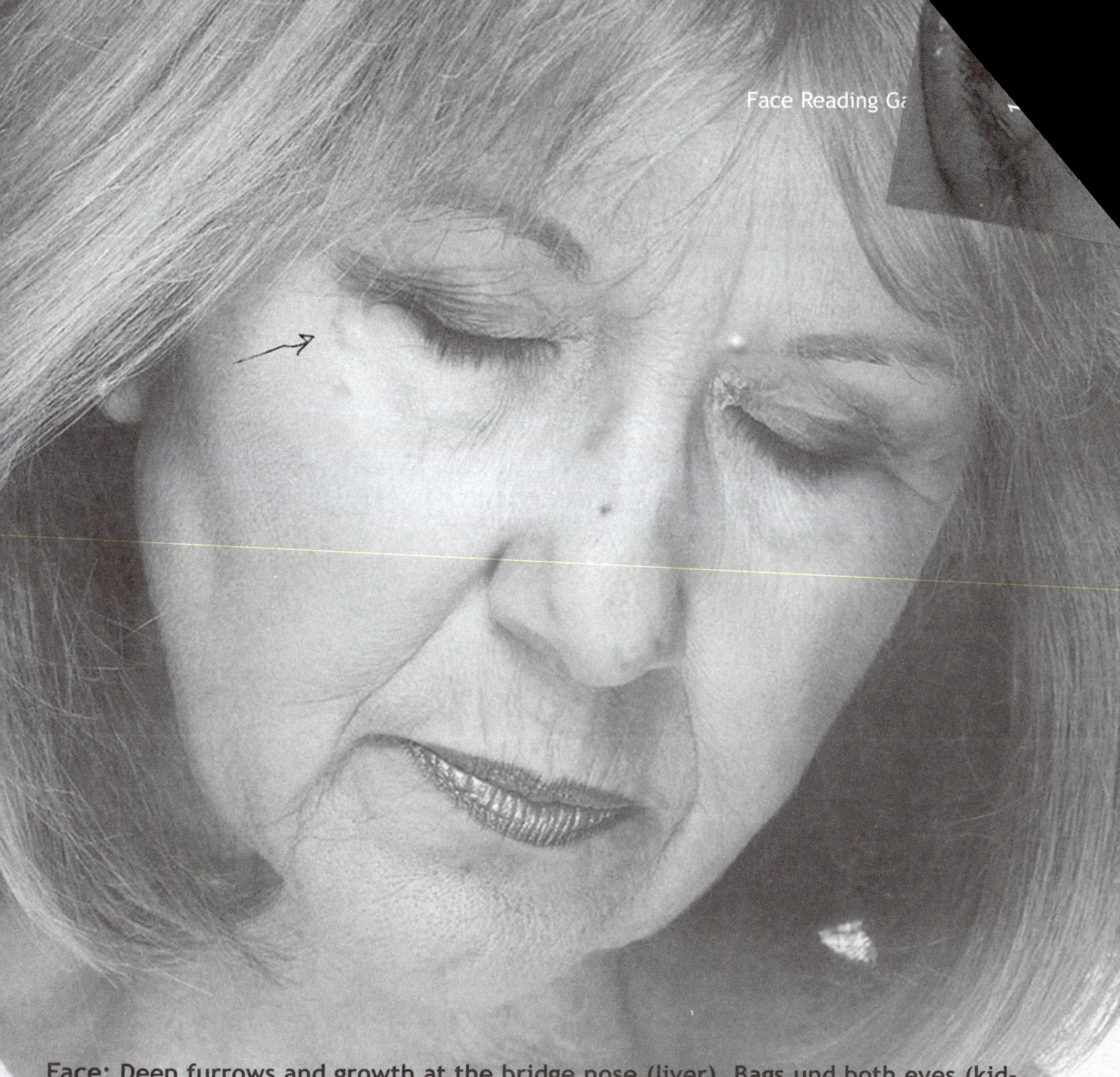

Face: Deep furrows and growth at the bridge nose (liver). Bags und both eyes (kidneys). The right corner of the right eye bag area is raised (adrenal gland). Notice the spots on the nose (heart). Notice the creases on the upper lip (heart from a mild stroke). Deep smile lines (colon). The chin area is puff and creased (reproductive issues). Hollow of the right cheek (right lung).

Problem: A mild stroke has affected her whole system and was brought on by smoking, alcohol, caffeine and a poor diet of processed foods. Constipation is also severe.

Solution: Eliminate caffeine, smoking, processed foods including dairy and replace with fresh fruit and vegetables with some egg and avocado protein. Use something to open up and repair circulation. Also use a liver, kidney and heart formula along with a good colon formula.

Face: Deep indentations at the flare of the nose (ileocecal valve), deep indentations at the lower end of the smile line nearest to mouth (descending colon). There is a slight irritation on the right endocrine strip (Immune system / virus issues). Including a small growth on the left side of the cheek (upper stomach).

Problem: Clogged ileocecal valve causing cramping above the right hip. Descending colon is weakened. Upper stomach and esophagus is irritated, including acid reflux.

Solution: Breads and cooked proteins must be eliminated. Water intake increased to 80-90 ounces a day (depending on activity level). Use of breads and caffeine eliminated.

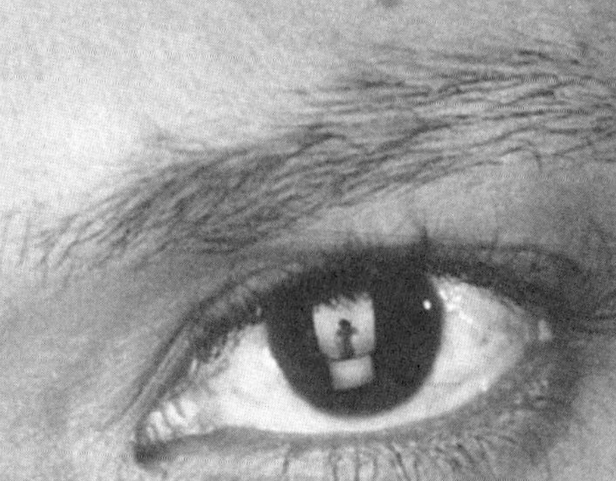

Face: Swollen endocrine strip (Immune system / virus issues). The hollow of the checks (lungs).

Problem: Viral / endocrine weakness due to parasites (Giardia). Chemical exposure and smoking has caused lung weakness.

Solution: Eliminate parasites and support lung function with turmeric, pleurisy root, etc.

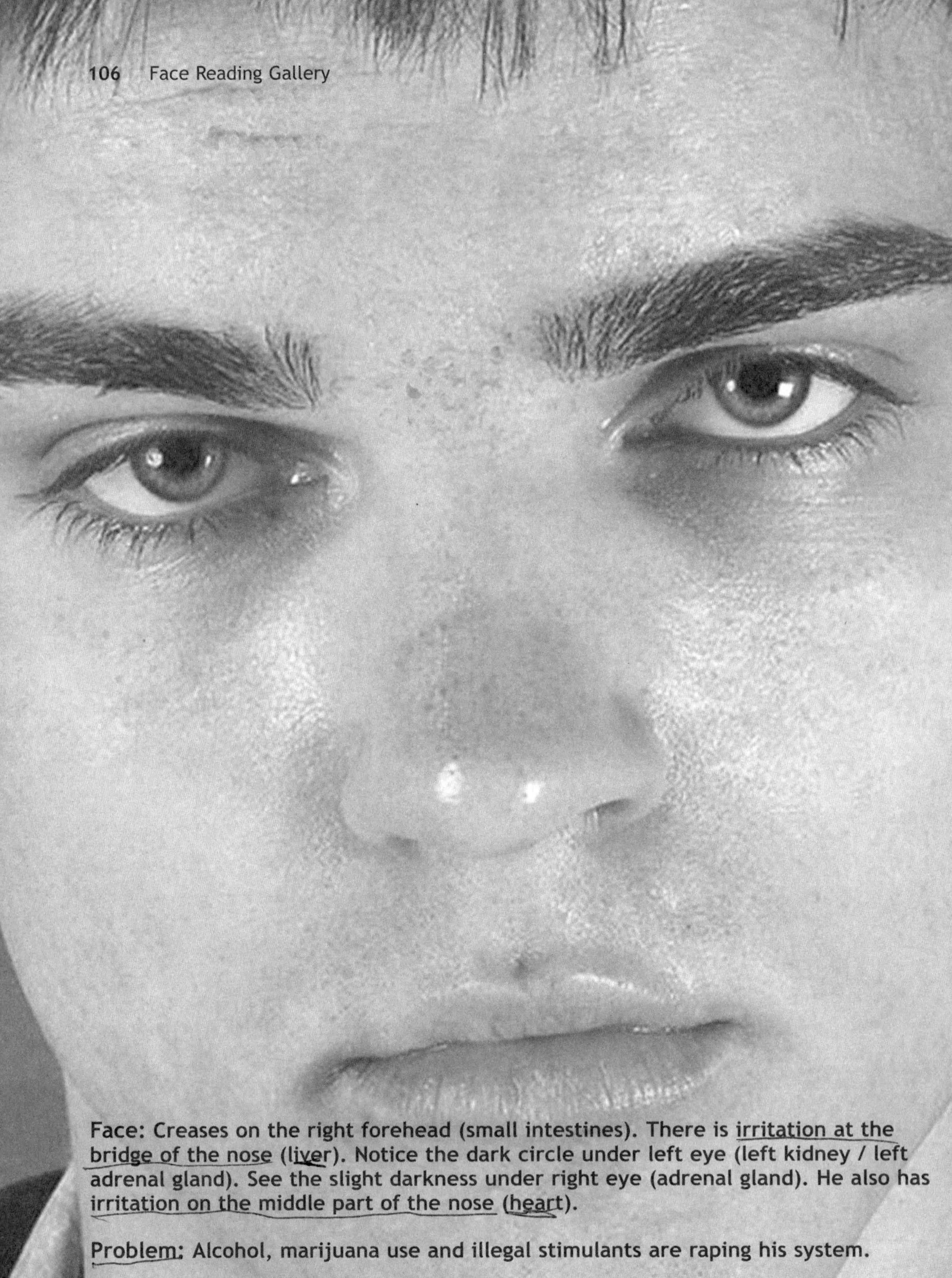

Face: Creases on the right forehead (small intestines). There is irritation at the bridge of the nose (liver). Notice the dark circle under left eye (left kidney / left adrenal gland). See the slight darkness under right eye (adrenal gland). He also has irritation on the middle part of the nose (heart).

Problem: Alcohol, marijuana use and illegal stimulants are raping his system.

Solution: Eliminate the items listed above and address the diet as needed.

It all starts with what we put in our mouths. If we feel bloated or any other conditions, ask the same question that the old wise man asked five hundred years ago. "What have I been eating"?

Correct the diet and the body heals.

Problems of the body are not caused by chemical or drug deficiencies.

Roger Bezanis

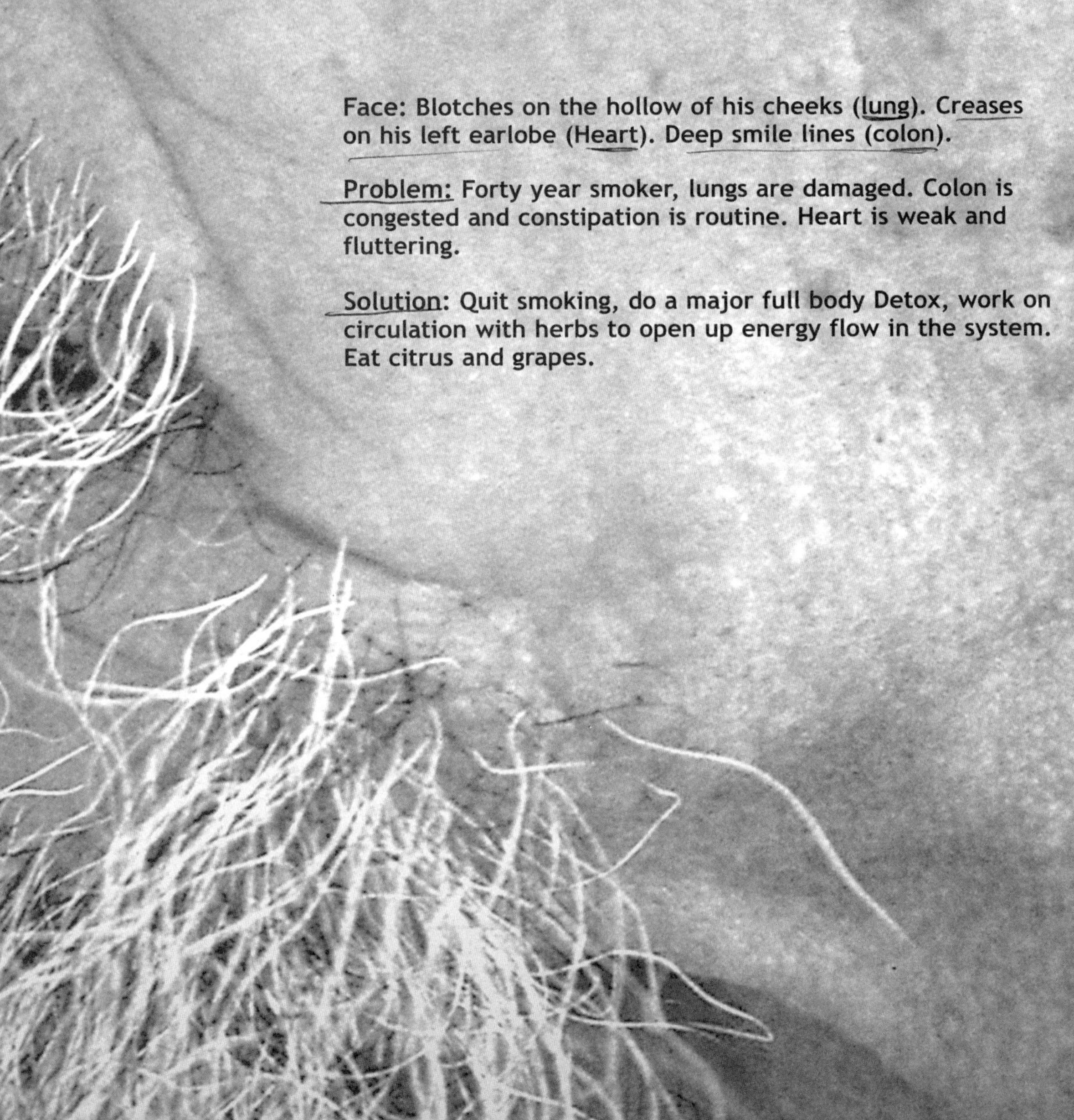

Face: Blotches on the hollow of his cheeks (lung). Creases on his left earlobe (Heart). Deep smile lines (colon).

Problem: Forty year smoker, lungs are damaged. Colon is congested and constipation is routine. Heart is weak and fluttering.

Solution: Quit smoking, do a major full body Detox, work on circulation with herbs to open up energy flow in the system. Eat citrus and grapes.

TEST YOURSELF / WHAT DO YOU SEE?

The answers are below upside down:

Severe colon impaction
Heart weakness from stroke (upper lip)
Weak kidneys very swollen
Severe reproductive issues
Weak lungs (hollow of the cheek)

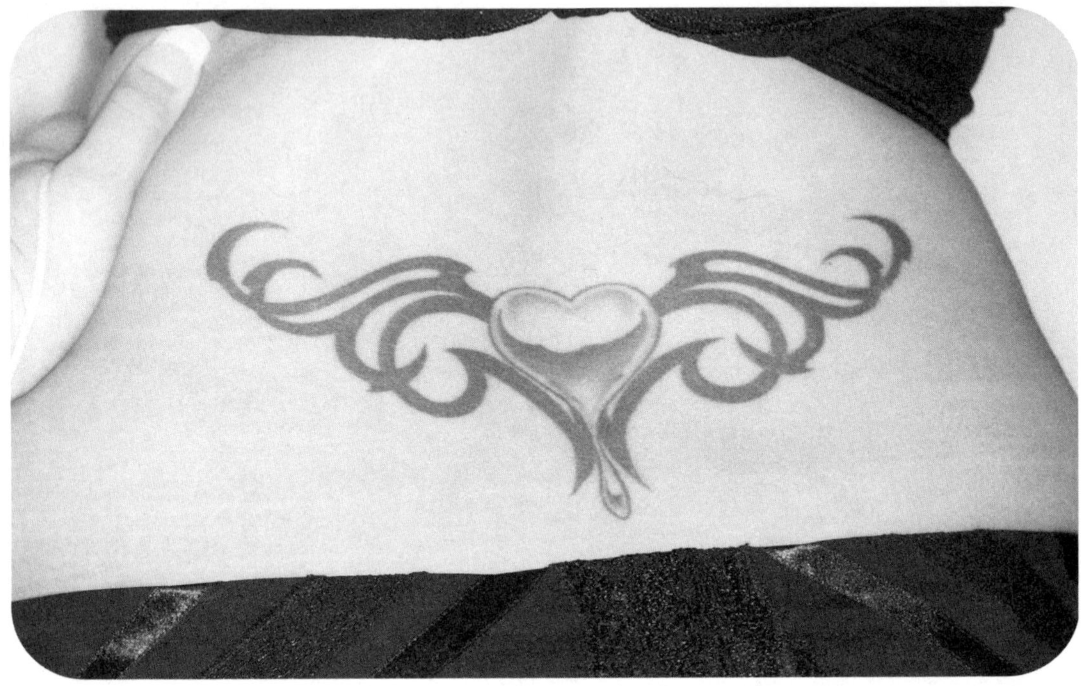

Tattoos attack the liver as it regulates the skin. Over time tattoo ink is absorbed via the skin and attacks the liver. Because the liver is slowly digesting tattoo ink, they eventually fade and disappear. Tattoo ink is so powerful that it alone can cause hepatitis.

in it every day. Every human on the planet is lactose intolerant. We are the only species that consumes milk from another species. We (and to a lesser extent primates) are the only species that eats solely for pleasure.

This is what poor circulation looks like on the fingernail moons. Notice there are none. Each finger (except the pinky on both hands) should have a moon. The largest is the thumb moon to the smallest at the ring finger. This problem is solved via a general detox of the system. It is best to include cayenne, wasabi japonica, cinnamon bark and turmeric along with B-vitamins, liver and kidney support.

circulation

This is what healthy circulation looks like as represented by the nail-moons. Notice that all the nails have moons except the pinky. This is what your nails should look like. To keep your nails and circulation strong it is advisable to take: cayenne, turmeric, wasabi japonica, cinnamon bark with liver and kidney support and B-vitamins.

half-moons on nails

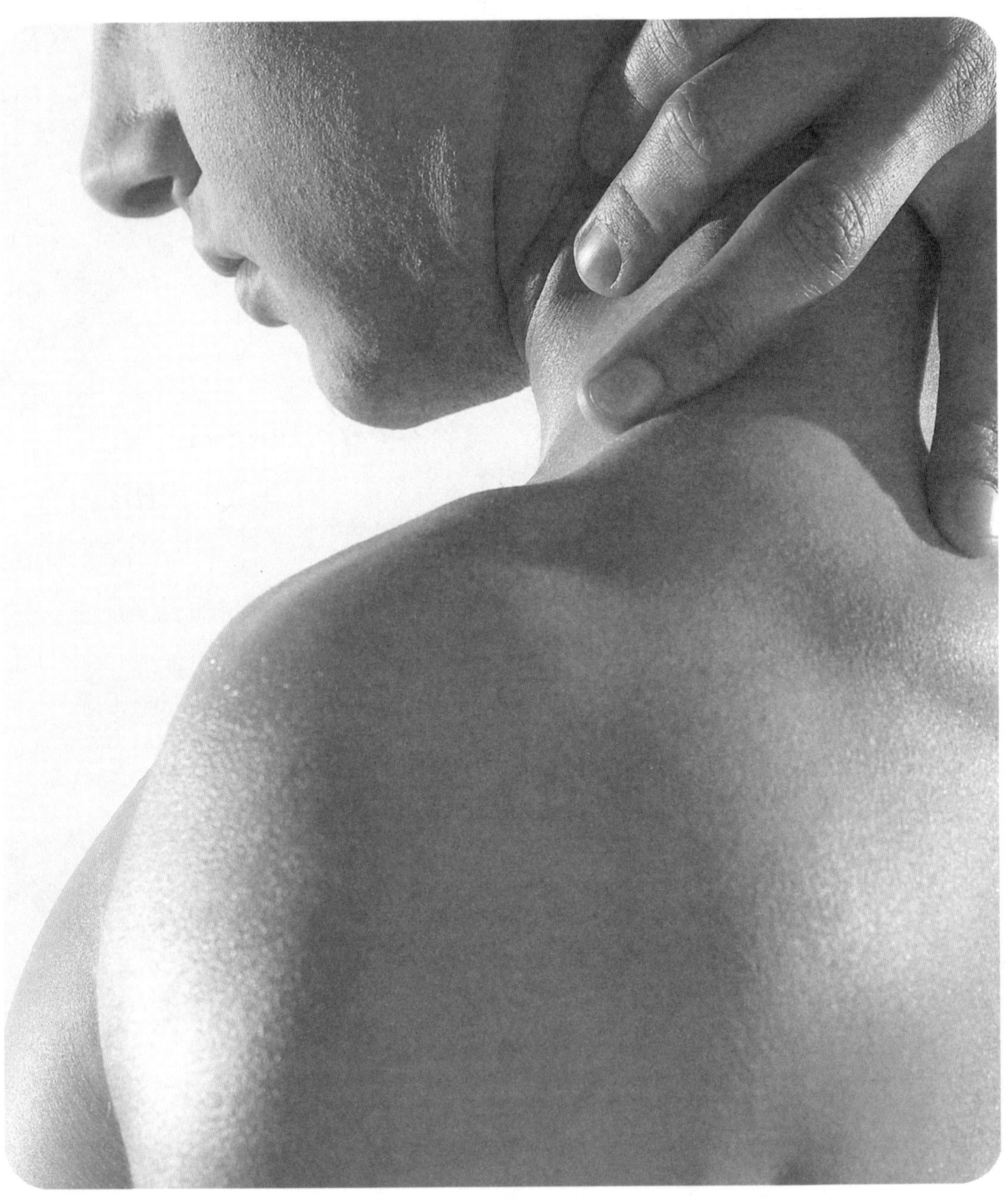

Upper left shoulder pain is always a current kidney issue. Kidney issues are demonstrated by upper left shoulder, low back, joint and various muscle pains.

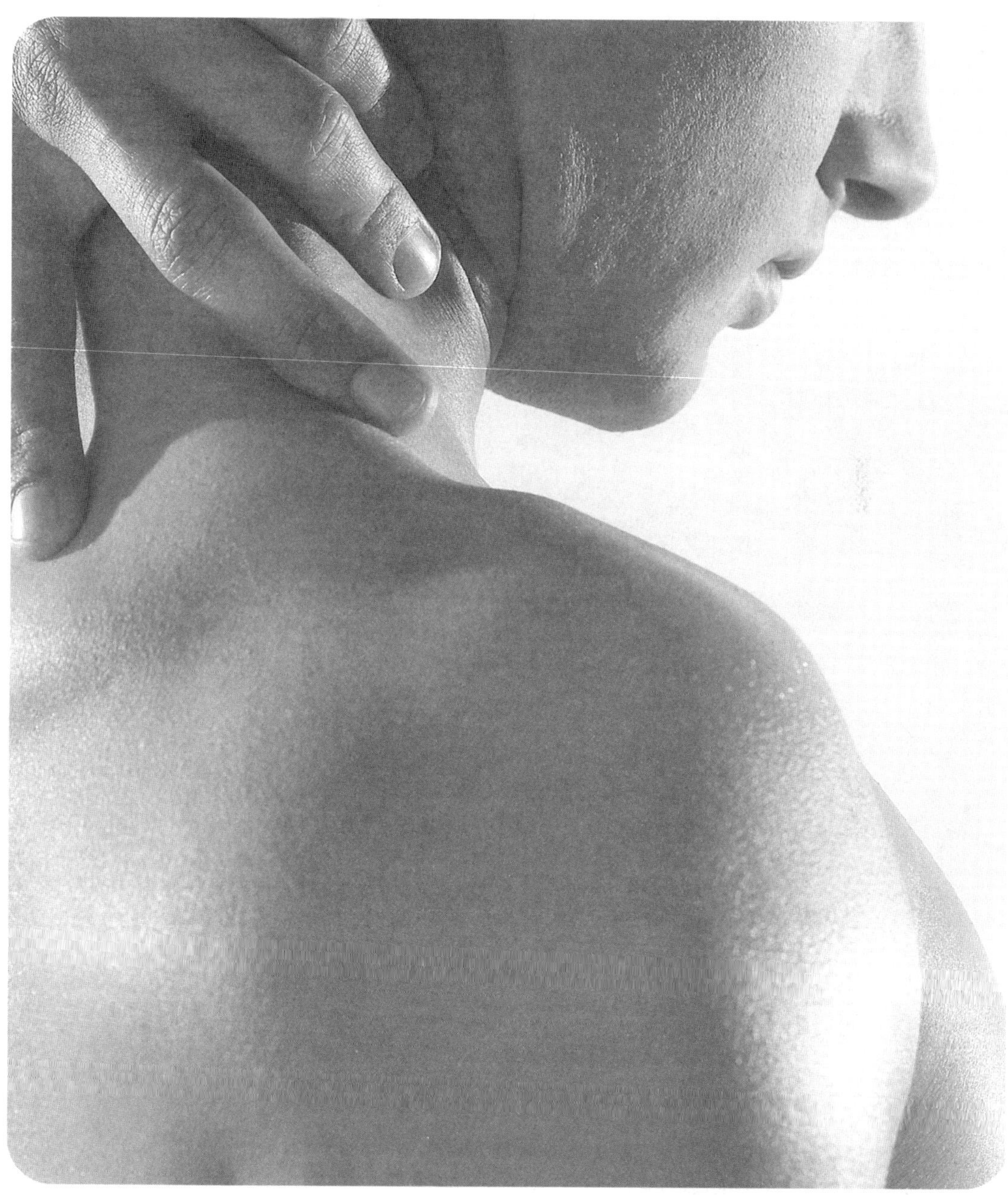

Upper right shoulder pain is always a signal of a current liver issue. Soreness can also be present in the right side of the neck, right pectoral, right bicep and triceps muscle.

Roger Bezanis

Who is the surgeon behind the mask? What motivates him? Is he a free thinker? Is he beholding to an organization that dictates what he does? Does he have your best interest in mind or a new Mercedes? Maybe you should see a chiropractor first.

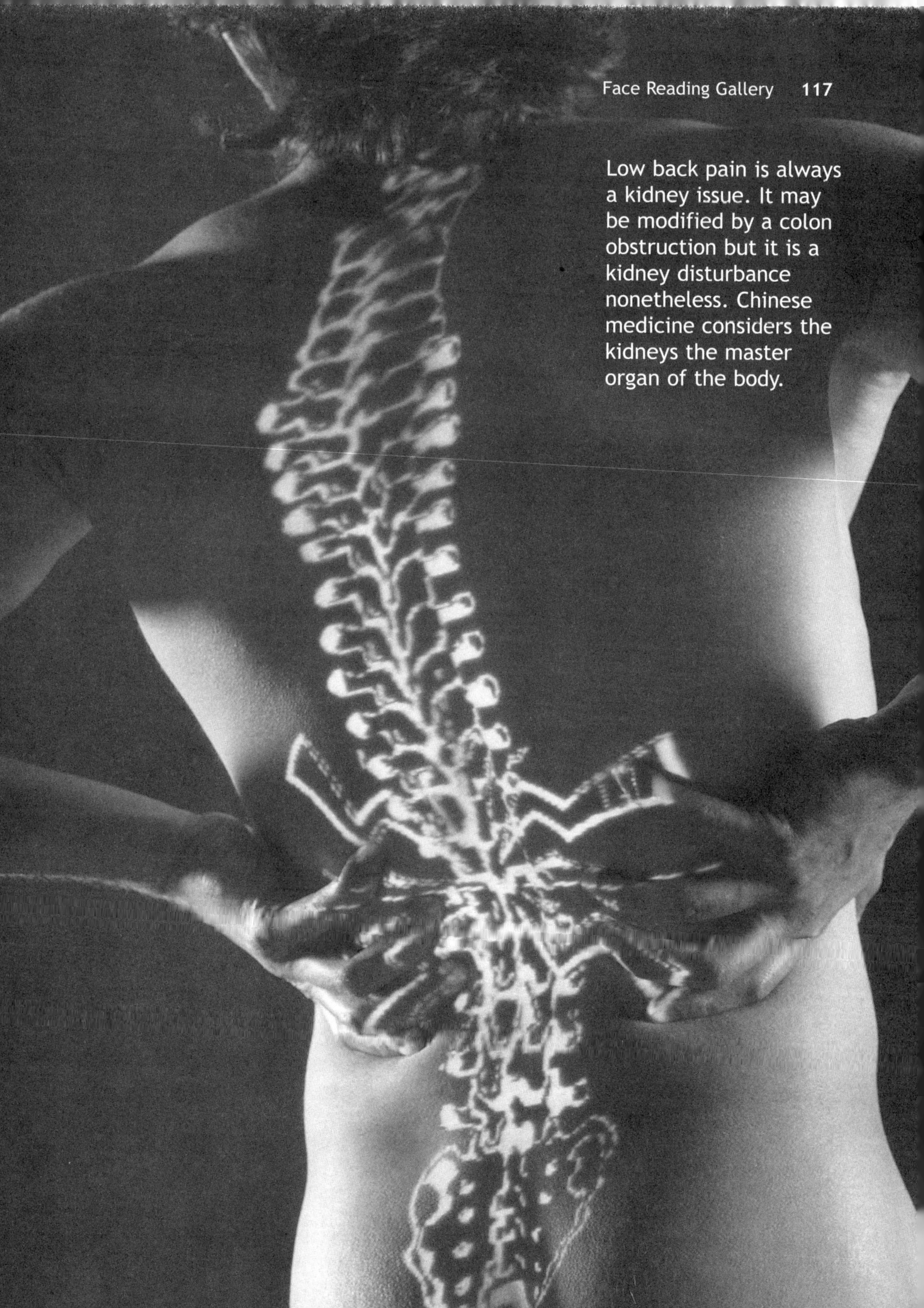

Low back pain is always a kidney issue. It may be modified by a colon obstruction but it is a kidney disturbance nonetheless. Chinese medicine considers the kidneys the master organ of the body.

This well-to-do gentleman was photographed circa 1887. Notice how poorly he looks. Privileged living means that he was able to afford and indulge in sugars, tobaccos and other 'treats' that were not as common to the general public. As you can see he has paid the price with a swollen stomach, poor kidneys, reproductive issues, endocrine / glandular trouble and liver upsets.

He was photographed circa 1879 Notice the lack of issues he had at approximately thirty years old. Not having the money to purchase the finer things meant he would have lived a better, less painful life.

This photo is from circa 1901. Notice how healthy he appears to be. His genes were strong and he appears to be showing no signs of a lifestyle lived in excess.

Look at what you can see from over one hundred years ago. His hair has receded (bladder / reproductive system), his kidneys are stressed (deep creasing under both eyes), he has a mole on his right eyelid and he has a huge mole on his chin (reproductive disturbance). Also notice the cleft in the end of his nose signifying heart issues. He is also clearly overweight and this seems to be facilitating his condition. With the right diet including kidney support and a full detox, he could have lost forty to sixty pounds. Looking at him, his weight was causing most of his problems, as the pressure in his body was crushing.

A doctor who does not listen to you and is not interested in letting you participate in your own healing is not a good doctor. You deserve respect.

A good doctor listens to you and cares about what you think. He is not anxious to send you in for surgery. Your doctor should be interested in alternative treatments and you should be willing to learn. Your doctor should never look down on you or belittle you.

kidney health

The most important food on the planet to eat for kidney health is grapes. They protect and feed the kidneys. They help the body correct the most dramatic problems imaginable including vertigo. The type of grapes consumed does not seem to matter.

grapes - vertigo

Digestion

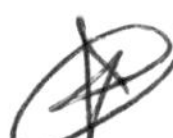

The best food for digestion is Clementine Tangerines. Indigestion is improved or made a non-factor within minutes upon eating them. They are also very good for liver health.

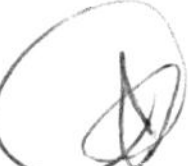

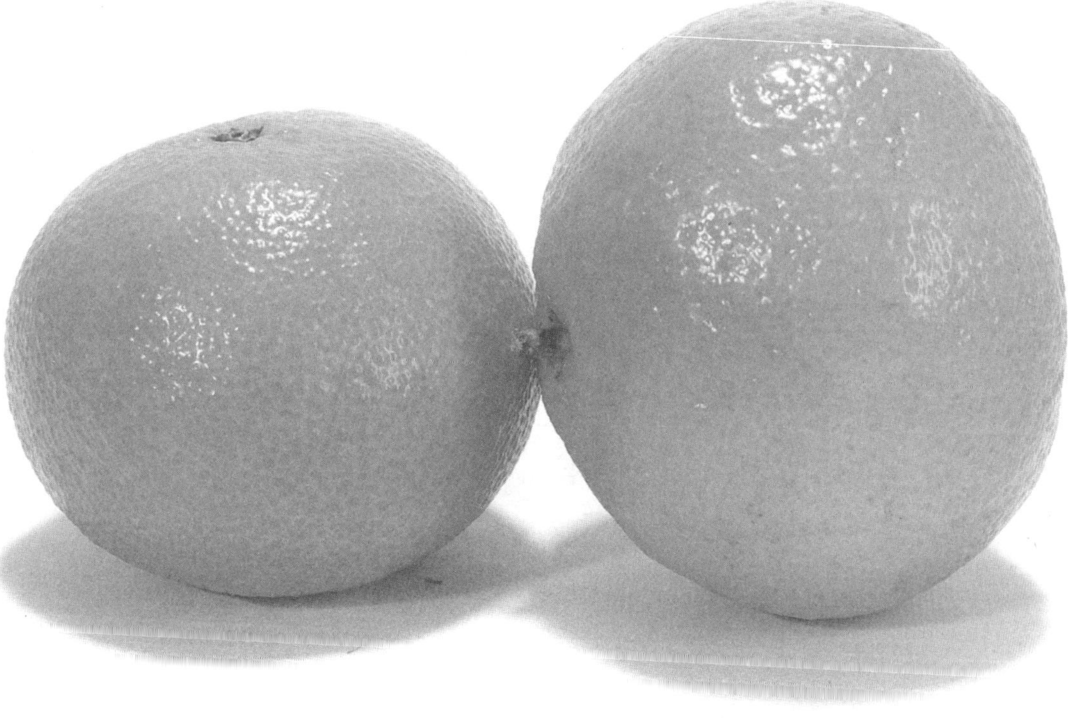

Alcohol is a mild solvent and poison that would never get FDA endorsement for human consumption if it were submitted for approval today.

Fresh vegetables are God's medicine and if consumed in plentiful amounts, they make the body almost impervious to sickness.

Meet the '3-Amigos' of poor health; sugar, flour and salt. Sugar is deadly in all processed forms as is flour which converts to sugar. Salt is a mineral that is only useful when it is ingested in a natural or whole food form. Table salt is not a natural form of salt as it was processed. Salt naturally occurring in a tomato, etc., is fine.

poor health : sugar, flour & salt

The best friend your body can have is 'nature's candy': fruit. Do not be afraid to indulge. If you can, get it organically grown. Nevertheless, eat fruit.

This so-called food is addicting and deadly to the system. We are burning-out our kidneys at an alarming rate thanks to poisons like these. More people are addicted to sugar than heroin and cocaine combined.

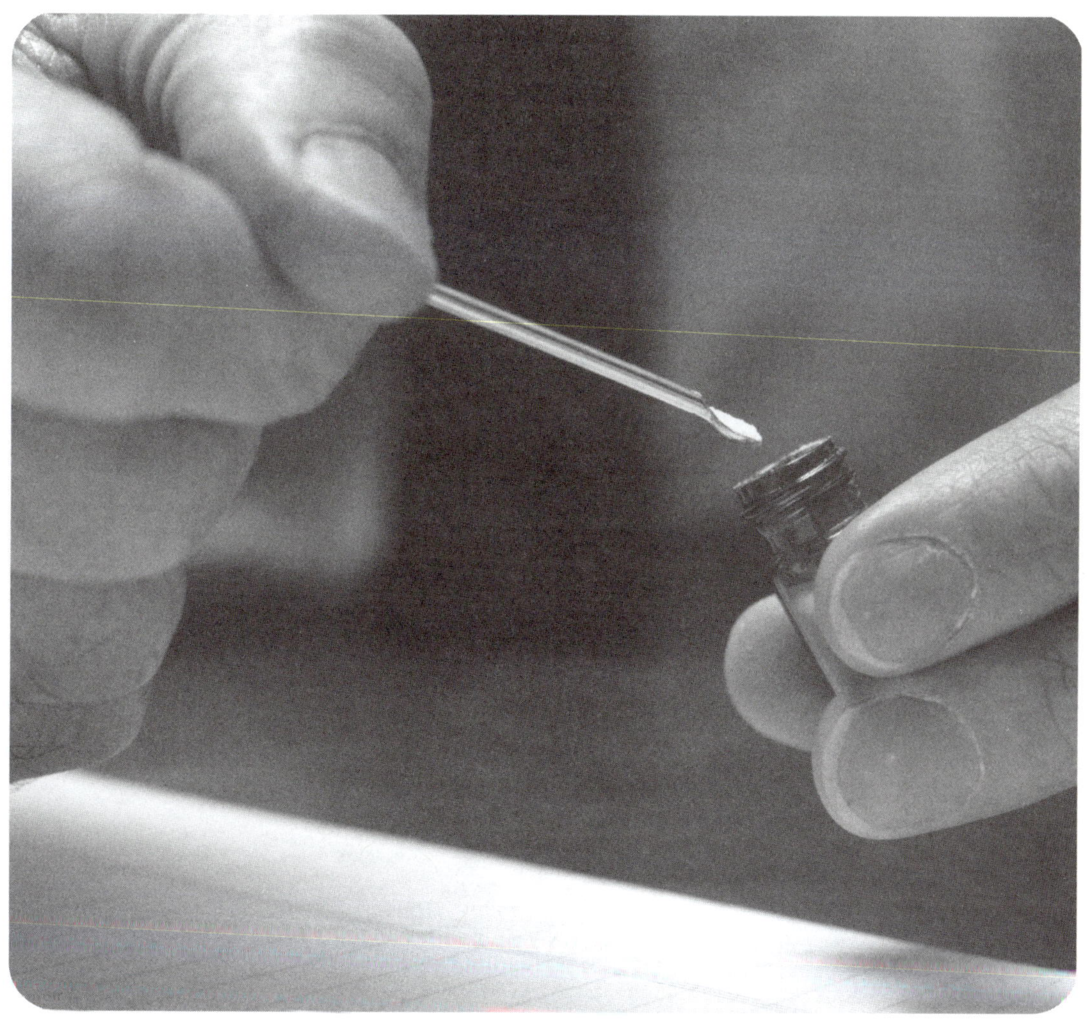

Cocaine is not the most addictive substance on the planet. But sugar, salt and flour are. Everyone you meet is addicted to the 3-Amigos of poor health.

Whole wheat bread is worthless to the body. Once grains are made into flour, they are toxic to the body. The cracked wheat you see adorning the crust of this bread is also worthless. Once the wheat kernel is cracked, the germ inside is dead. Bakers create bread by cooking flour until everything healthy in it is destroyed.

This is what whole wheat looks like. If you were really eating 'whole wheat' you would be gnawing on a stalk of wheat like this. If you planted a stalk of wheat, you could grow wheat. Planting bread may grow mold.

Caffeine is the most dangerous daily use substance on the planet. It is a poison and must not be consumed. Because of this my book will never be sold at Starbucks, Seattle's Best, Peet's or ___________ (fill in the blank).

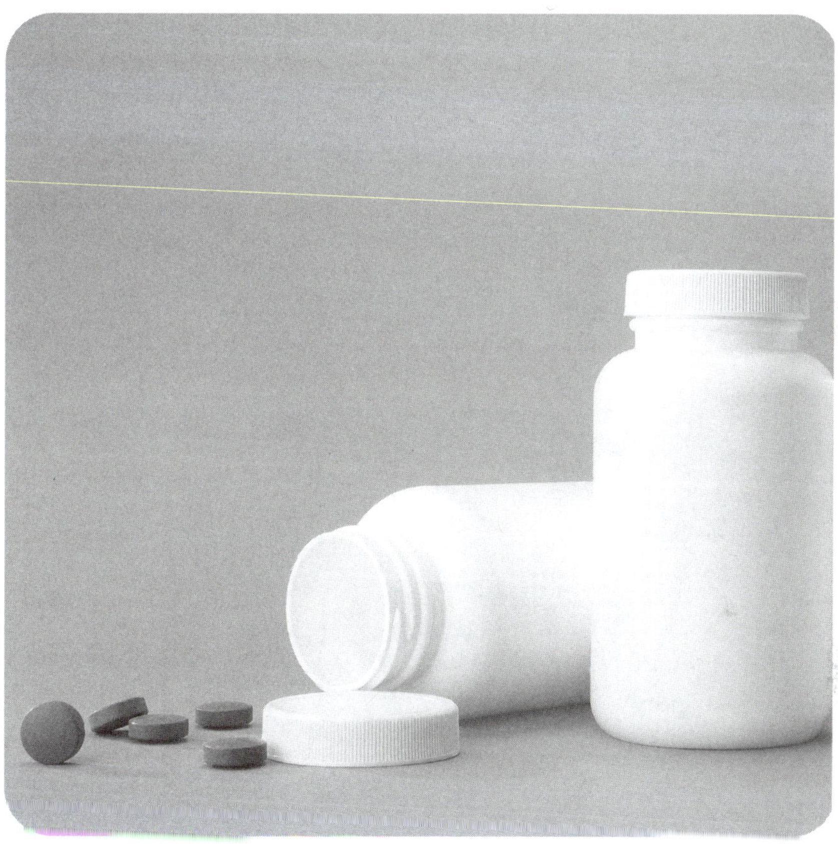

Herbal formulas are wonderful but whole food is the true medicine. Herbals are only temporary substitutes until you correct the source of your dietary issues. We eat ourselves into ill health. Caffeine is deadly and it is best removed from the body by a full 3-month detox.

Caffeine

The FDA (a government agency) takes 800 million dollars to approve a drug for sale. They issue a seven-year patent and then turn a blind eye to complaints until the patent runs out. To be truly useful to the government, you must be on drugs and in need of surgery.

Insurance companies, the FDA, AMA and American Psychiatric Association see you as a commodity. You health is worthless, your sickness is a priceless goldmine, your insurance is a treasure chest to be plundered, your free will must be controlled and your ability to think must be suppressed.

Psychiatry is an inhuman practice performed by insane doctors who want nothing more than to drug and control you. If you are taking drugs for a condition that is slowly made worse by their use, you will never recover. Remember Virginia Tech? Do you remember Columbine? Psychiatric drugs created all of the aforementioned.

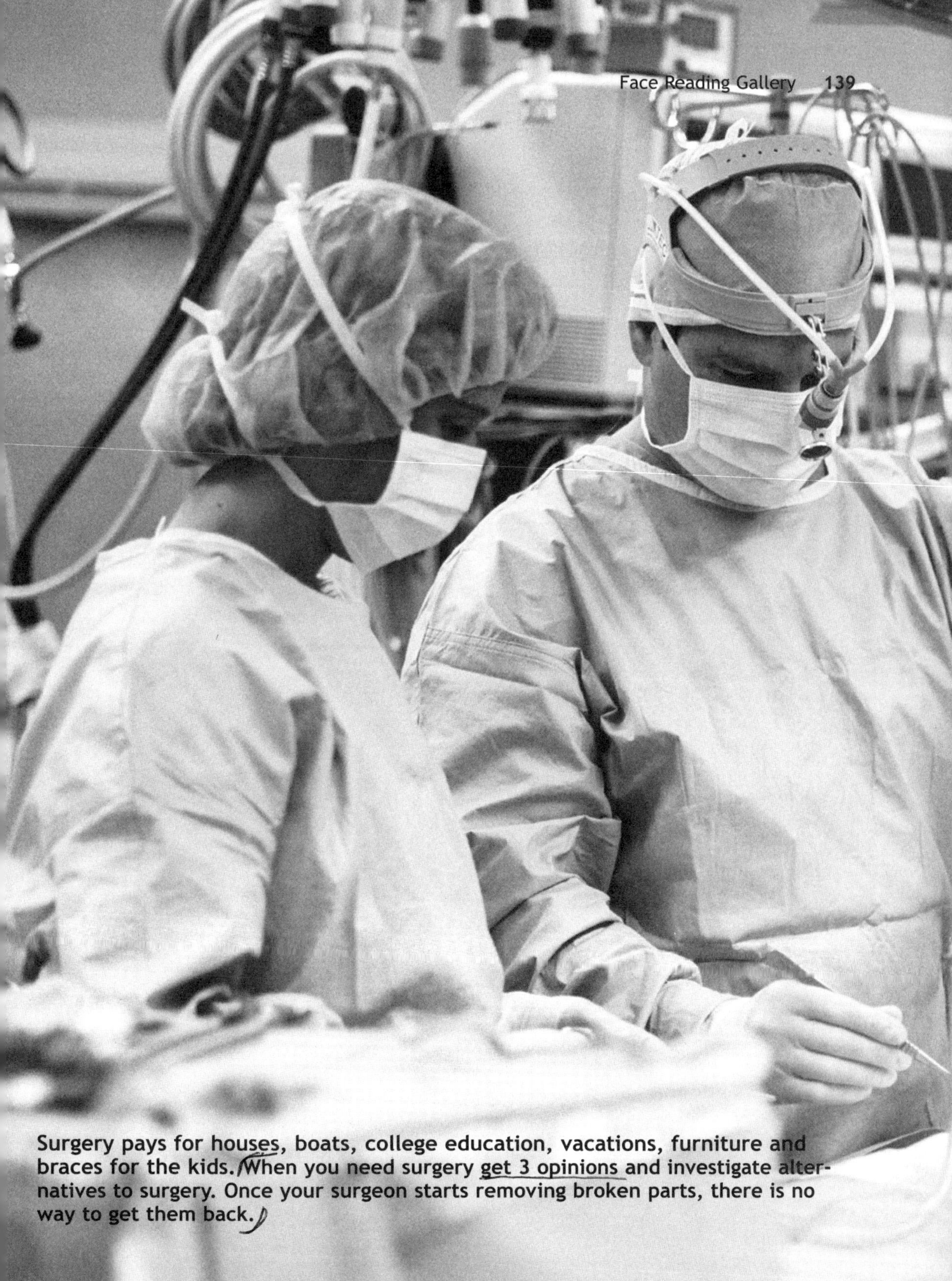

Surgery pays for houses, boats, college education, vacations, furniture and braces for the kids. When you need surgery get 3 opinions and investigate alternatives to surgery. Once your surgeon starts removing broken parts, there is no way to get them back.

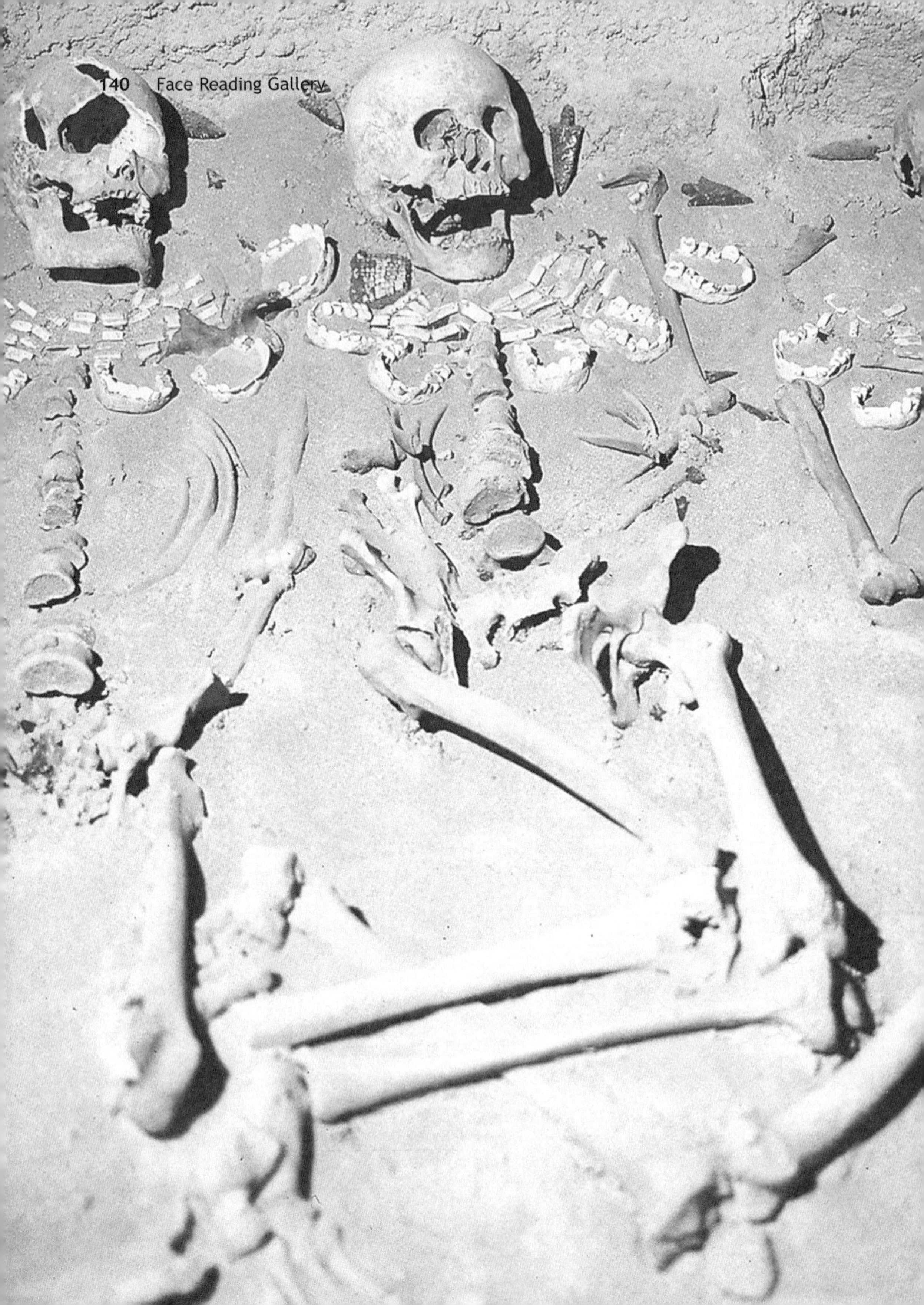

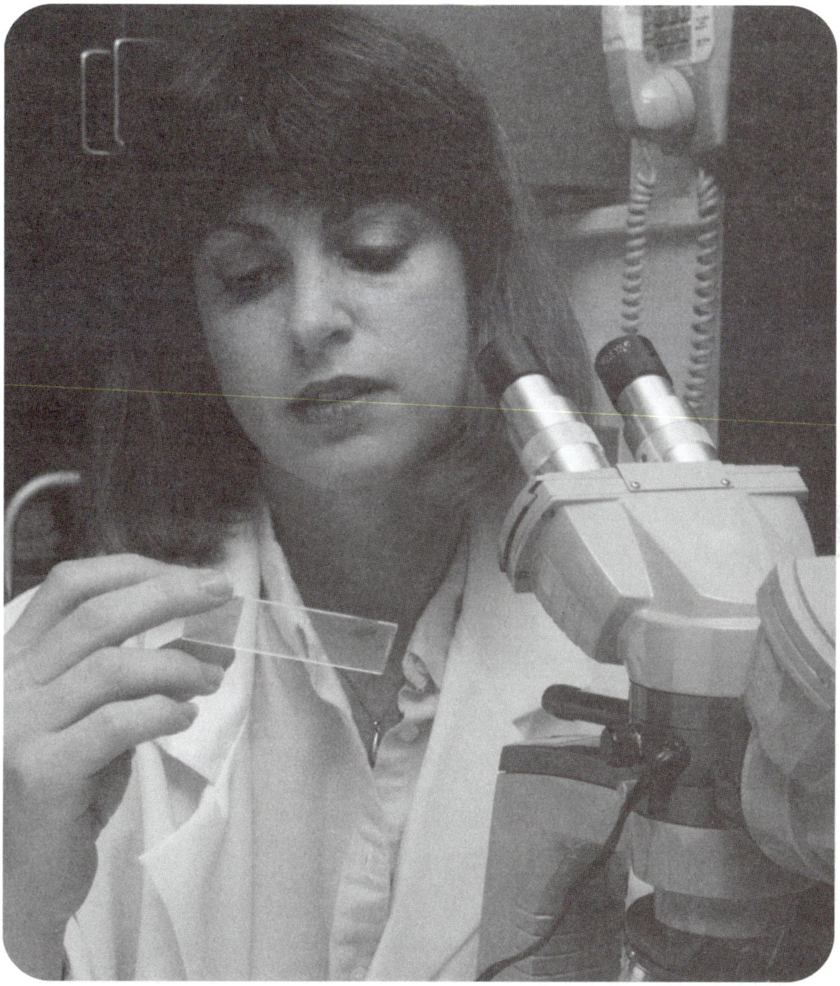

AIDS, Cancer, Flu and diabetes cannot be isolated under a microscope and are just a huge scary sales pitch. When you hear that x-million dollars is being dropped into research on some nebulous problem, the problem is all smoke and mirrors.

Man must be awake and not drugged to survive. To control his destiny and health he must not be a slave to substances and surgery. If not, he will become a footnote in earth's history. A drugged man is a controlled man.

This is not a healthy breakfast unless you only drank the juice.

Healthy Sources of Protein

Beef

Rare or raw steak (steak tartare) is fully bio-available to the body.

Avocados

Raw avocados are very friendly to the body. They also contain oils that when consumed raw are very healthy.

Eggs

Eggs can be readily consumed raw in fruit drinks or smoothies. Cooking destroys protein that then becomes an irritant to the kidneys, liver and endocrine system.

23 Validating Face Reading Effectiveness

Again, use these Diagnostic Face Reading photos in your office by simply directing your patients to really look at them. The effect of these photos and this book is really quite amazing. You will of course need to keep extra copies of this book at your office. When patients see these photos, they always want their own copy.

To really help your patients, use my Diagnostic Face Reading Charts (24 x 36) side by side on your wall with a good size mirror between the two charts.

- Point out the charts on your wall to your patients. Tell them to:
- "Look in the mirror and compare your face to the charts on the wall and tell me what you think is wrong."

They will turn to you and say

- "Doctor, is my _______ a problem?"
- It is then up to you and your patient to determine the best course of action.
- Get a full history of what symptoms your patient has present today (using the questions in the Energy Balancing Technique section or get an Energy Balancing Technique cheat card to help).
- Pick a therapy that will help your patient i.e. herb, diet etc.
- Take a picture (Polaroid or digital) of the patients face as it appears today.
- Put this picture and their current list of symptoms in their file.
- Send them home with what you two have decided is the best course of action.
- 30-45 days later have the patient return.
- Take a new picture and compare their new picture to the old one.
- Take a new patient full history of symptoms.
- Compare the new picture to the old one. Show the patient how they have changed.
- Do a new patient full history of symptoms; compare the new list to the old list. It will have reduced from 20 items to perhaps 9.

This simple approach validates that what you are doing is really working. In this day and age it is important to prove that what you are doing is safe and effective. Face reading and symptom reduction are the keys to your success.

24 Quantum Physics and the Body

About now you might be asking yourself "What does quantum physics have to do with face reading and the human body"? Your answer is EVERYTHING.

The body is an energetic organism made of material or mass. Read on.

Some of the greatest minds on the planet have toiled in the subject of Quantum Physics. The history of the study essentially started with quantum mechanics. This groundwork was the forerunner of quantum physics and took place in 1838 with Michael Faraday. Max Planck furthered it with the 1900 paper on blackbody radiation.

In a nutshell, Quantum Physics is the study of mass and its relationship to energy. In any structure (such as the human body), when there are equal amounts of mass and energy present, a state of optimum health is the result or balance is achieved. When there is an overabundance of mass or energy, the body gets sick and can die. If an imbalanced condition persists long enough, without fail the body will die.

Simple quantum physics formula: **Equal Mass + Equal Energy = Balance**

Quantum physics is so basic in its balancing aspect of life. It permeates all parts of life, even our language and government, stretching ad infinitum (infinity). For example black and white, hot and cold, dry and wet, forward and backward, soft and hard, acid and alkaline, etc. are all statements of balance.

On the road to further illustrate how mass and energy coexists, look at your dinner table or bed. Why do they not get up and walk away? The answer is; they do not possess energy available in sufficient quantity to accomplish the task of movement. All inanimate objects possess potential energy that can be ignited from an outside source. In the human body, a complete absence of energy would be called death.

A complete overwhelming amount of energy in the body can also cause death. This is commonly associated with a drug or chemical overdose. This is furthermore where we get the terms hyper-hypo and attack.

Organ overwhelm, caused by too much mass or energy, is different from failure as failing organs are experiencing very little or no energy.

The absolute expression of pure energy would be nuclear fission. A near absolute expression of energy would be a common fire. This is clearly only a near absolute expression of energy as this type of fire leaves ashes and cinders. The more complete the energy expression is, the more ability it has to destroy all mass.

This formula of mass versus energy explains why drugs are so harmful to the body. Drugs are, due to their processing, mass deficient and energy rich. Later I will dig deeper into this subject, with the focus on cocaine. You can now think with this concept; you are now starting to see mass / energy errors all about you.

Any organ or organ system that cannot process mass or energy / waste at its optimum capacity is failing and eventually will shut down. This fact is irrefutable and inevitable.

Consequently, is CANCER nothing but a mass that is not interfacing with and not being monitored by energy? That is exactly what it is. Hence, any health remedy for a so-called cancer must at its heart reestablish the flow of energy and mass at the affected site.

The body must be in communication with itself at every level 100 percent of the time to survive at an optimum echelon. All life is dependent upon these factors.

All life is trying to balance its mass and energy. The next chapter (Energy Balancing Technique) will explain this complex relationship.

25 Energy Balancing Technique (EBT)

Following on the heels of quantum physics is my energy balancing technique. EBT is the realization of real time quantum physics on the human body.

When I introduced the Energy Balancing Technique (EBT) almost 8 years ago, it was met with understandable skepticism. The technique was the outcrop of observations that I could not otherwise explain. Since I am in the business of explaining everything, I had to get to work.

First and foremost, I am an observer of life, and second, a formulator of herbal supplements. Testing my formulas almost a decade ago revealed that people claimed they felt better just holding the formulas before they even took them. I had not asked or probed for these observations. My test groups just kept offering them up.

Knowing that such "instant response" was impossible, I ignored the comments for weeks. Yet after 60-100 such comments I became very curious. Were these people all hallucinating?

Still not letting on that I was the least bit interested in these comments, I started testing the group with placebos. Suddenly the pleasant amazed comments detailing relief from aches, emotional improvement, enhanced vision, improved breathing, diminished pains and such, fell by 85%.

With instant response, I had achieved the impossible!

Still not sure what I had achieved, I began working on another formula. This mixture would be for the kidneys. I was certain nothing like this could ever happen again. Yet, I was not opposed to the idea.

A few months later I was back at it, with a new formula for kidneys. I was merrily testing away when I started hearing the comments again. Nevertheless, these comments were different. I checked my oriental medical references and in the descriptions were clues to what I was seeing.

Empirical data was proving that what was put in the LEFT HAND had a distinctly different affect than what was put in the RIGHT HAND.

Herbs put in the right hand affected all areas of the body directed by the liver. What was put in the left hand was directing all things regulated by the kidneys. When I switched formulas from one had to the other the affect would disappear. In other words, the hands were sensing for different systems of the body. This was the beginning of The Energy Balancing Technique.

Certainly what I have discovered is not something new. This must be very old. My guess is that it is more than 3000 years old as there is no mention of it. Regardless of its origins or how deeply it was buried in the sands of time, I present it to you now.

PRECEPT: The body has a constant flow of energy running through it.

PRECEPT: Whenever the flow of energy is interrupted in the body there will be a reaction of pain, discomfort, tightness, etc.

EBT AXIOM 1 - Your body is a sentient being (it is alive and conscious)

EBT AXIOM 2 - Your body is dependent on you for its survival.

EBT AXIOM 3 - Your body communicates to you 24 hours a day via sensation (pain, hot, cold, hunger etc)

EBT AXIOM 4 - Your body reacts in real time to all stimuli good or bad.

EBT AXIOM 5 - All aches, pains, swellings and other sensations are communications from your body to you.

EBT AXIOM 6 - Aches and Pains are requests for help from the body.

EBT AXIOM 7 - Man and his body communicate to the world via touch.

EBT AXIOM 8 - Touch is the most important sense humans have. Without it, man would perish.

With a few exceptions like hunger, and need for sleep, man & his body are not in communication.

At the moment of touch we will feel better, worse / hotter, colder, etc, instantly. If used, this technique evaluates any food or supplement in real time.

FACT: The body has two major test plates (or areas) that directly connect to our major organs for quick assessment.

TEST PLATE - RIGHT HAND (all organs and functions directed by the LIVER)

TEST PLATE - LEFT HAND (all organs and functions directed by the KIDNEYS)

SHORT LIST — RIGHT HAND LIVER — LEFT HAND KIDNEYS

RIGHT HAND LIVER:

- Liver
- Gallbladder
- Right shoulder / neck
- Stomach
- Small Intestines
- Colon
- Eyes
- Lungs
- Head / Brain
- *Lymphatic System
- **Parasites

LEFT HAND KIDNEYS:

- Kidneys
- Heart
- Left Shoulder / neck
- Most joints
- Low Back
- Adrenal glands
- Leg Muscles
- Prostate / Ovaries
- Bladder
- **Lymphatic System
- **Parasites

FULL LIST FULL LIST FULL LIST
LIVER / LIVER / LIVER
FULL LIST FULL LIST FULL LIST

RIGHT HAND
(RIGHT SIDE OF YOUR BODY ONLY)

Shoulder pain soreness or stiffness
Deltoid pain soreness or stiffness
Rotator cuff pain soreness or stiffness
Trapezoid pain soreness or stiffness
Neck (right side only) pain soreness or stiffness
Bicep pain soreness or stiffness
Triceps pain soreness or stiffness
Scapula pain soreness or stiffness
Latissimus Dorsi muscle soreness or stiffness
Right pectoral muscle pain soreness or stiffness
Fuzzy vision
Foggy vision
Irritated eyes
Stinging eyes
Watery eyes
Red eyes
Stinging tongue
Stinging or sore mouth (inside)
Congestion or pain in your nose
Congestion or pain in your sinuses
Congestion or pain in your chest
Bad moods
Mood swings
Irritable
Nervousness
PMS
Depression
Post partum depression
Obsessive behavior
Hot flashes
Insomnia
Trouble falling asleep
Trouble staying asleep
Headaches
Tiredness (is both a liver and kidney problem)
Itchy skin
Skin irritations
Skin tags
Strawberry spots
Acne
Boils
Numb skin
Tingling skin
Age spots
Liver spots
Lung irritation
Asthma
Pneumonia
Pain in the right side of your chest
Pain in the left side of your chest
Short of breath
Restricting breathing
Coughing
Emphysema
Tuberculosis
Lung cancer
Bronchitis
Pulmonary fibrosis
Sarcoidosis
Respiratory failure
Out of breath, easily
Gallstones
H. pylori (Heliobacter pylori)
Chronic fatigue syndrome
Epstein-Barr

FULL LIST FULL LIST FULL LIST
STOMACH / COLON / INTESTINES
FULL LIST FULL LIST FULL LIST

RIGHT HAND

- Right elbow pain
- Right elbow stiffness
- Right elbow soreness
- Right forearm pain
- Right forearm soreness
- Gas
- Bloating
- Acid Reflux
- GERD (Gastroesophgeal Reflux Disease)
- Acid indigestion
- Heartburn
- Indigestion
- Abdominal discomfort
- Abdominal spasms
- Ulcers
- Gas
- Upset stomach
- Abdominal distention
- Hiatal hernia
- Pain just above the right hip
- Soreness just above the right hip
- Cramping just above the right hip
- Leaky gut syndrome
- Polyps
- Ulcerative colitis
- Diverticulitis
- Diverticulosis
- IBS (irritable bowel Syndrome)
- Crohn's disease
- Sprue
- H. pylori (Heliobacter pylori)
- Hemorrhoids
- Candida
- Bloody stool
- Painful stools
- Foul smelling stools
- Abdomen sensitive to direct pressure
- Constipated less-than-one-elimination-per-meal-eaten

FULL LIST FULL LIST FULL LIST
KIDNEYS / KIDNEYS / KIDNEYS
FULL LIST FULL LIST FULL LIST

LEFT HAND

- Right kidney
- Left kidney
- Pain, stiffness or soreness in the left side of your neck
- Pain, stiffness or soreness in the left trapezoid muscle
- Pain, stiffness or soreness in the left pectoral
- Pain, stiffness or soreness in the left scapula
- Pain, stiffness or soreness in the left bicep
- Pain, stiffness or soreness in the left triceps

Pain, stiffness or soreness in the left elbow
Pain, stiffness or soreness in the left upper forearm
Pain, stiffness or soreness in the RIGHT lower forearm
Pain, stiffness or soreness in the left lower forearm
Pain, stiffness or soreness in the left wrist
Pain, stiffness or soreness in the RIGHT wrist
Carpel tunnel syndrome in RIGHT wrist
Carpel tunnel syndrome in LEFT wrist
Pain, stiffness or soreness in the left hand
Pain, stiffness or soreness in the RIGHT hand
Pain, stiffness or soreness in the left fingers or thumb
Pain, stiffness or soreness in the RIGHT fingers or thumb
Pain, stiffness or soreness in the upper left back area
Pain, stiffness or soreness in the center mid back area
Pain, stiffness or soreness in the left center back area
Pain, stiffness or soreness in the RIGHT lower back area
Pain, stiffness or soreness in the left lower back area
Pain, stiffness or soreness in the RIGHT hip area
Pain, stiffness or soreness in the left hip area
Pain, stiffness or soreness in the left hamstring area
Pain, stiffness or soreness in the RIGHT hamstring area
Pain, stiffness or soreness in the left front thigh area
Pain stiffness or soreness in the RIGHT thigh area
Pain stiffness or soreness in the left knee area
Pain stiffness or soreness in the RIGHT knee area
Pain stiffness or soreness in the left calf area
Pain stiffness or soreness in the RIGHT calf area
Pain stiffness or soreness in the left ankle area
Pain stiffness or soreness in the RIGHT ankle area
Pain stiffness or soreness in the left foot area
Pain stiffness or soreness in the Right foot area
Pain stiffness or soreness in the left foot toes
Pain stiffness or soreness in the Right foot toes
Dizziness / vertigo in the left ear
Dizziness / vertigo in the right ear
Ringing / tinnitus in the left ear
Ringing / tinnitus in the right ear
Kidney stones
Frequent urination during the night (more than once)
Frequent urination
Arthritis

Swollen joints (with or without pain)
Floaters (clear shapes) cross your field of vision
Weak nails that chip or break
High blood pressure
Gout
Diabetes
Numb or tingling muscles
Foamy morning urine (men only)
Exhausted a short time after eating
Exhausted from any time during the day (liver and kidney symptom)
Weak adrenal glands
Sexual performance issues
Difficult time staying aroused during sex
Lack of interest in sex
Lack of lubrication during sex
Lack of orgasm during sex
Unexpected pain during sex
Low sperm count
Trouble getting pregnant
Problems with fertility
Heavy bleeding during your period
Ovarian cysts
Uterine cysts
Uterine fibroid tumors
Unusual vaginal discharge
Heavy period cramps
Scrotum overly sensitive to the touch
Lack of sensation in the penis
Dull or sharp pain in the groin area
Heart double beat
Heart skips a beat
Heart flutter
Discomfort in the chest
Feel faint from time to time
Feel severe pounding in your chest during some light activities
Congestive heart failure
Heart attack
Stroke
Heart pound late at night for no apparent reason

When in contact with any substance, the body changes

Quantum physics clearly states this fact. We choose to ignore that a live organism (us) exists in a chemically hostile environment.

Man has neglected and denied this fact. Why?

Ergo, man believes he is intelligent and that his body to be stupid. He misunderstands the language the body speaks and finds these "communications" annoying. So much so that he suppresses these communications with painkillers and sedatives.

Imagine walking into your boss' office and telling him that the building is on fire. Ignoring you, he jabs a hypodermic needle full of morphine in your arm and depresses the plunger. You are now blissfully unconscious. Like your boss, you too are now clueless to the danger that the building is on fire.

Sounds silly doesn't it? Yet the above describes our relationship with our body. We constantly ignore and sedate it.

Man's instant response to stimuli is unavoidable, undeniable, unrelenting and irrefutable. You are going to test this and validate it for yourself.

Man reacts to:

- All Foods
- All herbals
- All chemicals
- Water
- Oxygen

In chapter four, I made mention of how the body changes when it is in contact with any substance. It will feel:

- Better
- Worse
- Neutral - No change.
- Get hotter
- Get colder
- Contract / tighten
- Expand / loosen
- Feel more pain
- Feel less pain
- Accelerate or speed up
- Decelerate or slow down
- Release waste
- Retain waste
- Release water
- Retain water
- Relax
- Become tense
- Oxygenate
- Deoxygenate
- Awaken / more energy
- Sedate / less energy
- Lighter
- Heavier

To test these phenomena, look at the KIDNEY LIST from this chapter.

Left palm

SHORT KIDNEY TEST

- Turn your head from the left to the right
  Notice how stiff and sore the LEFT SIDE of your NECK was just now
  Rate the irritation on a 1-10 scale, 10 being the worst____________
- Move your LEFT ARM over your head and behind you
  Notice how stiff and sore the LEFT SIDE of your SHOULDER was just now
  Rate the irritation on a 1-10 scale, 10 being the worst____________
- Bend your LEFT ELBOW all round, twist it and torque it
  Notice how stiff and sore the LEFT ELBOW was just now
  Rate the irritation on a 1-10 scale, 10 being the worst____________
- Turn and flex your RIGHT and LEFT WRISTS
  Notice how stiff and sore the RIGHT WRIST was just now
  Rate the irritation on a 1-10 scale, 10 being the worst (R)____________
  Notice how stiff the LEFT WRIST WAS
  Rate the irritation on a 1-10 scale, 10 being the worst (L)____________
- Flex your RIGHT and LEFT FINGERS
  Notice how stiff and sore the RIGHT FINGERS were just now
  Rate the irritation on a 1-10 scale, 10 being the worst (R)____________
  Notice how stiff and sore the LEFT FINGERS were just now
  Rate the irritation on a 1-10 scale, 10 being the worst (L)____________
- BEND AT THE WAIST left, right, forward back
  Notice how stiff and sore your RIGHT LOW BACK was just now
  Rate the irritation on a 1-10 scale, 10 being the worst (R)____________
  Notice how stiff the LEFT LOW BACK was just now
  Rate the irritation on a 1-10 scale, 10 being the worst (L)____________

You are about to repeat the same test again holding various substances one at a time in your left palm.

When you repeat these tests notice if you feel:

Better

Worse

The same (no change)

Continuing on, put three green grapes in your left hand and repeat the steps above (while still holding the three grapes).

Did you notice a change?

Were you?

- Better
- Worse
- The same (no change)

Continue testing yourself holding different substances; hold one at a time (in the left hand), while doing the flexing moves above. Keep this up until you are sure that you know what happens when the body comes in contact with a beneficial substance.

You may choose your own items to hold while testing as well.

At some point, test the items that are listed below: 

ITEMS TO BE HELD (one at a time)

Sugar
Water
Soup Mix
Salt
Tomato
Alcohol
Bread
Chocolate
Nail polish / or a solvent
Water
Vitamins
A formula for the kidneys

Repeat this test as often as you like against symptoms of your choosing.

NOW assess your body. Is some muscle, joint, tendon, ligament etc, sore? If so quickly check earlier in this chapter to determine if it is a liver or kidney problem.

RIGHT HAND = LIVER DOMINATED problem
LEFT HAND= KIDNEY DOMINATED problem

Once you know if your problem is a liver or kidney issue, you can continue on. Have you tested your current herbals and medicines? Did they make your symptoms go away by holding them? If not, those items are of very little value to you.

To test these phenomena, look at the KIDNEY LIST from this chapter.

SHORT LIVER TEST

- Turn your head from the left to the right
  Notice how stiff and sore the RIGHT SIDE of your NECK was just now
  Rate the irritation on a 1-10 scale, 10 being the worst____________

- Move your RIGHT SHOULDER in a rotating motion
  Notice how stiff and sore the RIGHT SHOULDER was just now
  Rate the irritation on a 1-10 scale, 10 being the worst____________

- Flex your RIGHT BICEP round, twist it and torque it
  Notice how stiff and sore the RIGHT BICEP was just now
  Rate the irritation on a 1-10 scale, 10 being the worst____________

- Flex your RIGHT BICEP & TRICEPS
  Notice how stiff and sore your RIGHT TRICEPS are just now
  Rate the irritation on a 1-10 scale, 10 being the worst ____________

- Take a deep breath and notice your lung's capacity
  Notice how much air you were able to get in your lungs just now
  Rate the irritation on a 10 best and 1 being the worst____________

(Energy can be tested; vision, emotional state, clarity of thought etc.)

Follow the same procedure that you followed for testing the kidneys. Substitute tomatoes, citrus, water or herbal formulas to evaluate how your body adjusts.

Test again.

Once you feel comfortable with this, use the technique all the time. You can even evaluate what to eat for lunch. You may appear rather interesting testing yourself (to others), but you will have certainty, regarding what you are about to eat.

Remember your body is a machine and is restricted by the same natural laws or physics that govern all machinery.

All machines:

React to stimuli

Need fuel

Need to be cleaned

Follow programs (or sequences of actions) no matter how rudimentary.

The body is systematic in its execution of its mechanical / life sustaining schedule. Think of this schedule as the combination numbers used to unlock a padlock. Numbers that when correctly entered, create a change. In the human body, the correct sequence can produce energy or reduce pain, etc.

A Master Lock Pad Lock will not open until the numbers are "dialed in" in the correct sequence. The right numbers "dialed in", in the wrong sequence, will leave the lock closed. This whole technique is designed to unlock your body every time it is locked up.

Your body will always want the following:

Every-body (all human bodies) needs Oxygen, Food & Water. From this we derive energy or life force. All bodies must produce energy to survive.

All bodies have the exact same numbers in their programming (the sequencing does change)

1). WATER (Always # 1 or 2 in testing)

2). FOOD (= Protein or Fresh Fruit)

3). REMEDY (a formula / herb or herb mixture / multiple mixtures as needed)

4). SOME COMBINATION OF THE ABOVE 3 POINTS.

The only variable in this whole equation is the order in which it wants these items. Often you can improve symptoms without the need of Protein or Fruit. The minimum you need to successfully reduce or eliminate any symptom is water (H_2O).

The roll of the Transverse Colon (TC): Do not negate the influence of digestion on your liver and kidneys. As the TC stretches across the abdomen, in front of the kidneys and below the liver / gallbladder, it can play havoc on all three.

A stressed TC can push up on the liver / gallbladder and back on the kidneys causing all manner of symptoms. When symptoms persist, always check water, remedy, protein, and transverse colon (one at a time, stopping when there is an improvement)

If you are not making the headway you want, introduce a colon herb, formula or citrus to the RIGHT hand, and while holding the other items you were testing test again. Again, a simple colon herb, formula, tangerine or orange in the right hand is all that is needed to repeat this test again.

This simple maneuver can produce miraculous results. Upwards of 98% of all humans suffer with constipation or a bowel problem; therefore, check the Transverse Colon as necessary. If you are having problems with this technique, your doctor can help or you can always call me.

Man's environment requires he interact with it via touch. This being the case, it explains why this technique is so basic. Man must in a moment's notice quickly evaluate cold, hot, sharp, dull, soft or hard, etc.

This sense is so refined it has dominated our being. Yet, this is an ancient protection mechanism that has been neglected. It has taken me decades of testing to re-establish this technique. I am giving it to you here.

Use it. Use it often.

Anyone who has ever seen me work at a convention or do weekend training is amazed at how adept I am at EBT. Doctors stare in wonder as doctor after patient walks away from me feeling better and not fully knowing why.

EBT is not Kinesiology. Do not make that mistake. Quantum physics deals in mass and energy. Problems of the body are either out of balance mass or energy. When the body contacts anything containing energy the body will either balance mass, energy, or both.

Muscle testing or Kinesiology involves the use of touching or holding something to the body while another person (the practitioner) tests the strength of the body. This reveals whether the item being tested is good for the body or not.

The last paragraph explained just why I do not do kinesiology or any of its offspring's. That type of testing requires one energized being (YOU) being in contact with another energized being (THE TESTER).

This kind of test is inherently faulty as there is an energy exchange between the tester and the testee. Unless you intend to live the rest of your life touching the tester (the other individual), the energy exchange between the two of you skews the test completely.

The EBT is by its purity, 100% accurate. The only factor being, the creativity awareness and detective work of the tester to unravel what they are working with.

Do not be fooled

Should the person you are interviewing try to take control and jump ahead or starts telling you

"Nothing hurts", "I'm fine", "This is silly" or some other variation of arguing, tell this person, "Thank you, but if you are not going to cooperate, I am going to stop and we will be done. If you want my help, I need you to help me. If you do not want my help, tell me now so that I can stop."

If you are working with someone who has an expanded / descended abdomen and who insists that they do not have issues of their colon or intestines, stop. When this same person insists that they are not constipated (less than, 1 elimination per meal eaten) stop. You cannot help this person, as they do not really want help. If that same person claims to never have been constipated, stop. See the chapter later on HELP.

In order to do face reading and EBT, you must be brave / confident and persistent. Do not get discouraged if you get a couple of no answers.

Remember, the EBT questions do not treat anything. It is up to you to use the right formula or herbs that will alleviate these symptoms. If you use the right formula or herbs, you can expect to see an immediate change in these symptoms. Note: an improved diet will also alleviate these symptoms, as diet is the most destructive aspect of our lives aside from drugs and surgery.

Accurate Strength Testing

While I discourage you from doing muscle testing with another person, I am including a test that involves testing strength, which you can do by yourself.

You are going to test yourself against dead weight.

Establish which side / hand is your strongest (left or right hand).
Get a 3-5 gallon unopened bottle of water (for a water cooler) or dumbbell (5-30 lbs.).
Place it directly next to the outside (not in front or behind) of your knee (four to six inches away).
Using your weaker hand, hold a substance to the center of your chest.
Squat down (at the knees) and grasp the neck of the water bottle or the dumbbell handle.
While gripping the bottle or handle, slowly stand up.
Notice how heavy the bottle or dumbbell appears.

Repeat the above 7 steps while holding nothing to your chest and then again while holding the substance to your chest. Notice that your strength is altered by what you hold to your chest.

This test reveals the invisible effects of quantum physics on the body. Certain substances will make the body stronger by unlocking energy. While others will interrupt this energy flow and the body will be weaker.

IMPORTANT NOTES IN STRENGTH TESTING

- First establish WHICH is your dominant side, right or left (stronger side of your body).
- Pick an item to test sugar, candy, cookie, supplement, fruit, vegetable, etc.
- Hold the item to your chest with your weaker hand.
- With the closed water bottle or dumbbell on your stronger side (next to the side of your leg).
- Bend down once or twice and lift the bottle or dumbbell without holding a substance to your chest.
- Repeat the above step while holding bread corn chips sugar or a cookie, etc. to your chest.

Was the bottle heaviness of the bottle or dumbbell affected by what you were holding? You are experiencing the simplest of communications from your body.

These tests reveal what your body wants and are otherwise (weakened) harmed by.

Repeat this test until you are certain of how it works. Test with the items below. Simple tests like this will uncover foods and chemicals that make the body stronger or weaker.

Your body never lies. Learn to trust its signals and you will be healthier.

Phase 1: acquire the following items:

A). 1 closed 5-gallon bottle of water (like for a water cooler)

B). 1 candy bar made of chocolate, unopened

C). 1 small bottle of tomato juice or vegetable juice

D). 1 lemon

E). 1 apple

F). 1 packet of artificial sweetener

G). 1 packet of sugar

With the seven items listed above, do not unwrap, open or eat any of the items you are going to test with. Leave the items closed and undisturbed.

Phase 2: next, with all of your items a few feet away, do the following:

1). Stand next to your 5 Gallon bottle of water on your dominant side.

2). Bend at the knees and grasp the bottle comfortably around the neck with your dominant hand.

3). Using your knees, stand up erect and notice how heavy your water bottle appears to you.

4). Notice how easy or hard it was to pick up the bottle a few inches off the floor.

Phase 3: Pick up an item like the candy bar and hold it to your chest with your weaker hand. Stand next to your water bottle and repeat the above 4 steps.

Repeat this test over and over again with different items held to your chest. Frequently do this test with nothing in your hand and notice how it affects your strength. Notice if your grip is weakened by what you are holding. Continue to test with various items, noticing what makes you weak and or strong or has no effect.

Dr. Wayne Dwyer recommends use of this type of test to demonstrate that negative thoughts make your body weak.

This is a very pure way to test the body and supplements. It is far better than Kinesiology, Muscle Testing and Resistance Testing. If it is utilized, it will give you amazing information.

26 Fingernail, Hand and Finger Analysis

The fingernails display the state of the body as regulated by the kidneys.

Every organ system of the body is dependent on fluid for its survival. Therefore, each fingernail displays the water table / circulation / energy level of the systems of the body.

There are hundreds of techniques for healing and detecting the health of the body. I have focused this book on giving you tools you can utilize and get very good at. Fingernail analysis is an extremely good tool that can be used with the other techniques to further validate and cement your earlier findings.

Like my face reading technique, my fingernail analysis method is not exactly like other practices heretofore found. Yet all techniques attempt to give you a window to your health.

Fingernail analysis has been with us for almost 4000 years. Each finger of your hand has a story to tell. Before I tell you the story of your fingernails, I should mention that every problem of the body has three similar factors: lack of oxygen / lack of circulation and lack of energy. This is why supporting your energy is akin to supporting your life. Think of these factors as life support for the body.

If an organ or area of the body is oxygen starved, then bacteria will spread and the body will falter even further. Again oxygen / circulation and energy are the answer.

When there is a broken bone, if not enough oxygen reaches that area, it will take an extended period of time to heal. Therefore, if oxygen consistently saturates an area of the body, the body will be more resistant to so-called disease, and when problems do occur, the body will heal quickly.

One of the best herbs that can be used to increase circulation is cayenne. Cayenne stimulates circulation and has a very distinct effect on healing.

Your nails should not:

- Easily split
- Easily chip
- Have ridges
- Have bumps
- Be yellow

Revamping of your lifestyle and diet is a sure way to start correcting any condition of the body. Here is what each fingernail represents.

Thumbnails: Represent the colon and intestinal tract.

Index Fingers: Represent the state of the liver and gallbladder and therefore represent your emotional well-being.

Middle Fingers: Heart, lungs, circulation.

Ring Fingers: Kidneys, adrenal glands, pancreas, sex drive and reproduction.

Pinky Fingers: Represent the lymphatic system, endocrine system, spleen, the brain and spine; all influenced by the kidneys.

What the nails should look like or WHAT IS A MOON:

At the back of your fingernail, NEAR YOUR FIRST FINGER JOINT, is a white (or light colored) half moon shaped area. All of your fingers should have a moon except the pinky finger. The moon represents the circulation as related to the organ associated to that finger.

All fingers should have moons except the pinky fingers.

If you have a black or partially black tongue combined with no moons on any fi
pinky, this can portend a very toxic condition.

Not a death sentence, yet if this condition persists, a very oxygen-depleted condition can spread in the body. The condition is often called cancer. Remember quantum physics states that a blockage is caused by little or no energy, circulation or oxygen. Repairing these factors repairs this condition.

When healthy, the moons should progress biggest to smallest from thumbs to ring fingers.

1). Thumb = Largest moon

2). Index finger = Second largest moon

3). Middle finger =, Third largest moon

4). Ring fingers = Fourth largest or smallest moon

5). Pinky fingers = No moon at all

Beware of moons that take up almost the entire nail, as this can be indicative of severe liver problems. Memory problems are often present when there are less than four moons per hand. The other accompanying problems often presented are poor circulation and cold hands. Low energy is also very likely.

No Moons At All on Any Fingers or Thumb

This is indicative of very poor circulation. The kidney and liver and therefore the entire system are under attack. This is the result of heavy toxicity in the system that if left unchecked could lead to cancer. The person will have most of, if not all of the liver and kidney symptoms listed in the liver and kidney chapters.

TONGUE NOTE: Look at the tongue. At this point examine the edges of the tongue. Have the person open their mouth and flop or lay their tongue out of the mouth relaxed without strain. It should just lay relaxed out of the mouth.

Look to see if there are tooth indentations on the sides of the tongue; If there are, this combined with the lack of moons can signal heavy toxicity in the system or even cancer.

Two Large Moons On the Pinky Fingers

This condition indicates an overworked heart / endocrine system and possibly high blood pressure. The kidneys will normally be severely overloaded. Look at the face. Are the eyes puffy or dark? If so, you will also find low back pain, stiffness or soreness as well as sore muscles. This can include a thyroid problem / endocrine problem, which again has bad kidneys at its base.

TONGUE NOTE: Have the person stick out their tongue; if, when the tongue is relaxed, it is pointy and red tipped this validates a heart problem.

Short Wide Reddish Nails / Short Wide Nails

This condition indicates a cardiovascular issue (i.e. heart condition), high blood pressure and problems of the arteries. The moons on fingers and thumbs may have a "halo" of white silhouetting or separating the moon from the rest of the fingernail.

This just further validates the condition of heart.

Dark Spot on the Ring Finger of the Right Hand

If you notice a black oval spot on the right hand ring finger, this can indicate a liver problem that can even indicate liver cancer.

Arched Nail That Rolls Down Over the Tip of the Finger

A nail with this condition indicates that the kidneys are not processing protein. The individual may suffer with low energy throughout the day. They may be on a kidney-irritating high protein diet. This individual may be taking iron that is not being processed. This individual has kidney issues and needs to clear their kidneys and open up the channels. clear my kidneys

A Flat Nail with No Curvature

This indicates that there are digestive disturbances or possibly an inflamed chronic stomach condition. This also includes nails that are blackish or yellow in tone.

A Spoon Shaped Nail That Dips in the Middle and Grows Up at the Tip

This is a red flag and indicates the presence of parasites in the system. The nail may also be hazy looking or unclear. You may feel fatigue and crave sugar. All of this signals parasites. Cancer patients also can have nails that meet this description.

White Spots under the Nails

Should you develop white spots underneath your nails, it indicates you are dealing with excess hormones. You may also see white horizontal lines on the nail. These lines further indicate kidney issues. They are not caused by protein or calcium as is commonly believed. There is one cause for these spots and one cause only, hormones, but where are these hormones coming from?

(See the HORMONE WARNING AT THE END OF THIS CHAPTER)

Red Spots

If the middle finger has a red spot on it, this can indicate a heart condition.

Nails That Split or Are Easily Broken

Nails in this condition are lacking nutrients, as are the systems the nails represent. Normally, all nails will be in this condition but isolated chipping, breaking and splitting do occur. This is always indicative of kidney challenges. Vitamin B-complex could be being eroded by parasites or just not getting into the system due to toxicity in the kidney. Alcohol consumption, caffeine intake, drug use and excessive protein may cause the same condition.

Slow Growing Thick and Hard Nails

This again is a kidney issue regardless of the nail or nails involved. Tobacco use, heavy industrial chemical exposure, which directly leads to endocrine system overload, also crafts this challenge.

Yellow Nails

Often comes with years of smoking. The lungs are very overwhelmed and oxygen is not reaching the cells at a sufficient rate. The person may have a chronic cough and digestive tribulations. Yellow nails can occur due to years of chemical exposure as these compounds have settled in the lungs. The liver supports the lungs; therefore anything that can be done to improve liver and lung function will be a benefit. Other common symptoms will include insomnia, poor energy, itchy skin, irritated eyes and extreme poor moods. Again, this condition is greatly aided by simply improving liver / lung and kidneys as these dynamos are in a weakened state.

Vertical Black Lines under the Nails

Indicates internal bleeding associated with the organ that corresponds to that finger. This is also an excellent test for parasites as parasites ingest quantities of blood. Often this condition is facilitated by a diet high in sugar, breads, manmade starches, caffeine, unhandled stress and constipation.

Black Splotches on the Nails

If a black spot is seen on the nail that does not move with nail growth this can mean cancer. Examine the tongue for color (should not be black). Notice the presence of the fingernail moons (no pinky moon) and look to see if the tongue has teeth marks on the edges, when it is relaxed and laying out of the mouth.

HORMONE WARNING: The two hormones that show up under our nails can be either testosterone or estrogen or faux versions of either one.

We live in a chemical happy "life better through science" society. Business needs to get every dollar it can from its products. The thrust in the poultry, beef, fish and dairy industry has been to deliver product to market that arrives faster and is more profitable. In the last 40 years hormones have been increasingly used to "plump up" the average animal targeted for slaughter. If the average meat yield is increased by just 3 percent per animal, this is worth hundreds of millions of dollars in profit annually.

Added Hormone (steroids) Impact on Society

- The average age for a first period is now 12?, up from age 14 in 1900.
- Teenage breast size has increased at an alarming (1.3 cup size) rate in the last 20 years.

- The number of breast cancer cases reported annually approached 900,000 in 1997, up from 572,000 in 1980.
- Juvenile diabetes (virtually unheard of 40 years ago) is on a steady rise.
- Male muscle mass is increasing while scalp hair is decreasing. Hair replacement has become a billion dollar a year industry in the last 30 years.
- Since the advent of hormone infusion into the food supply, the average height of humans has jumped by more than 4%.

Correctly you should be asking how this has happened.

The answer is both alarming and maddening: beef, poultry, fish, chocolate and dairy products are your culprits. Earlier I mentioned that our meat and dairy is infused with hormones to make it bigger, meatier and therefore more valuable. Money is the answer.

Steroids are pumped into our food supply not for our benefit but the benefit of the seller.

These hormones are much like seeing a doctor and getting steroid injections. We are participating in a chemical experiment at this very moment. The only permission you gave was based on what you chose to put in your mouth.

Another source of hormones is from chocolate. Chocolate mimics both testosterone and estrogen hormones in the body and offers a double dose when you consume milk chocolate. Have you ever wondered why you feel so good when you eat chocolate? If so, the chocolate confectioners of the planet would prefer you did not mention the next paragraph.

Chemistry class 101

Chocolate creates noticeable euphoria when consumed due to hormone mimicry.

On contact with the system, chocolate quickly converts to synthetic estrogen and testosterone. Your body starts to react to this chemical cocktail. The body goes into the reproductive and growth cycle. Suddenly we are swept up in a chemically induced cloud of aphrodisiac sensation. Blood flow increases as temperature rises. Breathing quickens, as does the pulse.

The euphoria derived from chocolate has been well known by Valentine's Day marketers for decades. Did you think it was love? Did you think you had found your soul mate? Perhaps you did, but you were also drugged in the process and didn't know it.

Whenever you eat chocolate you will feel some degree of euphoria, sexual urges, and brief but quick burning energy. Long consistent exposure causes kidney / endocrine and liver failure. Now that you know where the bodies are buried, there is no hiding from it.

Unless you change, you are giving your tacit compliance to participate in an experiment where the long-range results are not known. The choice is yours. To prevent hormone overload and the resulting failure of your system, eliminate chocolate, dairy and eat only free-range meat and poultry from your health food store. Not heeding this warning your body (via steroids) will take on mass (height / breast size / muscle) and mutate in ways that cannot be predicted. Imagine your heart swelling in size, or masses growing in your brain or vital organs. These conditions are under your control but if not controlled by you, you may start living a nightmare every day.

Free-range

adj. 1 a: Of, relating to, or produced by animals, especially poultry, that range freely for food, rather than being confined in an enclosure: free-range chickens.

verb 2 a: The raising of livestock and domestic poultry; permitted to graze or forage rather than being confined to a feedlot
Synonym: unenclosed

A Word or Two on Your Fingers

Another way to detect INHERITED kidney issues (and there are many) is to look at finger length.

INDEX FINGER—–-	1st finger closest to the thumb
MIDDLE FINGER—-	2nd finger (the bird flipping finger)
RING FINGER——-	3rd finger (where a wedding ring goes)

Your ring finger (3rd finger) of your dominant hand should be longer than your index finger (1st finger) of the same hand.

If it is not, there is an inherited kidney issue. A predisposition to a kidney problem (or any problem) does not have to manifest. If you are aware of potential problems, potential problems can remain potential.

Now a Word on Your Hands

Another way to check for current kidney challenges is demonstrated on this test.

Do the following.

- Stand in front of a mirror and close your eyes.
- Now lightly shake out your arms and let them fall to their full length and dangle at your sides.
- Without moving your hands or arms, open your eyes and look (in the mirror) at where your palms are facing.

Are they facing?

A). Behind you?

B). Toward your thighs?

C). More forward toward the mirror?

(Right hand = Right Kidney / Left hand = Left kidney)

A = Weak - low energy kidney on that side of the body

B = Indicates the kidneys are healthy and running well

C = Indicates hyper-condition as the kidneys are running hot

You may also notice that the hand that is facing more directly behind you is on the side where your kidney is worse today. The results of this test change on a daily basis as your kidneys run better or worse.

To further validate your findings, compare the bag or dark circle under the eye to the hand that is more directly angled behind you or in front of you,

Did you notice that your eyes agree with your hands in this test? Did you also notice other kidney symptoms such as low back pain, kidneys that feel warm (even slightly)? These tests are simple yet very useful.

27 About The Tongue

The tongue does not get much attention in western medicine yet it speaks volumes about your health. Usually it is just in the way during dental work and examining the tonsils. In the early 1900s the tongue was far more important in diagnoses. Today it is still accepted that a white coating indicates immune system activity.

Tongue basics

Tongue Cracking

Should the tongue have cracks in it, it is due to a kidney problem. Regardless of anything else you know or that might come up, at the basis of it is a kidney problem. If the cracking is very deep then the stomach is also involved. Regardless, digestion and kidneys are at the source of this issue.

Red Spots On The Tip Of The Tongue

Indicates heart issues; the denser the spots are, the worse the condition. Compare this with other tools from earlier chapters. Read the chapter on ear piercing, as this section reveals much data. If the tongue is pointy at the tip, this is also an indication of heart issues.

Stinging Tongue (Burning Mouth Syndrome)

The totality of this problem is a liver running hot. The sensation can spread all over the mouth. The diet is at issue. Eliminate oils, spicy foods and salty food. Eat citrus, use a good liver formula (without milk thistle), drink more water and avoid caffeine. Like most problems of the body, BMS is the result of an ineffective / poor diet.

A Slightly Black Tongue

This is the forerunner to serious oxygen depletion in the body. The endocrine system, liver, kidneys, etc, are overloaded. There is never a kidney problem that does not include a liver problem; both need support. Remove sugar from the diet as well as sodium and correct the problem. See your health care practitioner and with his or her help, you can improve this situation.

A Predominantly Black Tongue

When the tongue is predominantly black, this is very serious as the system is in a shut down mode. The kidneys and liver are in very great trouble and since they support and regulate the entire system, the system is under great stress as well. Poor circulation will make the hands, feet, legs and arms cold. In later stages the body will become very hot as the immune system struggles forward. The person may have a dull, constant headache, labored breathing, dizziness and confusion. This is not a death sentence; it indicates that much must be done to immediately increase CIRCULATION / OXYGEN and ENERGY to the body.

They may be manifesting all the symptoms of kidney and liver overwhelm. If this condition is allowed to continue, the body will get weaker and show more signs of shutting down. This condition does not have to signal the end. It just indicates that to reverse the condition it will take a lot of time and work. Again, repair CIRCULATION / OXYGEN and ENERGY to the body and, of course, eliminate all manmade sugar and as many processed foods as possible.

A Pink Clear Healthy Looking Tongue Without Spots or Teeth Marks

Everything is fine and the system is working properly. If you had conditions of the tongue and they have changed, beware that the condition may return. Therefore you must be diligent.

The healing of the system, and the corresponding tongue changes do not necessarily occur gradually. The tongue will improve its look as unhealthy conditions reduce and the body gets stronger. The body may feel better on contact with certain remedies and stimuli, but chronic conditions will take time to fully heal themselves.

About Your Hair

Hair gets a lot of attention in our society but for all the wrong reasons. Sure it looks great and can be colored, dyed, made curly or chopped off. More importantly, it reflects the health of our kidneys. When the kidneys are running well, the nails and hair are strong.

Hair that is thin and getting thinner indicates that the kidneys are in trouble. If the hair has thinned but has stabilized, then kidneys were a problem and have also stabilized. Graying hair is indicative of kidney weakness. It is true that we inherit our health tendencies from our parents; yet, it is what we do with these tendencies that matters.

Repeating, hair should keep its color; if it does not, it is due to weak kidneys. The door of health swings both ways. Hair that grays overnight or over a few days is directly due to overwhelmed kidneys. But the hair can return to its natural color if the problem is caught early enough.

I have corrected my own hair color twice (at this printing). Others are working on the same target.

The mechanics of it work this way. Due to kidney blockage or overwhelm, the kidneys are not getting or are not processing B-complex and other nutrients (which supports kidney function and hair color). When this occurs, the hair loses its color. The hair can also start falling out.

The other factors are of course decreased oxygen, circulation and energy. Repair all three and kidney function and any condition can change even hair color.

Correct any problem of the body with the same 5 steps:

1). Determine what you are being exposed to that is facilitating the problem (this is the stimulus).

2). Eliminate the stimuli causing the problem.

3). Strengthen or clean via detoxification the organ affected by the stimuli.

4). Don't re-introduce the stimuli that caused the problem.

5). Repair circulation, oxygen and energy flow in the body.

28 Eyebrows

Eyebrows are not just for plucking and /or decoration. You may have noticed that eyebrow color does not always match hair color exactly.

*Darker eyebrows foretell an excellent kidneys probability factor. Your eyebrows should be darker than the hair on your head.

*If your eyebrows are naturally light in color, then it will take more work to keep your kidneys healthy.

*If the eyebrows grow sparsely and are lighter in color, this again indicates kidney challenges.

*If the eyebrow hair of either sex grows straight up and does not lie against the skin, then the liver and the kidneys are problematic.

As I said at the beginning of this chapter, the better circulation of the body, the better the health of the body will be. Do not be afraid to incorporate cayenne capsules, turmeric, cinnamon bark and wasabi japonica into your life. Take enough to create the kind of effect that you are looking for. Do not ignore your diet, as some people like to do. If diet is never addressed, your condition may return.

Summation: Oxygen must consistently saturate the body. Bodies resistant to disease are oxygen / circulation and energy rich. Utilizing the previous three factors can heal any problem.

29 What Your Body Really Needs and Wants

Albeit short, you are embarking on one of the most important chapters in this book. It unveils itself in the next several paragraphs. If you understand and apply the following data, you will almost certainly never have a weight problem again. You will be able to heal the most serious of problems. You will be almost impervious to sickness.

Imagine your body as a warehouse business. The job of a business like this is to receive goods at the receiving dock, process the items and then redirect them out the shipping door to a waiting truck. Your staff can handle 25 packages a day without too much trouble.

Your business is open from 8 to 5 pm daily. Processing delivered items takes 3 hours per item from delivery to shipping dock. Given that your warehouse staff needs to take breaks, lunches and go home at 5:00 pm, it is important to make their job as simple as possible.

Otherwise, you risk them not getting home on time for dinner and thus not being rested for the next day, Should they be required to work overtime, it would be expected that they would show up for work the next day late, feeling tired or sick or all three.

With these factors in mind, when would you want your deliveries?

You would, of course, want them in the morning and no later than 2 pm in the afternoon. Deliveries that come late means your staff cannot go home on time. Tired workers are not effective workers.

Imagine a tired staff trying to keep up with the day's work after one, two, three or consistent late night work. Imagine your order department going a little overboard with crazy or unusual items that need loads of processing just to be understood.

Delivery packages would start to stack up, your warehouse will start to have to store all of these unhandled packages.

This is the state of the human body. This analogy is accurate to how we must run our days. Eating in the morning is vital to start the day. Eating the majority of your meals no later than 3:00 pm, while not social, is very healthy.

If you do eat in the afternoon or evening (and you can), it is best to eat fresh fruit or a light salad. You will be amazed if you adapt this approach. You will be energized and alive all day. Your body can heal itself much quicker. You will drop weight (if you need to) and look younger.

Your shipping and receiving department, in order to work well, needs to handle packages that need little or no processing. It also needs those packages early.

A Short Play

Congratulations! You have just been elected to the new hamlet of Toeville. It is a sleepy little community of manicured front lawns, picket fences, bike lanes, dog walks and bouncy people. Amazingly, it is a neighborhood inside your own body.

This morning is like any other morning. The sun is up and people are happy. All of your residents (the joints, tendons and ligaments) put out their Uric Acid Trash in their tidy little cans for pick up.

Like every morning, the cans will be picked up promptly at 7:00 a.m. But unlike the other days, the UATT (Uric Acid Trash Trucks) are not going to show up. Back at the waste dump the crews must have been partying all night and are all hung-over.

The next day comes and goes. Then the next day and stills no trucks. The tra stack up. Imagine no pick up for 3 days! The crews must have passed out on a suga else can go wrong?

Trash is everywhere and the Toeville residents are so upset they are not even showering. The residents can hardly stand up without pain. They cannot take out any more trash, as they are too exhausted to move. Then the pipes in Toeville start leaking. There is sewage and water everywhere. Remember Sara Cynthia Sylvia Stout? Toeville can't take the garbage out.

Toeville is an absolute mess! The problem that was a local one has now become a statewide disaster. Everywhere in the state trash is out of control with no relief in sight.

Modern medicine would say it is a toe problem and treat the toes, never getting to the source of the problem. They would tell you that the residents need Prozac or Zanax. Psychiatrists would insist that the garbage is in the heads of the residents not on the streets.

The genuine problem is at the city dump (the Kidneys). The kidneys (city dump) are so backed up with waste yet unprocessed, trucks cannot get in the gates. 17 blocks of backed up trucks, not able to off their loads is a nightmare. Until dumping takes place, Toeville remains a mess.

Under ideal conditions, the toes can put out their collected uric acid garbage and know it will be picked up several times a day. Toeville's city dump problem, which has now become a joint, muscle and sleep problem, is now a body wide severe pain problem.

Uric acid irritates the delicate cartilage of all joints. It must be quickly removed. But, due to conditioning and big business selling the next new magic bullet, you are left without answers. Pain is killing you, but you are told there is nothing really wrong except the pain. Logically in this scenario you must use painkillers.

Unless you learn how to use nature to heal the body, it will get worse and worse. You are not a bad person just misled, lied to and drugged.

The FDA, AMA and Big Pharmaceuticals need you to be medicated and spending every dime you can muster to alleviate your woes. They want direct access to your insurance and life savings. Is there a natural solution?

Something as simple as grapes or tomatoes reset your kidneys. The most severe problems may be reversed with use of green grapes. Tinnitus, including vertigo and arthritis can all see relief. Joints can regain their smooth pain free moment by just changing the diet.

Again, you are not a bad person, just one of the billions who have been misled, lied to and drugged.

30 Sugar: Love It or Flee From It?

There is very little that I can say about SUGAR. It is the biggest business on the planet and the most addicting substance man has ever created. You have never met anyone without some form of addiction to it.

Sugar is so dangerous that the mere removal of it from the diet can spell huge changes. Researchers believe that removal of sugar would eliminate 99.5 % of all health complaints.

So debilitating is sugar and the sugar lifestyle that receptacles used for insulin needles are now common in busy public restrooms. Diet is the key to health and life. Business today is not in agreement with being healthy. Money is all that matters and money equals sugar, unless you chose the alternative.

Try to order a salad with nothing processed on it and the server will look at you like you have 6 eyes. Turn down bread with a meal and you are practically a leper. Read the quotes below and you decide if sugar has a place in your life.

"The average person loses more than 90% of their immune function within 15 minutes of indulging in this poisonous substance. This deficiency lasts for about 2 hours after the stress occurs." - Dr. Stoll

"The bottom line is that sugar upsets the body chemistry and suppresses the immune system. Once the immune system becomes suppressed, the door is opened to infectious and degenerative diseases. The stronger the immune system the easier it is for the body to fight infectious and degenerative diseases." - Nancy Appleton, Ph.D.

"Intensive research during the past twelve years on the relationship between diet and susceptibility to infection, not only in polio but also in common respiratory infections and tuberculosis, has convinced me that the human organism can protect itself against infection virtually completely by proper nutrition." - Dr. Sandler, 1952

"TB (Tuberculosis) increased dramatically in Japan, shortly after the Japanese acquired a cheap source of sugar on the island of Formosa (aka, Taiwan), in 1910. Britain experienced a dramatic increase in deaths from TB during the 1700s, especially among workers in sugar factories and refineries." - William Dufty (Sugar Blues, p. 77)

"If only a small fraction of what is already known about the effects of sugar were to be revealed in relation to any other material used as a food additive, that material would promptly be banned."
- John Yudkin MD, Ph.D., F.R.C.P., F.R.S.C., F.I. Biol., Prof. of Nutrition at London University.

The average American consumes an astounding 3 pounds of sugar each week. The average teenager is eating up to 5 pounds a week. If you don't think that advertising aimed at children is working, just consider the rising incidence of obesity, rabid rate of diabetes and childhood disease. Between 90 to 95 percent of these problems are due to the ridiculous amount of refined sugar we as parents allow them to eat.

None of this should be surprising, considering that highly refined sugars in the forms of sucrose (table sugar), dextrose (corn sugar), honey and high-fructose corn syrup, are in practically everything.

Making matters worse, foods such as bread, cereal, crackers, and rice convert to sugar in a few minutes of ingestion. Mayonnaise, peanut butter, ketchup, spaghetti sauce, and a plethora of microwave meals are loaded in white sugar. All of this attacks the kidneys and pancreas, which instantly kicks insulin production into overdrive. Insulin promotes the body to store fat. Eating manmade sweets can cause rapid weight gain. Recently it was reported that abdominal fat was directly linked to cancer, heart problems, kidney failure and even rapid tumor growth.

In the last 20 years, we have increased sugar consumption in the U.S. from 26 pounds to nearly 160 per person per year! Prior to the turn of last century (1887-1890), the average consumption was only 5 lbs. per person per year! Cardiovascular disease, cancer and morbid obesity were virtually unknown in the early 1900's. Look at crowd photos taken in 1900 compared to 2000 and witness the amazing fattening of Americans.

Being healthy is a choice; as long as we believe we are the victims, we continue to be victims. When you decide to be healthy, you have taken the first step to achieving that goal. Perfect health is a goal to be worked toward. It may never be reached, but the journey is well worth the trip. The alternative equals a life of constant aches, pains, and oddball diseases, compounding weight issues, excuses, denial and premature aging.

Do you want your health to improve or worsen? If you answered improve to this question, then the work I have put into this book is beginning to stick. The first step to making changes is changing your thinking process. Read this book as many times as you need to in order to know it.

In early 2007, the New England Journal of medicine reported, "Sugar suppresses the immune system by up to 95% for as much as 8 hours after ingestion."

Compare that with the popular notion that sugar feeds cancer and parasites. Consider that sugar does not feed anything, but makes the body bankrupt in defending itself. All forms of sugar prevent the body from utilizing vitamin C. Some camps believe that Glucose (a simple sugar) coats tumors, making them impervious to damage. Regardless, sugar suppresses the immune system, leaving it moot.

Sun, Sloth and Kinkajou bears are all known as Honey Bears. These three bear species consume large amounts of honey as part of their diets, which gives them their name. Honey bears are the only animals in nature that suffer with tooth decay.

In other words even nature is not immune to the horrendous affects of the raw sugar coming from honey. Some research shows that honey derived sugar is even more damaging to tooth enamel than white table sugar. Do not make the jump to believe that raw fruit sugar is damaging, as it is not. Yet, fruit sugars found in pasteurized juices can be harmful.

White / brown / honey / molasses sugar is credited with creating the following problems:

- Mineral imbalance
- Hyperactivity
- Anxiety
- Depression
- Anger
- PMS
- Learning difficulties
- High blood pressure
- Liver cirrhosis
- Hypoglycemia
- Heart trouble of all types
- Ulcers
- Obesity
- Grey hair
- Wrinkles
- Colon problems of all types
- Joint problems
- Insomnia
- Respiratory trouble
- Spontaneous abortions
- Fertility trouble
- Prostate trouble
- Skin disorders
- Circulatory issues

Medical Nobel laureate (1931) Otto Warburg, Ph.D., discovered that cancer cells have a fundamentally different energy metabolism compared to healthy cells. They live on vast amounts of glucose (simple sugar). Cancer is anaerobic (in absence of oxygen) and sugar and lactic acid create an environment that is oxygen free, which allows tumors to spread. The key is that the body has become acidic due to processed food that is starving the system.

Tumor cells cannot exist in an oxygen rich alkaline environment. They need sugar and acid to starve the area under attack of oxygen. The body becomes fatigued and this is an early sign that something is wrong. Chronic fatigue or no energy can exist years before tumors are actually seen.

Keeping ones weight under control and within 5-10 pounds of their ideal is important to keeping the body from becoming acidic and toxic. Tumors are starved in the correct environment.

Sugar and Holidays

We are in a vast sugar cesspool and have no idea we are. How bad is it? Is it really true? Can it really be that bad?

Yes.

Consider what you are up against. The following all are built around sugar:

Halloween
Desert
Birthdays (yours and all your friends and co-workers)
Christmas
Christmas Eve
Hanukkah
Kwanzaa
Thanksgiving
Easter
Celebrations (general)
Weddings
Divorces
Engagements
Father's day
Mother's day
Funerals
Bar Mitzvahs
Bat Mitzvahs
Anniversaries
Valentine's Day
St. Patrick's Day (alcohol converts directly to sugar)
Cinco de Mayo
Retirement
Promotions
Bridal showers
Baby showers
New year's Day
New Year's Eve
Super Bowl
Boxing Day
Save the Eagles Day
Amelia Earhart Day
Ben Franklin Day
Martin Luther King Day
Chinese New Year
President's Day
Purim
Girl Scout Week (Girl scout cookies)
Passover
Labor Day
Veteran's Day
Boss Day
Rosh Hashanah
Yom Kippur
More...

All of the above celebrations practically beg for sugar. Is it really a surprise that the United States is the fattest country on Earth? Is it a shock that kidney problems, i.e. diabetes, hypoglycemia, gout, fibromyalgia, etc., are spiraling out of control?

We have a reason to eat sugar every day. We have to use discipline not to.

31 Food vs. Poison / Drugs

Question: What is the difference between food and poison?

Answer: Freshness and cooking or distilling.

Now I will tell you the rest of the story. Later in this book I will explain the importance / need for raw food. I am now going to explain this in such a way that it will probably change your life. The coca plant is very popular in South America and is used even today in religious rights.

Mate De Coca, sometimes called Coca Tea is made by slowly brewing coca leaves over a low flame. When made correctly it has the stimulant effect of strong coffee. It has been and remains a popular South American drink.

The tea can be made stronger (via longer brewing at higher temperature) for healing applications. In the heights of the Andes its leaves are not only consumed via liquid ingestion, the leaves are also chewed to release their benefits. So common is the tea derived from the Coca leaf (and its benefits) that guides working on the Trail of The Inca (on the way to Macchu Picchu) recommend it for mild altitude sickness.

In parts of South America, it is considered a wonder concoction. It is revered as almost magical in its attributes. Interestingly, with such a fantastic reputation, how can a derivative of this amazing leaf be considered the lynch pin of world drug addiction? How can one compound so useful be at the apex or pinnacle of the war on drugs?

The Coca Leaf, if processed long enough, becomes cocaine!! Cocaine may very well be the most feared drug on the planet. Coca leaves, if distilled long enough, become so dangerous they become a pure poison. If you were elected World Drug Czar, you would want to eliminate cocaine from production and use. But if you did, tens 10s of millions of people worldwide would be out of work. This would be a worldwide catastrophe. Illegal drugs, drug addiction, drug enforcement and drug treatment is a trillion dollar a year business.

But back to our story about Coca leaves. If you were to travel to the Andes and participate in a ceremony that employed the chewing of Coca leaves, it wouldn't be long until you felt the effects of a medium stimulant. Locals exposed to the leaves more often would feel an effect similar to that of strong coffee or black tea. Now imagine that you, in your eagerness to fit into this new culture, went a little overboard and chewed a pound of Coca leaves. What would happen? Would you die, get sick? What would become of you and your high Andes leaf experience?

At worst you would get an upset stomach, vomit or get diarrhea as your body rejected this over use of the leaves. They are placed between the cheek and gums (in front) just like chewing tobacco. This may also be the origin of chewing tobacco, as tobacco was not native to Europe.

At the end of your Coca Leaf experience, you would be in a state of slight hyper stimulation or highly energized but not dead.

Balance that against the amount of cocaine you would need to create a fatal experience.

Perhaps a gram of cocaine will kill. Why? Because that gram of cocaine is cooked residue of perhaps 3000 leaves. Is it more understandable why drugs are fatal in small amounts?

All drugs follow this same path from something natural to something dangerous all due to the intense distillation process. A gram of cocaine powder can kill, verses pounds of the leaves that will not.

This process of distillation is repeated to a lesser extent on a daily basis in kitchens and restaurants all over the planet. Heat kills most organic life. The longer anything is cooked, the less it resembles food and the more it resembles a drug. This explains the medicinal affects of mom's chicken soup when it is slow cooked all day.

To get a feel of just how bad cooking in a microwave oven can be, feel free to look up the following test. Its results were placed on the Internet. The test was conducted with houseplants and can be easily replicated. Testing was conducted with identical houseplants over a one-month period.

The test: Two identical houseplants were given equal amounts of water at the same time on a daily basis.

One plant received water that was boiled on the stove and cooled and the other received water that was micro waved and then cooled.

After one month of the exact same care, the plant that received the micro waved water was dead. Does this mean the boiling of food or water is better? This test would have to be repeated and studied with tap, purified, spring, microwave and boiled water to be fully relevant. It nonetheless proves that microwaving is harmful.

It is generally accepted that microwaving alters the molecular structure of anything it is targeted at. Consequently, it should not be a surprise that micro waving anything, should be avoided.

32 Deadly Carbohydrates and Your Body

For a datum to really be understood and be useful, it must be repeated. Reinforcing your belief that the standard American diet equals death is a tragic thing to have to do. Electronic media continues to brain wash you, the reader, every day. Because of that, this little book needs to roar like a lion to even be noticed. Help me beat the drum. If you don't, we all die a little bit.

We are now going to consider the staple of the American diet, BREAD!

Bread and all processed carbohydrates, but especially bread, immediately swell in the stomach. It then starts breaking down into sugar. Temporary euphoria takes over as you begin to feel wired and finally you crash. Metabolism comes to a roaring stop the moment that sugar and yeast collide with your system. That is why the body swells, instantly feeling larger.

Swelling is why men loosen their belts after a meal with bread. If you were to measure your waistline on a Monday morning and then eat bread several times during the day and for dinner, you would notice that your waistline has expanded by 1-3 inches by Tuesday morning.

When the body's metabolism is shut down or slowed, it cannot flush out waste. This causes the body to become acidic, which leaves the body open to disease and bacteria. Reduced circulation, lack of oxygen and limited energy makes living in a body difficult. Burning Mouth Syndrome and indigestion until all hours of the morning is not uncommon. Eliminate processed carbohydrates and live a leaner, healthier life. Eliminating bread is one of the more easy vices to give up. When you do, you will be shocked by the results.

Indigestion and the Acid Pump

Time for another pack of lies served up to you by your wonderful AMA and advertisers, "You have acid indigestion and it is caused by too much acid production in your stomach."

This statement is an ABSOLUTE LIE!

If you acted on this statement, you would forever have indigestion as the statement is backwards. Lipitor commercials for high cholesterol are no different. High cholesterol is a product of an overwhelmed or poorly functioning liver. Yet in Lipitor commercials, they warn you not to take it if you have liver problems. Hundreds of thousands take it every day and get worse. Still Lipitor is being sold and will continue to be.

It is the equivalent of adding gasoline to a fire in an attempt to put it out. I am just doing back flips on that one.

Do you realize that over the counter antacid sales exceed 20 million dollars a week? Do you realize that too much acid in the stomach is not the problem but the opposite of what is really going on? Here are the facts. Your stomach produces a small amount of hydrochloric acid to help soften food so that it can be digested. When the food is like slurry (a watery mixture of insoluble matter, mud, etc.), it passes on to the small intestines. Food that is poorly chewed eventually enters the small intestines as well.

When we eat breads, pasta, pizza, crackers, cakes, cookies, popcorn, sweets, etc., we overwhelm the acid producers and our stomach is shut off. All of these foods convert to sugar and in doing so leave the stomach a compost bin. The result is the body signals you by giving you an acid indigestion symptom. This is just the stomach asking to be made acidic again.

The solution is not to desensitize the stomach or try to block acid production, but to turn it back on. Here are a couple of things you can do to facilitate this. Eat an orange or tangerine (the juice alone will not help); a lemon or other citrus can work as well. The enzymes in the pulp of the fruit work to switch back on the pumps and acid indigestion is instantly reduced.

Try this; you will be amazed at how well this works.

What Are You Putting in Your Mouth?

We all like to eat. It is one of those simple pleasures that have spun out of control. We can eat 24 hours a day and have anything we want. We have more choices than ever before. Yet we are eating less real food. We are surrounded by food yet we are starving. We diet constantly, but we are the fattest nation on earth.

Oh, and eating is fun too. Science has improved our lives to the extent that we can mix our breakfast in a glass and eat protein bars all day long. Welcome to the future. Welcome to the Star Trek world of nutrition. Progress via science has really improved our lives. How did we ever get along without instant orange flavored drink, chicken nuggets, gummy bears, hot chocolate, self-heating soup cans and coffee? We all need microwave popcorn and frozen food. Don't we?

Clearly, we were in dietary hell before science came to our rescue and saved our lives, right?

Not even close. Look it up. You will see that the fattening of America continues. Some of our foods are closer to being plastic than food.

Do you realize that imitation crab is not actually a fish at all? It does not swim. It is closer to rubber than fish. Grab a bag and look at it. Read the ingredients: Sugar, sorbitol, meat or tapioca starch, egg whites, and vegetable or soybean oil. Natural and artificial crab flavorings are added. Carmine, caramel, paprika, and annatto extract are often used to make the crab's red, orange, or pink coloring.

There you are, eating imitation crab and trying to lose weight and you can't figure out why the weight is not coming off. It is not coming off because this imitation crab is not just imitation crab it is imitation food.

Eating imitation crab is like chewing on filet of tennis shoe sole. Mmm, mmm, mmm, 'gotta get me some of that'.

Eating rubber fish, what could be better? How about chicken nuggets? That is clearly better! Why? How? Well, they're actually chicken! But it is special chicken, very special chicken, made up of all types of chicken. And it is all mechanically separated from the bone. In other words, ground up, then mixed with, you guessed it, artificial ingredients and then PRESSED into the cute little fun-to-eat-shapes.

Then what do we do? We smother all of these delicious chicken-like bites in barbeque, honey mustard, or ranch sauce, with the main ingredient, you guessed it again, SUGAR.

I really want this book to sell, so I am going to coat the pages with sugar. Not only will this book sell because you can read it, it will sell because you will eat it before you finish reading it. Ha! When the book is gone you will have to buy another one! And another one!

Then I can advertise on Nickelodeon and show happy kids eating my book. I could be bigger than Dr. Seuss! Unsuspecting kids will love me!

I will be #1 on the New York Times Best Seller list and no one will actually be reading my book! The public will eat me right to the top. Sugar is a wonderful thing!

Why have they not invented Sugar-Salt? That way it will soothe all parts of the palate at the same time! Go ahead, tear out a page of this book and eat it.

I assure you this book is made of sugar! Just lick the page and you will see.

I am just joking.

Consider this; a body consuming sugar will have numerous symptoms including tendonitis.

33 Tendonitis, Bursitis and Arthritis

No doubt you have guessed by now that tendonitis is just a name an AMA researcher invented one day in the hopes of selling drugs and surgery.

Whenever an expert is presented with confusion, they must by definition of "who they say they are", come up with an answer. The honest response of "I don't have any idea" somehow sounds too unprofessional. Such is the case with tendonitis, bursitis and arthritis (**'the itises'**). With what you know right now in reading this book, you can discern more than the expert. You recognize that **'the itises'** are a kidney symptom, liver symptom or combination of both.

This is not to say that pulled muscles, torn muscles, strains, ragged ligaments and frayed tendons don't happen. They do, but what facilitated the pull or strain was a dirty filthy street that forced the back up of our Uric Acid Trash Trucks. All of this is due to overwhelmed kidneys. The fact that healing takes so long is also due to kidney weakness. Damage in a body with healthy kidneys heals at a sensibly fast rate. Filthy systems often never heal completely.

Because of this waste, all healing processes are slowed and injuries don't heal satisfactorily. In the end, a slight sprain, which should hurt a day or two, becomes a chronic problem due to constant stimuli of uric acid or lactic acid lingering in the area.

There is zero difference in how the body approaches Arthritis. It **'the itises'** is just an irritated joint due to waste accumulation. Arthritis does not exist. Corroded joints exist but arthritis is just a name for "I have no idea." Perhaps they slap a pseudo prefix on the symptom and call it "inflammatory arthritis" which equals "it hurts and there is swelling."

The CDC (Center for Disease Control) reports on their website that:

1998: Doctors told 33 million patients that they had some form of arthritis, osteoarthritis, rheumatoid arthritis, gout or lupus.

2005: Doctors told 46 million patients that they had some form of arthritis, osteoarthritis, rheumatoid arthritis, gout or lupus.

They project. That in 2030, Doctors will tell 67 million patients that they have some form of arthritis, osteoarthritis, rheumatoid arthritis, gout or lupus.

What is going on here? We are eating / poisoning our kidneys into failure. Diabetes statistics (another kidney issue) show the same trends.

Overworked kidneys cannot catch up. Therefore you are in pain. If you have concluded that you should not feel sore or stiff very long, you are right.

This is the simplicity of the body that I am continually speaking of. The attitude in the world today and for centuries to come will be to mask the symptom. This book and you can have a major affect in changing the minds of those in power that promote such archaic thinking.

Big business and Wall Street advertisers are not interested in this book. They want to sell you pain relievers. Sore backs equal big bucks. Pulled muscles equal bonuses and big houses. You do not have to buy into what the Wall Street advertisers are saying. They are making big money (billions) and they of course do not want to give that up.

Billions of dollars are sunk into arthritis research, a diabetes cure, etc. Because we are looking for a culprit outside of ourselves, nothing will change. You can change. But until you change, big Pharmaceuticals will keep doing business as usual.

The therapy is as simple as changing what you put in your mouth.

The culprit is what you sweeten your tea, cereal and muffins with. Including your coffee (a known diuretic) and all of those colorings, dyes, drugs, chemicals and preservatives that enter in our faux food supply, Lack of water, protein overload, poor diet, deficient sleep and 24/7 life styles can all cause these chronic problems.

It will take time, but you can master these issues and change your life.

In essence, when your kidneys are functioning at top capacity, you will notice the following body traits:

1). Better flexibility.
2). Better strength.
3). Better endurance in all exercise.
4). Faster recovery time after workouts.
5). Resistance to pulled muscles.
6). Better sex drive.
7). Better sexual performance.
8). Better reproductive performance. Soreness & Stiffness of the Body 57
9). Better heart function.
10). Better balance or equilibrium.
11). Corrected blood pressure; if it is high or low it will correct.
12). Better afternoon and early evening energy.

13). Better sleep.
14). Better lymphatic system function.
15). Better bladder function.
16). Little if any cramping of any type.
17). Freedom of diabetic symptoms.
18). Freedom from Gout symptoms
19). Freedom from arthritis like symptoms

With use and understanding of this book, you place yourself firmly in the driver's seat in your life. You are in charge of your own health care. Use this book and teach those around you.

34 All About the Liver

You have read that the liver and emotions are linked. What does that statement mean? It means that 4000 years ago in China the physicians to the emperor started noticing strange behaviors emanating from "His Highness."

He would get emotional, i.e. angry, sad, depressed, nervous, edgy, fearful, paranoid, etc., after coming in contact with different substances. Shakespeare, Francis Bacon, Jean-Baptiste Poquelin (Moliere) and other dramatists knew of this relationship, as did medicine of the 14 century.

With that in mind, look at the definition below of melancholy. It is very revealing as this emotion was directly tied to the liver and the gallbladder function. The exact location of the gallbladder can be found attached to the right underside of the liver. It produces bile, which is a digestive aid and stool softener.

1mel·an·choly
Pronunciation: \?me-l?n-?kä-lē
Function: noun

Inflected From(S): plural mel·an·chol·ies

Etymology: Middle English malencolie, from Anglo-French, from Late Latin melancholia, from Greek, from melan- + cholē bile — more at GALL

Date: 14th century

1 a: an abnormal state attributed to an excess of black bile and characterized by irascibility or depression B: BLACK BILE C: MELANCOLIA 2 a. depression of spirits: DEJECTION B: a pensive mood

It was believed that when the gallbladder produced too much bile depression would follow.

It was believed that when the gallbladder produced too much bile depression would follow.
We now know that the liver regulates all emotions not just depression. We have also mapped out the direct relationship to substances ingested and our liver function and therefore moods.

It is further observed that as his immune system goes mans emotions follow.

4000 years ago in China the Emperors physicians started to fully appreciate how delicate the liver was. They noted that the liver's (the center for detoxification for the human body) ability to do its job was directly impacted by the food or chemicals the emperor ate or absorbed.

Cleansing the body of impurities is the liver's job. Based on the construction of the body, the liver via one of its channels (colon, lungs, skin or mouth) comes in contact with every substance the body contacts first. This means the liver is the hub of your body. All roads lead to the liver.

Keeping the liver clean and free of waste was of paramount importance to these physicians, as the emperor's mood would not only affect all of China, but their lives directly. If he was in a foul mood, he could have had them removed from his circle of court physicians or even beheaded.

Either way you would certainly lose status (headless or jobless) by being disciplined. To simplify and add clarity, the body, being perfect has several built in alarms that we are supposed to react to.

Such as:

Hunger = Eat

Thirsty = Drink

Tired = Sleep

Pain = Bad / Avoid

The above four points are accepted and non-arguable. The following five points have been neglected:

Itchy skin	= Liver
Watery eyes	= Liver
Emotional stress	= Liver
All bad moods	= Liver
Coughing	= Liver

When the Emperor's physicians gave him certain mood enhancing drugs, his mood would alter, but when he came down from the drugs, he was worse off than before. Therefore, what was happening? The physicians had inadvertently increased the load on the liver. Yes, the drugs initially made the emperor feel better (as he was somewhat sedated). All the while his liver was working overtime to break down the substance to drive it from the body. They found that the best way to control his mood was by being sure that the emperor had a healthy, fully functioning liver.

Healthy liver function with no drugs was paramount to keeping the emperor in the pink. His diet was the key. Water, seasonal fruit and herbs (food) were the best approach. Waste not processed by the liver dispenses into the system. Escaped waste lodges in the fatty tissue, connective, tissue or muscle tissue. There it will stay until such time that the liver can process the waste.

When we get moody, it is the liver signaling us that it needs help. The irritant can be hormonal; yes, testosterone and estrogen can cause liver overwhelm. Therefore, menopause and your period are especially brutal on the liver and, as a consequence, your emotions. But, it is all a liver issue. Improve liver function and you will feel better.

The true source of fear demands a special note. It is believed by many that "fear" is controlled or regulated by the kidneys. This is not true or the Chinese would not have written "liver and emotions are linked." This belief is derived from the observation that terrified people often lose control of their bladder. Therefore, it is easy to conclude that fear equals fluid release and is directly caused by "fear" hitting the kidneys.

The correct sequence is fear-stimuli cause the body to release a hormone or chemicals. The liver must quickly address this substance but fails in the attempt. In response, the liver goes into crisis mode and attempts to flush the substance from the system and releases water to the kidneys. If you recall, the liver is the "washing machine" of the body. The Released fluid rapidly hits the kidneys. The kidney as directed by the liver flushes the fluid and the person, in "fear", urinates.

Please correct anyone who you discover has this common misconception.

Weight Loss and the Liver

Weight loss has been a mystery since man became physically and socially aware. The liver must wash the body free of waste. When the liver is impaired or running slow, it will not be able to flush waste out of the system. Efficient liver function is paramount to wash toxins and fat from the structure of the body.

Steroids and the Liver

Steroids suppress the immune system yet are given for poison ivy and poison oak. These two irritants cause the body to itch and swell. The reason why is because your body has been attacked by an acid irritant. Treating it, your practitioner will tell you that you must take steroids to prevent this inflammatory response.

Please understand that your liver regulates your skin. When you have stumbled onto poison ivy or oak your body is fighting an irritating poison. The last thing anyone should ever do is turn off the immune system when there is an immune system challenge.

Therefore, do-not-take-steroids-ever. Understand that your immune system is under siege (via your liver) and support it with liver herbs, water and citrus.

Steroids will keep you sick longer as your liver will not be functioning.

Support your liver. Do not shut it down.

Mad Men in White Coats

One has to then ask, why did psychiatry start giving people psychiatric drugs for liver issues? The answer is simple yet complex.

Every field of endeavor on the planet is trying to help everyone all the time. That being said, psychiatrists had an intention to help. But, by not knowing structure and function of the body, they only added to the problem and made things worse and worse.

The problem with psychiatry started with its roots. The term "psychiatry" literally means the 'doctor of the soul', coming from the Greek, "psych" meaning soul, and "iatros" meaning doctor.

This term acknowledged a fundamental truth:

"That man has a soul."

Man was not a piece of meat that could not think, he was a spiritual being. Johann Christian Reil (1759-1813) coined the term psychiatry in the West in 1808. Reil clearly recognized that the soul was what animated the body. He called it the "Vital Force" that separated living organisms from inanimate objects.

But in his own work while championing the "Vital Force" (which we could call the soul), he also called for the dissecting of the body to better understand the vital force. This immediately creates a problem as he had just combined the soul and the body into one mechanism: a piece of meat.

In the following statement, he inadvertently created a stage where the future dissection of the body would be acceptable.

Reil wrote:
"It would be advantageous for theoretical and practical medicine if we could analyze the different kinds of degrees of organization, if we could reduce their most complex tissues to their most simple elements and if we were able to, we would then be able, more happily, to analyze many phenomena and to reduce them more accurately to their principles."

Reil's rambling and effusive observation may very well have been misunderstood and taken to mean that man was an animal and therefore without a soul.

He concludes with:
"Follow them (the systems) from the original most elemental organ to the most complex animal organs."

All of this came to a head in 1811, two years before his death, as a professorship of "psychiatric therapy" was established in Leipzig, Germany. A similar chair in Berlin followed this. That same year, 1811, the first laboratory opened up designed to study the human mind via dissection of the brain. This idea is as ludicrous as dissecting a TV to look for the actors.

Germany spun out of control as it was involved in a political chess game that would affect every class of people in Europe. Germany needed to control larger masses to be successful. If experts (there is that word again) claimed it so, it would be accepted as true.

This need for control was part and parcel behind these oddball observation and postulations:

Psychiatry As A Political Tool

Psychiatrist C.T. Groddeck, 1850, psychiatrist, awarded a doctorate for his dissertation entitled: "**The Democratic Disease - A New Form of Insanity**." In Groddeck's view, every democratically inclined person was insane.

Psychiatrist C.J. Wretholm (Groddeck's colleague) 1854, "discovered" the still shocking "**Sermon Disease**". Wretholm believed that anyone who enjoyed church was disturbed or insane.

Psychiatrist P. J. Mobius, circa 1854, extensively lectured in Germany and in Europe on the "**Psychological feeble-mindedness of woman.**"

Psychiatrist Adolph Hoppe chimed in with his contribution to mental disorders with "**Political and reformatory insanity.**" Therefore: All political reformers were insane.

Psychiatrist Adolph Hoppe later added the politically damning and World War I stimulating

"**French mental illness**" for those born in France, as he considered France cursed.

The above observations while primitive and laughable by today's standards are not laughable at all. They are horrifying. These ideas were believed and acted upon.

Otto Von Bismarck (World War I Chancellor) used these twisted ideas as justification to start World War I. Hitler had the groundwork laid for WWII with the rest of these works and many more. Germany, being racially pure, had as its divine right to purify and direct the people of Earth.

Kind of like a global policeman. Sound familiar?

Anytime one group sees itself as senior / smarter / closer to God or more righteous than another, war follows. The masses will pay the ultimate price. Every war fought in history had this idea at its core.

These observations / hypotheses served as a useful tool to squash dissidents to the military and political opponents. With a mental program explaining that man was indeed an animal (a twist on Reil's work) Bismarck - the leader of Germany - did indeed use this "science" as a cause for a justifiable war.

No doubt, Wilhelm Wundt (1832 - 1920), the future father of psychology, read Reil's papers. Later Wundt would theorize that man was an animal and that all thought was brought about from the result of chemical reactions in the brain. Today, Wundt is still highly revered in the field of psychiatry.

It was one of Wundt's students, Emil Kraepelin, who became known as the "Father of Psychiatry."
He believed that mental symptoms were hereditary and he supported the sterilization of certain "mentally ill", so defective genes could not be passed on. Ernst Rudin was a student of Kraepelin, and he was a rabid eugenicist. His racial theories were sold to Hitler. The resulting "Master Plan" for a pure Aryan race was created. Hitler was often correctly described as the "most evil man in Nazi Germany."

35 The Chinese Liver vs. the Psychiatric Brain

PROBLEM: Ragged emotions

1993 BC - China , Chinese doctors conclude:

- The liver is the center of body detoxification
- The liver modifies emotions
- The brain is a nerve center
- The spirit is not housed in the body

Result - Fix the liver and emotions will balance

1854 - Leipzig Germany, Psychiatry concludes:

- Man has no sprit
- Man is an animal
- The brain is a nerve center
- Slicing and medicating the brain disconnects emotional response

Result - Fix emotions by dissection and drugs

Because the Chinese saw the problem as a simple organic problem of waste management, it was straightforward to solve with liver support. Both groups saw the same thing. Psychiatry even had the benefit of the earlier Chinese work. They, in essence, ignored it.

4000 years ago the Chinese saw a chemical overload of the LIVER with a resulting symptom of heightened emotions. They discovered it was easy to "cool" the emotions by addressing the liver.

2120 years later Psychiatry saw a chemical overload of the BRAIN. Read on to find out what the psychs did besides help to start world wars.

In 1897, German legislator Julius Lenzmann attacked the psychiatric community in a speech on January of that year. In part, he said, "Most, if not all of the doctors of the insane are extremely nervous individuals. I have knowledge of the trials where all of the participants were of the opinion that the only insane one was the doctor." Lenzmann saw the writing on the wall but was ignored.

Thanks to that blind eye and all the ones before his, unspeakable atrocities would follow.

Soon to come were brain experiments, including medications (or poisons) such as calomel (a colorless, tasteless compound, Hg2Cl2), which was originally used as a purgative and insecticide. Also used were leather gags, hand mitts, straightjackets, restraining chairs, solitary confinement; electro shock, insulin shock; frontal lobotomy and ice pick surgery.

You have been introduced to the players from the beginning. The players from Germany and France are all on the play list, but what was happening in America? We now jump across the pond and into North America. Meet John Fulton of Yale, Egas Moniz of Portugal and Walter Freeman, an American psychiatrist. They all met in 1935 while attending a neurological conference in London. Imagine the stories they must have had to share!

Fulton completely removed the two frontal lobes from a pair of chimpanzees, a "Lobectomy." The procedure had radically altered their chimpanzees' behavior. Fulton could no longer generate experimental forms of neurosis in the animals. They were seemingly proofed against agitation.

The maniacal symposium droned on and on. Finally the discussion about the significance of the frontal lobe removal arrived. The assembled company hedged gently around the delicate issue that Fulton's chimpanzees raised. Eventually, Egas Moniz asked the question that Freeman had wanted to ask. "If frontal lobe removal prevents the development of experimental neurosis in animals, and eliminates undesirable behavior, would it be possible to relieve anxiety states in man by surgical means?"

A year later, Moniz attempted this butchery on a female patient and eventually several more. By 1945, Freeman developed the Ice Pick or Transorbital Leukotomy, a slash across both frontal brain lobes using an ice pick. The pick is shoved up through the top of the left and right eye sockets. The surgeon then uses a sweeping motion to destroy the two frontal lobes. The Transorbital Leukotomy replaced or pushed aside the Lobotomy.

Psychosurgery was on its way. By 1955, Psychosurgery was common, as were the drugs to combat mental disorders such as Thorazine, the precursor to psych drugs including Prozac, Zanax, Zoloft, Paxil and Haldol.

Eventually, brain operations were banned. But, amazingly, shock treatment never fully was and it is still practiced today. The new brain surgery is completed with the Gamma Knife / Radiosurgery (emotion altering brain surgery done with radiation).

Complaints against psychiatry are not new. In 1882, reports on psychiatric treatment methods, which were sadistic, had prominent German individuals such as the parliament, journalists and scientists, protesting. One statesman said, "One of the most pronounced problems with psychiatry had been its inability to recognize what the problem actually is with the mentally ill."

However, psychiatry did not disappear. I hope you are outraged reading this. You may be able to prevent psychiatry's next victim if you speak up. Psychiatry in the United States has the backing of the government and is expanding the same way it did in Germany. There was a time when the psychs were on the run. Since the mid 1990's, they have been gaining strength. We must fight, and fight hard. Drugs do not belong in schools. Columbine and Virginia Tech did not have to happen. Psychiatry remains one of the most evil tortures known to man.

You thought electro shock and insulin shock have been banned?

In 1993, Dr. Steven Rasmussen became the first U.S. physician to treat OCD with a surgical tool known as the gamma knife, which focuses 210 gamma-ray beams into a single point. A tiny hole is burned in the brain creating irreversible damage. The brain is still ripped apart with less mess. Patients are left violently and grotesquely damaged. Yet they *are* meek, manageable, quiet and docile. Patients may be docile and quiet, however they are still angry and suicide is very common.

I have successfully aided individuals diagnosed with OCD to become normal by just repairing their liver. Anyone can do this. It is not just I; we can all make a difference when we decide that we can.

Again slicing up the brain to improve emotions is akin to cutting open the TV to look for the actors. Now wouldn't it be safer to just clean up the diet and then the liver? The answer is yes and, over the last 16 years, I have helped thousands of people get off their psych drugs, thousands more to not get started on them, and thousands more to feel good every day without drugs or dangerous surgeries. Toxins and emotions are a liver problem.

Every day the AMA (American Medical Association) working in concert with the APA (American Psychiatric Association) invents new names / diseases for behavior that is either normal or fixable with nutrition, herbs and vitamins.

Sweaty palms are now a disease called Palmer Hyper Hydrosis. Post Partum Depression didn't exist 20 years ago. RLS (restless leg syndrome) wiggled on to the radar five years ago. All of these reactions are *now* **diseases**. Not to mention ADD, ADHD and more. Imagine crowded AMA / APA conference rooms full of executives 'brainstorming' the newest malady to *sell* to the public.

Thanks to our dedicated and hardworking AMA / APA we have a never-ending reason to drug ourselves. These labels with peer and employer pressure force people to seek out Psychiatry, which means they will be buying drugs and stimulating the economy. They will also be dying a little more every day.

Remember the absolute roots of psychiatry can be found earlier in this book, in the sections on Phrenology and Physiognomy.

When you treat your body like it is whole, complete and perfect, it heals. If you believe that bad moods are calls for Prozac or a Prozac deficiency you have been brainwashed. Treat the proper organ the correct way and begin to love life again. A headache is not an aspirin or pain killer deficiency. Remove the offending poisons and the body always heals.

You can choose to be healthy. So can your friends and family. Anyone who is on the fence about psychiatry or psychiatric drugs needs to read this chapter; you may save their life.

36 Truth About the Brain

In the last chapter we discussed the brain in roundabout fashion. Does the brain deserve all of this attention? Does this nerve-filling piece of meat that allows you to perceive smell, see via the optic nerve and coordinate the functions of the entire body deserve this? We all know that it is the human nerve center. But do we know what it really does?

Hippocrates thought it was the center for personality as has been stated thousands of times by poets, doctors and scientists.

Good news. They are all wrong. You are the center of your personality. Not to be religious, but there is a force running your body that is separate from your body. Some call it a soul. It has been called the Élan Vital (life force) and many more names.

Your personality therefore is not housed in your brain; it is wherever it is, at any one moment around your body. But you are not a body or your brain.

If your brain is not you, and you are not your brain, then why does it get the focus of so much mystery? As a relay and coordination station, it is unsurpassed.

The preceding paragraphs fly in the face of modern western thought. In this country (USA), the government is very interested in supporting psychiatry. Why? There are any numbers of reasons, from the very evil to the really very, very evil.

The most logical answer is that there is money or kickbacks in it for someone somewhere. I am not going to show you a paper trail that I have established over 10 years of investigation. Why—because, I don't have such information. Therefore, I will not be blowing the lid of off psychiatry. "Psychogate" (the funding of psychiatry by government to control the people of earth) has yet to be revealed, if it ever will be. Although it would be fun to be at the heart of such an investigation, I would probably not live to see my 95th birthday and definitely not my 50th.

It is just the pursuit of money that drives psychiatry, or should I say the drug industry that supports psychiatry. Or is it the other way around? First, the AMA (American Medical Association) working in concert with the APA (American Psychiatric Association) names a new disease, then drug companies race to invent a drug for the invented disease, and then they pay the FDA (Food and Drug Administration) gads of cash.

Follow the bouncing check.

Imagine that the following story is true. For sake of argument sake, let's just say that the AMA occasionally gives inside information to its favorite drug company or two. Once armed with this valuable data, these companies have the ability to develop a new drug for a heretofore non-existent disease that the AMA is about to invent.

If it sounds like I am saying that the AMA actually names new diseases, complete with symptoms, it is true. This disease may be a common problem that until now never seemed like a problem or disease. Diseases are not diseases until the AMA alerts us that it is a problem, such as sweaty palms.

Dare I repeat? The AMA invents a new disease, passes the data to a favorite company. Maybe this company gives KICKBACKS to the AMA? Then that company beats the others to the punch by delivering the new drug. This means said Drug Company makes a gigantic payout to the FDA (a government agency).

Now with a check for $800 million dollars in hand (not counting KICK-BACKS) the FDA grants a patent for seven years of exclusive rights. Armed with an unchallenged drug, it is off to the races to make claims and sell as much of their drug as possible before people start dying.

Death equals a slap on the wrist, a wink, a nod and a "Don't do that again."

The unsuspecting public starts buying this new drug to solve their sweaty palms. The subject of FDA dirty dealing is such an obsession that there are several books on the subject including "The $800 Million Pill: The Truth behind the Cost of New Drugs" by Merrill Goozner.

The FDA accepts and rubber-stamps the formula on the promise that the drug company (XYZ or Pfizer) has proof of safety and efficiency of their drug.

If this isn't clearly a money problem, I don't know what else is. If all of this is true and, believe me, I have seen the documents (of course this is all lies, the FDA will tell you this), what else is there to know?

Money makes the world go around. Beware, at any moment, there could be an announcement in the news that, "If you like the Simpsons, South Park or American Idol, you have an Obsessive Compulsive TV Addiction (OCTVA)." Be very afraid, you could be arrested at any moment and pumped full of a drug that your health insurance will support while your body turns to jelly.

What about so Called PSYCHIATRIC PROBLEMS?

Over and over I have stated that so called "Psychiatric Problems" are treated (and made worse) with drugs. Emotional issues are not a brain problem they are liver issues. The list below can be completely handled every day by changing the diet and fixing liver function. See the section on liver herbs.

- Panic attacks
- OCD
- ADD
- ADHD
- Depression
- Fear
- Agoraphobia
- Social Anxiety Disorder
- Anxiety
- Bipolar disorder
- Intense Sadness
- Palmer Hyper Hydrosols
- Dysthymia
- Paranoia
- Delusions
- Apathy
- Asperger's disorder

With a little self-control and understanding, everything that you have read in this chapter can be successfully treated with improving liver function. Yes, you can and must get off your psychiatric drugs. You have been reading this and you should re-read this chapter again. It is vital that you learn this information for yourself and others. No one should be on psychiatric drugs regardless of who prescribed him or her, your family doctor or a psychiatrist.

You can be the cause over your body and emotions.

Share this chapter with all of your friends and they will be better for it. Again, re-read the chapters on the liver, and brain and tell everyone you know about what you have learned. Make these issues your issues. If you are sickened by what you have read that's good.

The truth that you have read in this chapter can save lives if you speak up.

37 The Liver and Milk Thistle

Most people have heard about the wonders of milk thistle, an herb commonly used for all liver problems. The majority of people do not know how it works or if it actually is effective. Yet we all have the idea that it is the crème de la crème of liver helping herbs. Where does this hoopla come from? You may remember that earlier in this book I promised not to recommend any company or product; well, I am not going to. What I am going to tell you is an interesting story.

Who is this ancillary character to your life story?

Your liver is a vast storehouse of chemicals that can efficiently break down most matter. Basically it's a mobile chemistry platform that goes everywhere you do and is performing lab work 24 hours a day. It protects you from harm and helps produce food around the clock. Regardless of what it is, or when it is, your liver is there as your protector.

Be it challenged by cat dander or the most toxic substances, your liver is ready to rumble.

Summation: When running at capacity, your liver patrols your body like an infrared, motion-triggered- laser guided and rabid bulldog hopped up on steroids. Should it be off line for any length of time and you are exposed to danger, death slithers a little closer every passing second.

Imagine being in charge of this mind-numbing 21-century security system! Like it or not, you are.

If your body were a country, the liver would be its army, navy, air force, marines and Special Forces. Again, your liver meets, greets and designates for assignment all matter that enters your body. All chemicals lodged in your fat (and there are thousands), when metabolized by diet, exercise or pure luck, are spirited off to your liver for a safety check and then excreted. That is the way your body is supposed to work.

Today we are knee deep in toxins and your liver is a very behind in its work. Yet every organ of your body depends on your liver being active to stay healthy. If your body is breaking down, look to the liver and the kidneys as they support each other. YOUR LIVER MUST PROTECT YOU. If this relationship is altered in any way, you suffer.

Therefore, why is Milk Thistle all the rage for liver cleansing? Milk Thistle is a LIVER PROTECTOR. If you have researched as I have, every description of milk thistle includes the note "liver protector." Over thousands of years and continent to content the message is the same: Liver-protector.

The liver is the most unusual organ we have in our body. Up to 25% of it can be removed and it will still repair itself.

The liver is basically a disinfecting sponge that rejuvenates as it is worn out. The only organs in the body that repair themselves are organs deriving their power from the liver. The quicker the body repairs itself, the closer that organ is in its association to the liver.

With the liver so well armed, why does it need to be protected? Remember the most popular liver herb on the planet is milk thistle. Remember that milk thistle is a known liver protector. This all makes sense until you consider what the liver does for you and what milk thistle does for the liver.

The liver is supposed to protect you. If milk thistle is isolating it from harm (by protecting it) this is cause for alarm.

Again, the liver is the only organ in the body that can actually repair itself (up to 25% loss). It is meant to take a beating and keep on ticking.

My research reflects that Milk Thistle is, without question, one of the most damaging herbs currently being used for liver issues. If you only judged by the simple yardstick of feeling better or worse while using it, you would never use it again.

Milk Thistle does just the opposite of what you would actually want it to do. Milk Thistle builds a wall around the liver and prevents it from doing its job by protecting it. If your liver is off line or being protected, it cannot do its job and you are made the victim. There are practitioners who do "Milk thistle therapy."

The following is a condensation of several conversations that I have had with doctors offering such "therapy."

Q: How long do you do milk thistle therapy?

A: Up to 3 years and 3 years ideally.

Q: What can the patient expect during therapy?

A: They will notice various things, sleeplessness, irritability, low energy, headaches, fuzzy vision & congestion.

Q: Really, all of that?

A: Yes, because as the liver throws off all of its waste, you will feel it.

Q: How long does that phase last?

A: The detox phase?

Q: Yes, the phase that includes feeling badly.

A: The entire time.

Q: 3 years?

A: Sure.

Q: How do the folks feel when they stop or are done?

A: They feel great.

To summarize, the patients feel horrible during the entire length of the therapy. Th ter" when the therapy is over. Therefore this "therapy" is kind of like putting a vice on your head and every day tightening it just a little bit. It should be no surprise to anyone, that the patients feel better when the "therapy" is over. Who wouldn't?

There is a huge misunderstanding about where the body harbors toxins. The liver is not holding them. It only processes them. Toxins are lodged in the fatty tissue, muscle and connective tissue of the body. Cleaning the liver is like cleaning purified water as it pours out the spout. The liver is already clean.

I have stated again and again and now again, a liver formula or liver herb should make you feel better right now. If you have a headache and take a correct formula for liver function, you should notice that your headache is better right now.

When taking any formula for any purpose you should notice one of these three things:

A). You should immediately feel better and more emotionally balanced.

B). You should immediately feel worse or more emotionally frayed.

C). You should immediately feel nothing. Either you do not need it or it is not working.

If you feel worse (B) ask yourself, what are you taking? It is what is causing you this discomfort, especially if the discomfort comes within seconds of taking it. To be sure, wait until you feel better again and take half the dose you took that made you feel bad. Should you again immediately feel bad, or feel nothing, eliminate that formula or herb from your self-treatment. It is not working.

If you feel nothing, the formula is too weak or you do not need it. You can test again at a later time, but if you had liver symptoms and felt nothing taking your liver formula, it is junk.

The herbs I have found that perform best for liver issues are:

Bupleurum: (Chinese liver herb. Considered the best herb for liver)

Beet Root; (common, found everywhere, it is one of the few herbs that support both liver & kidney)

Dandelion: (considered an American herb, it is greatly effective)

Hyssop: (gets little fanfare but is a very good herb)

Gentian: (another favorite and often ignored, but is an excellent herb)

False Unicorn: (actually assists the liver with handling all hormones)

Tribulus Terrestris or Puncture Vine: (not really a sex enhancement herb, unless improving liver function makes people sexually active)

Cayenne (long considered too hot for the liver yet in very small amounts it is beneficial as turbo booster for all herbs)

Wasabi Japonica has been used in Japan for the past 25 years for all forms of cancer. It is also great circulation, and the elimination of parasites.

Turmeric (known as an anti-inflammatory herb, it opens channels to the entire system as well as the liver)

Remember, a correct therapy for the liver opens up channels and does not block or limit them. You should never feel worse while taking any formula. Please also understand that feeling worse two hours after taking any formula usually means your body needs more at that moment. The test would be to take more when you start feeling bad and find out for sure.

I have gone on and on about just how bad milk thistle is. So why is it being used?

There are six very good reasons why it may be sometime before the world catches up with my work.

- Habits, old ones die-hard
- Monkey see monkey do. If one company uses it, it must be good for every company
- Lack of imagination and or personal research; most companies are not even looking
- Money: launching new products is not cheap; neither is reformulating them and marketing them
- Expectation, the general public is conditioned to believe that milk thistle is the herb for liver
- Volume of noise I make to have a real impact must increase by 250 – 350%

The statement regarding milk thistle being a liver protector is a powerful one. Liver protection sounds like a good idea, yet it is completely backwards.

There are those doctors who insist that milk thistle is the only herb to use if Hepatitis is to be treated. They claim to have helped numerous patients and they may have. But the expense was to the detriment of the system. When the liver is off, the body is always at risk. Sure one problem was solved (hepatitis), but again, the rest of the system was poisoned for 5 to 9 months of treatment.

The reason the liver was swollen in the first place was a toxic load of some severity. The swelling may very well have been due to long accumulating damage. Or, was it from drinks yesterday and rich desserts for dinner last night? Hepatitis is a far easier condition to solve than people think. It is just a call from the body to make changes.

The solution is not to take the liver off line and sacrifice the body. The correct approach would be to reduce its load via dietary change, increased water consumption, while escalating circulation, energy and oxygen in the body.

What about high cholesterol? Cholesterol is strictly a liver congestion problem that is routinely solved in 30 days with use of the right herbs.

Atrophied liver:

Extended Milk thistle exposure (isolating the liver) is dangerous, as the liver loses its ability to function. Imagine breaking your leg, and not being allowed to walk for 3-7 months, while someone carried you around. Your leg would heal but it would also atrophy, as lack of use would lead to smaller, weaker muscles, all because you allowed your leg to be "protected."

What exactly are liver enzymes? Should you worry about them? Will liver enzymes kill you?

Relax; liver enzymes are just the result of the liver doing its job. The result of fighting is a little blood. When the liver is doing its job it is sacrificing itself to protect you. The enzymes are just the sloughing off of dead liver cells. That is all liver enzymes are, DEAD LIVER CELLS. The solution is to give the liver the food it needs, citrus of all types, fresh fruit, less sodium, no caffeine, salt or white sugar. With these changes, the liver heals rather fast.

Summation: The liver is always sloughing off dead liver cells. Liver enzymes are just another name for dead liver cells found in the blood. Use of Milk Thistle should be prohibited. Eat a healthier diet full of citrus. Do not protect your liver; help it with more foods that support it and do a body detox as soon as possible.

When you do the investigative work as I have, you will discover all of the evils of Milk Thistle. In the end, practically anything short of a bullet is better for your liver than Milk Thistle.

The liver enigma

Statement: "The liver is the filthiest organ in a cow's body and should not be eaten."

Statement: "Cow's liver is full of vitamins and nutrients and is very healthy to eat."

Which statement is incorrect?

ANSWER: They are both partially incorrect.

FACT: The liver is NOT corroded with poisons. It is in fact a processing warehouse / plant loaded in raw chemicals. It does not harbor toxins it breaks them down. The body harbors toxins in its fatty tissue, muscle tissue and connective tissue. When the liver is given too large a load to process it allows the body to store the overflow waste for later dispensation.

CONCLUSION: You would not eat the tablet-making machinery of the Twin Labs vitamin company to acquire the benefits of their vitamins. Buying several bottles of the finished product at their front door would make more sense.

Stating it another way, (sorry for this) eating Bill Gates to understand your PC better is pointless. It does not make much sense. I am sure Mr. Gates would agree.

Getting healthy should not include eating a nutritionist, a doctor, this book or cow's liver.

Remember: Avoid eating anything laden with hormones and antibiotics. Otherwise you risk raising havoc with your body. These chemicals play havoc with your system and increase the toxic load on your liver.

Remember: Should you start taking any formula created for your liver, and upon taking it, immediately start feeling worse (within 1 minute of taking it), it was the formula you took that made you feel that way. If you feel worse 2 hours later, it was something you ate or were exposed to in the last few minutes.

Remember: *Cause* and *effect* = you cause the effects good or bad in your body.

What ultimately happens to your health is 100% your responsibility. You need to be in your best possible health or you become a burden to those around you. Once you seize the horns of your own health, anything is possible. If all you can think about is being sick, do something about it. Some people call this tough love. I call it, self respect. You deserve the best possible life you can have.

Start now, or if already have started, push for greater success. You matter; we are all counting on you.

38 The Liver and Your Skin

Earlier in this book and again in the last few pages, I have indicated that the liver monitors or regulates the skin of the body. What is often forgotten is how delicate this relationship happens to be.

Anything that gets on the skin immediately affects the liver. Taking a shower or a bath is actually a bath a simple technique for washing of the liver. When you rise in the morning, you are washing your liver and jump-starting your immune system. If you have insomnia (a liver issue) and take a shower prior to bed, you usually sleep better. Why? You have drawn toxins out of your liver that might have kept you awake.

Hepatitis is a swelling of the liver. It is believed that the dirty inkwells of tattoo artists cause numerous cases of hepatitis B & C every year. This is not true in a direct sense. There is no question that tattoos and hepatitis are linked. There is no question that the inkwells of many tattoo artists have Hepatitis in the mix.

Yet the equation is backward. One does not get Hepatitis from inkwells, as it cannot be passed from one person to another. What does happen is that tattoo ink is a strong poison and brings on a swollen liver. Then those who come back again and again for their next tattoo fix leave Hepatitis markers in the inkwells of the artist.

Those with tattoos have a 75% higher chance of contracting hepatitis than those without tattoos. The more tattoos one gets, the higher the probability that Hepatitis will be contracted.

The problem, while obvious, is usually ignored. The ink is a poison and it is directly applied in a very dense fashion to the skin. In essence, you are indirectly attacking your liver with tattoos.

Another very interesting aspect of tattooing and liver function is, that the liver fades or eats your tattoos. The liver is constantly eroding the dye of the tattoo. If given enough time the liver will remove tattoos completely.

Remember the last time you accidentally smeared permanent marker on your hand? The color faded even without washing. The color was not rubbing off or "wearing off"; it was being absorbed into your body.

Most people believe that washing was what removed the stain from their fingers after an episode of "oops, I got that all over my hand." Washing did help. But a huge part of what happened was your skin absorbed the foreign matter and (hopefully) sent it to your liver for processing.

As for tattoo ink, this is the simplicity of why they fade. Again, with the right formula of herbs and diet (or some combination of the same) tattoos can and will eventually become a faded memory.

Migraines

Migraine headaches like all headaches are a product of liver overwhelm. The odd element of the migraine headache is that it does not act a run of the mill headache. Normal headaches are not affected by usual liver supplements or foods. Why don't Migraines react like other headaches and easily resolve?

General run of the mill headaches respond to good liver formulas, water, food, vitamins, rest and various combinations of the above. The answers as to what makes Migraines so different come from their traits.

Traits of a Migrane

Sensitivity to light (liver issue)

Sensitivity to sound (kidney issue)

Throbbing pain in the head (liver issue)

Head pain may be localized or involve the entire skull (liver issue)

Can be accompanied by nausea (liver issue)

Odors can make them worse (liver issue)

Blurry vision is common (liver issue)

Foods can make them worse (liver issue)

May last for several hours

Equilibrium problems can occur (kidney issue)

Another interesting and telling fact about migraine headaches is that they will affect women at a rate of four (4) to one (1) over men.

The above pieces of data are all very telling and start to paint a picture of what is at the heart of debilitating problem.

How can migraine headaches affect more woman than men? What could be pushing these statistics?

There are factors that affect many women but not men as the list below will illustrate. Women due to advertising, culture and thousands of years of conditioning have become a test plate for the latest musings of the "woman recreationist mind." If men were required to adapt to the habits and requirements that we impose on women, there would be revolt of a global proportion.

The following list delineates what separates men from women. Keep in mind that much of this list is self-imposed.

In the 21st century women participate in the following:

- Makeup
- Earrings
- Nose rings (95% more women have this than men)
- Tongue rings (97% more women have this over men)
- Acrylic Nails
- Nail polish
- Nail cleaning and preparation chemicals like acetone
- Birth control pills
- Contraceptive jells
- IUD's
- Hair colorings / dyes
- Perfume
- Tampons
- Panty Liners
- Perm solutions
- Implants
- Face lifts
- Botox
- Cleaning solvents (some women clean with these far more than men)
- High heels
- Moisturizers for the face
- Cleansers for the face
- Moisturizers for the body
- Cleansers for the body
- Douches
- Fertility drugs
- Hysterectomies
- Tubal ligation
- Nylons
- Bras
- Eating disorders (reported only) affect women by upwards of a 7 to 1 clip over men
- More

During the bygone days, there was a time when Lysol (popular bathroom and house cleaning solution) was used as a douche. As you might have guessed, some women died from this practice.

Considering the list above, every item on this catalog has the potential to be toxic to the human body. Many of them are very toxic to the body.

The items and habits above can block the system interfering with liver and kidney function. They all have the potential to cause system wide irritation. When you study human function as I have, this conclusion is apparent.

Tremendous liver and kidney-overwhelm causes migraines. The solution is reduce as many of these irritants as possible and then support liver and kidney function via diet and supplements.

Otherwise woman's' wellbeing will be affected on a daily basis and wreak further migraine issues.

Migraine culprits or facilitators are in the above list without fail. The sooner we can address these problems and start eliminating them, the sooner we will be able to not only address migraines in women but better health for women up and down the line.

A mystery remains as such until the light of observation is shown directly on it. Then the pieces fall together as they do above. Assay yourself against this list and see if, at the moments of your worst pain there was something that "set it off."

Now imagine that all of these factors or a good portion of them are attacking the immune system of our challenged young woman

Therefore, the recipe for handling migraines would be to return function to the liver and kidneys with various herbal formulas, herbs and foods while eliminating as much of the above list as possible.

The foods that activate the liver and kidneys can be found earlier in this book. Please look them up and employ as many as possible.

39 Showering and the Liver

You know that the liver regulates the skin. One of the easiest ways to affect change in the liver is to take a hot shower! Why? Because the skin is part of our excretory system thus taking a shower opens up these channels and aids the liver.

This is also why taking a hot shower to start the day is so vital. Simply, this activity jump-starts the immune system by activating your liver and kidneys. The kidneys are activated with your shower water as well via water absorption.

The results on sleep can be seen the first night.

Taking a hot shower before bed insures better sleep as insomnia is just due to an overworked liver. The same process that activated the liver in the morning helps to calm down the system at night.

Dry skin brushing is another way to insure better liver function.

The practice of dry skin brushing is very old and dates back thousands of years. But when employed in a daily routine is very beneficial. The ability of the skin to excrete toxins is of paramount importance for good health.

It is a fact that skin brushing is one of the optimal ways of TURNING ON the immune, endocrine system and all the glands of the body very quickly. In addition, at the same time, it triggers an increased physical and mental well being as the liver that regulates the skin is now very active.

The Benefits of Dry Skin Brushing

Dry skin brushing helps the body to shed dead skin cells, which helps to improve skin texture and cell renewal.

Skin Brushing encourages the body's discharge of metabolic wastes, which greatly aids the lymphatic drainage of the entire body. When the body rids itself of toxins, it is able to run more efficiently in all areas.

Brushing also helps to tighten the skin because it increases the flow of blood. Increasing the circulation to the skin can also help lessen the appearance of cellulite.

Dry skin brushing stimulates the lymph system to drain toxic matter into the correct channels, thereby purifying the entire system. This enables the lymph to perform its house-cleaning duties by keeping the blood and other vital tissues detoxified.

Skin brushing may help with muscle tone, and a more even distribution of fat deposits.

Because of direct liver function improvement, skin brushing aids the nervous system by resetting the connection to the skin via the liver.

(Note: using a good strong brush in the shower is very beneficial in cleansing the liver via the skin)

Waste cannot persist in a body teaming with circulation. Help your body improve circulation by removing its waste with skin brushing. Try it and find out for yourself.

Final note, the skin can be brushed wet (via shower or bath). If it is done in a wet environment, it must be brushed harder using something that is semi-stiff, such as a loofah sponge. Exfoliate can be used but must was completely off. If you have been paying attention, you will agree that the fewer chemicals used for the cleansing of the body the better. Remember, soap is manmade and therefore has little place on the body for any length of time. Soap does have its place as a disinfectant and abrasive scrub, but a little goes a long way.

40 The Liver and Oil

Even before man learned to write, the importance of oil was well understood. Without question, oil has been sought after, hoarded and fought over long before recorded history. Archeologists and scholars agree that in man's vast panorama of existence, he has had many obsessions, from fire to microchips but none more consuming than oil.

Even though much of the early record has been submerged, lost, buried, burned, or forgotten oil has left its indelible stain. Oils of all types have been coveted at one time or another. Olive oil may have been the first vegetable processed where the end result was a valued lubricant. The Yom Kippur story from the Torah is a celebration of oil and its importance. People will die for oil and have throughout earth's history.

World War II was fought over oil. The Germans and Japanese didn't have it, and needed it to expand. Expansion based on a national thirst for oil was what started and ended the bloodiest war on record. Regardless of what we are being told, we are now in the Middle East for the same reason.

The "black gold" has been used as a food, lubricant, and fuel, for anointing of kings, protecting warriors, an additive in the manufacturing process and in medicines. How important is oil to religion? The word Messiah literally means "the anointed one." The name Christ comes from the Greek, khristos, "the anointed one," a literal translation of the word mashiach.

Translation: "Our savior is the one anointed with oil!" Oil has been given a lofty place in the story of man.

Oil in the body is very mysterious. During youth we do not want it (oily skin). Aging, we cannot get enough of it as our skin has "dried out." The obsession grows as we hydrate moisturize, slather, soak and paint on masks.

Cosmetic companies indoctrinate us into the belief that the body is too stupid to run itself. The right question would be, is oily skin the cause of blackheads, pimples and skin disorders, or is it something else?

Television, radio, newspapers and the Internet tell us that, to be healthy, we must override our body's natural oils with all manner of creams, salves and washes.

By the age of five we morph into little automatons that suddenly NEED to run right out and purchase the next new and greatest thing! Advertisers understand this and now target huge parts of their budgets at pre-teens. Begging, pleading and cajoling leads to pestered parent purchases.

Our shopping mantra is:

"TV, radio, internet and newspapers do not lie... Buy!! Buy!! Buy!!

"Ignore the body"

"Science knows best"

"What is new IS better"

"Own it first"

Our oil obsession, like the shopping mantra, is deeply rooted in our psyche.

Do humans really need TO ADD oil to their diet? The answer is NO. Read on.

Anatomy 101: The liver is a chambered organ that filters much like the air filter found on your car. Everything you ingest quickly arrives at the liver for processing. Without processing, your body would be swimming in poisons. Remember the liver is the lynch pin of your immune system.

Hepatologists have long studied the oil and liver function quandary and unflinchingly acknowledge that the risk for damaging the liver is extreme when oil is ingested. Understand that all oils coat your liver, leaving it inoperable for hours immediately after ingestion. Warnings about the dangers of oils on liver function are not new, just ignored.

The "inhale and exhale" of the liver must be steady and constant. It must (much like your lungs) take in and then release, take in and then release. Like a sponge, it wipes up and rinses out, until it gets congested or immobilized. Sucking air out of a brick is of little use, as is a tired, overworked, oil coated liver.

The body has no defense for processed oil. None! It can only try to release it into the bowel. Have you ever noticed an oily stool? Oil is the last element to leave the stomach. It floats in the stomach as it floats on water. Does that mean there is no human use for oil at all? Under strict supervision, while utilizing a detoxifying sauna program, exercise, and proper vitamins, oil creates untold benefits. This type of program is the finest approach to detox that has ever been found and is now offered around the world. Under these conditions oil has a purpose and aids the tissues to release waste. Unquestionably, using this approach with supervision creates amazing results.

But the random taking of oil supplements can be very irritating and potentially damaging if done willy-nilly. Remember, the liver is the hub of your immune system and cannot go offline or be slowed.

Today, many women take Evening Primrose (EP) oil to help with menopausal symptoms. It is commonly used to relieve hot flashes, neck pain, shoulder pain, sleeplessness, poor concentration, low energy and bad moods. In an oil preparation it is useless. Those who take EP routinely notice that moods and other symptoms actually get worse with its use.

Why? Because processed oil is the carrier or delivery system for EP.

EP in a dry form is very beneficial to the body. After sixteen years of investigation and years of personal firsthand experience, this fact has been borne over and over again.

When the body does need some oil, how should it get it? The body distills all the usable oil it needs from our fresh fruit and vegetables. Have you heard of orange oil or avocado oil? Oil is so prevalent on earth that it is a component in all-organic life.

Yet, once we process the oil out of its original whole source, it becomes useless to the body.

Here is the rule to follow:

- *Never, ever, use oil supplements unless under supervision as part of a detox program.*
- *Derive your oil intake from whole food alone and then it is 100% bio-available to the body.*

The following is a list of problems that can occur with the use of processed oil:
(This includes cold processed olive oil):

Looking or feeling bloated
Gassy digestion
Gallstones
Hepatitis- like symptoms
Itchy eyes
Burning eyes
Watery eyes
Itchy Skin
Tingling skin
Poor concentration
Poor moods (anger, depression, etc.)
Hot flashes
Right side neck pain or stiffness
Right pectoral muscle pain or stiffness
Right deltoid muscle pain or stiffness (round part of the shoulder)
Right rotator cuff pain or stiffness (inside of the round part of shoulder)
Right scapula pain or stiffness (large flat bone behind your shoulder)
Right elbow pain
Low energy between 9 PM (night) and 3 PM (afternoon)
Fuzzy vision
Headaches
Congestion (nose, sinuses or chest)
Fidgety
Restless
Hot tempered
Confusion
Sleeplessness

Again, if your body does not derive its oil under its own power, through its own processes, the body cannot use it.

Avoid these foods:

Popcorn
Butter
Margarine
All nuts processed and raw
All seeds processed and raw
Mayonnaise
All oils (in bottles)
Fish oils (in capsules)
Oil supplements (in any form)
Vitamin E-oil supplements (except dry vitamin E)
Salad dressings (pour off the excess oil and you should be fine)
Sardines
Cheese

If the worst thing you eat is a little salad dressing, so be it. Remember, if you eat a salad dressing that separates in the bottle, pour off the excess oil, as it adds nothing to taste and is only filler.

You can regulate your health with the information found in this book. It is up to you to use it.

41 Dangers of Salt and Sodium

Salt and sodium are more insidious than sugar, as we never expect them to be so undermining to our health. Practically all-manmade food is a mix of sugar and salt and sodium. The reason, as "food / taste engineers" will tell you, is taste. Sugar is acidy on the PH scale, whereas salt is alkaline on the PH scale. Any chef will tell you that pleasing the palette is about balancing salt and sugar, as they are the most powerful sensors on the tongue.

Interestingly sugar is the hardest of the trio to give up, as it is the most addictive substance on the planet based on sheer numbers. You do not know anyone who is not addicted to sugar. Even if we have given sugar up, we will always be addicted to it. Diabetes numbers prove this as its incidents climb steadily higher every day. Being an exaggerated or extreme kidney condition, this should not be surprising to anyone. Contact with any one of the three will produce the list of problems below:

A) Water retention

B) Increased or high blood pressure

C) Accelerated heart rate

D) Low back pain, muscle pain and joint pain

If you do the above, you will naturally eliminate all processed carbohydrates from your life. Yes, you are going to have to eliminate the terrible JUNK FOOD MONSTER as well. What makes up junk food? Junk food is basically a slang term for food with limited nutritional value, also known as empty calories. If you look on the label of some "so called food," you will see a chemistry lab concatenation of ingredients including:

Sugar
Sucrose
Dextrose
Honey
Fructose
Corn syrup
High fructose corn syrup
Corn sweetener
Maltose
Lactose
Glucose
Molasses
Brown sugar

Many of these ingredients are listed as the first 5 ingredients on the label. What is the common denominator in all of these? S-U-G-A-R!

Sugar is wildly addicting, and junk food makers, knowing this, feed it to you by the tablespoon full.

FDA Food label law requires ingredients to be listed in descending order of amount used. The first item on the list is the most prevalent down to the least prevalent on the bottom of the list.

Pay attention to the amount of saturated fat, unsaturated fat, hydrogenated oils, peanut oil, soy oil, and olive oil and canola oil. These processed oils are some of the worst things you can put into your body.

A few more words about bread:

If you want to see an immediate change in your weight, give up, breads of all types, crackers, rice, grains of all types, pastry, cookies, doughnuts, muffins, pizza, pasta and rolls. If you cannot quite grasp this, just ask yourself, "If I planted_________ (fill in the blank) in the ground, would it grow?" If the answer is no, then you should not eat it.

"This week's topic is bread, a supposedly harmless subject, and a supposedly innocuous food item that we partake as food almost religiously two to four times a day. Bread, a supposedly harmless food, that when consumption is stopped, detoxification begins. It is common for people to experience severe cravings for refined grain products and often binge on them. There are more words of acute understanding that undermine the necessity of bread. There are more words that deplore why bread is so anti-health and its many implications when eaten. When starches are consumed, people wake up the next day and go through unpleasant periods of feeling foggy, hung-over, or sedated" - Grain Damage by Douglas N. Graham, D.C.

The information on bread is nothing new; it just has been conveniently ignored. Man has been making bread for thousands of years. Well documented in ancient Egypt, common workers were given bread and beer (derived from yeast) as the centerpiece of the Nile diet.

Prior to settling in Egypt, nomadic ancient man ate a diet richer in protein as planting and harvesting was not an option. Farming and tending the land is a natural development of putting down roots. Ensuring survival requires life to adapt to the changing environment or go extinct. Whereas animals are forced to adapt to an evolving planet, man alters the planet to his needs. No water? Start building a canal. Perhaps a large mountain in is your way obstructing your view? Dynamite a way through. No rain? Start cloud seeding.

Moving away from a powerful nomadic hunter-gatherer to a more tranquil, cultivation and domesticated lifestyle, spelled mutation for man. Egyptians settling on the Nile 5200 years ago developed written language, monoliths, shipping and religion; they cultivated crops, created bread and ate grains. Because of the sugar conversion from grains and breads, for the first time in the archeological record, man developed chronic physical problems.

Tooth decay became rampant, malignant cancers appeared while he was losing inches off his height. His lifespan was noticeably shorter, his skull brittle and his brain tumors grew. Was Neanderthal man really as superior a being as his tremendous stature and physical strength would indicate? How did a smaller, weaker, sugar-craving smarter human oust this pre-historic superman? We may never know, as the Neanderthal gentleman is no longer here to defend his choices.

Summation: *Man mutated or evolved in response to his dietary choices and lifestyle developments.*

Consider the following:

"The milling of wheat destroys 40% of the chromium, 86% of the cobalt, 68% of the copper, 78% of the zinc, and 48% of the molybdenum. By the time it is completely refined it has lost most of its phosphorus, iron and riboflavin, as well most fiber. Wheat flour has been plundered of most of its vitamin E, important oils and amino acids. White bread also turns to glucose as quick as white sugar (This is the staple diet of the majority)."
– Klenner, Southern Medicine & Surgery. April 1951.

"It (sugar) ought to be against the law - and white bread also."
- Dr Kelley DDS, Sunday afternoon, November 7, 1971.

In simple terms, milling insults the kernel of grain via the grinding process. Milling grinds these kernels to a fine powder that is then renamed, flour. Why is milling so horrific to all grain? Because once a kernel of wheat is broken and the germ or enzyme exposed, it is now no longer alive and thus bio-unavailable to the human body.

The germ or enzyme is nature's way of un-stressing the digestion of the body. It serves a dual purpose of pushing forth future generations of wheat stalk by carrying the genetic code necessary to sprout. Planting a scoop of even the best flour under the finest conditions will produce a yield of absolutely nothing.

Flour is dead in all forms. Planting a whole and complete wheat kernel produces wheat. Planting flour results in zero = dead substance.

Therefore, what is cracked wheat bread or whole wheat bread? A sales pitch, strictly a sales pitch. Cracked wheat is dead on grinding and then cooked to be certain of its destruction. Not to mention whole wheat bread has not one bit of whole wheat in it. If you were actually eating whole wheat, you would be gnawing on a stalk of wheat.

All foods carry enzymes prior to processing (as stated before).

Take a raw piece of steak and cook it "well done." Leaving it on your kitchen table for 6 months would produce a hard piece of leather. Natural drying out guarantees this expected affect.

Raw steak, if placed on your kitchen table for 6 months produces dust as it slowly disintegrates. The active enzymes assure this result.

Why does this happen? In raw food, enzymes are as vigorously energetic as nature intended. They are actively degrading tissue for later fertilization and seeding of the planet. To be sure, enzymes guarantee future generations and healthy soil. What happens to apples when they fall off a tree, if left alone? They rot (this is enzyme action) as the result of a robust ecosystem in action.

Ignoring natural law and building an environment to meet his whims has poisoned man.

Enter big business as supported by your government. Here are your friendly U.S. Government food pyramid recommendations from 2003,

Per day serving suggestions are to eat:

6-11 BREAD (dead), CEREAL (dead), RICE (dead), and PASTA (dead)
3-5 servings of vegetables (lots of vitamins)
2-4 servings of fruit (sweet and good for you, also lots of vitamins)
2-3 servings of milk (source of calcium)
2-3 servings of meat, fish (source of protein and iron)

After scanning the above five points, if you can't see a connection to who is making "contributions" and is receiving favors from our government, then you are not looking hard enough.

Someone apparently has a vested interest in you staying fat, as the commerce of this country is dependent on what you eat.

If you followed the above guidelines, you would blow up like a balloon.

Addicting breads / ground grains and flours are "food-like" substances and must be eliminated from your life for you to achieve any kind of success commencing any diet. Processed carbohydrates are also known as simple carbohydrates. Simple carbohydrates quickly turn to addicting sugar in the system and then store as fat.

Complex carbohydrates such as tomatoes, oranges, grapes, onions, broccoli, apples, tain natural sugar that is digested yet does nothing to contribute to "sugar poisoning." They convert from sugar to usable components in the body. The reason is because the enzymes contained in the fruit allow the body to utilize the sugars as fuel.

Manmade sugar-based carbohydrates are empty shells of energy, behind which there is nothing but vacant calories. Processed carbohydrates are guaranteed to become fat in the body. Bread is so free of any nutritional value; the makers embolden it with vitamins and minerals as a matter of course. Even with this bolstering, bread is still noticeably barely north of ingested cardboard.

Survive Better, Cut out the following:

- White Bread
- Whole Wheat Bread
- Squaw Bread
- Pumpernickel Bread
- Unleavened Bread
- Rice (white and brown)
- Kasha
- Tabouleh
- Pasta
- All cereals
- Oatmeal
- Shredded Wheat
- Crackers
- Cookies
- Cake
- Protein Bars
- Food Bars
- Potato Chips
- Corn Chips
- Pork Rinds
- Puffed Rice

If you cut out just the list above you will feel a difference.

The above 21 items are just the beginning. If you are starting to think with the content of this book, then you are aware that cutting out the processed carbohydrates is not enough to fully change the lines of your body. Cooking food kills or destroys enzymes.

Therefore, the more raw food you eat, the better you will feel.

What to eat, FRESH OR RAW

- Tomatoes
- Onions
- Cabbage
- Lettuce
- Spinach
- Broccoli
- Cauliflower
- Asparagus
- Radishes
- Celery
- Zucchini
- Squash
- Cilantro
- Cucumbers (not pickles)
- Sprouts
- Garlic
- Beets
- Kale
- Green beans
- Eggplant
- Mustard greens
- Okra
- Potatoes
- Hot peppers
- Pumpkins
- Turnip greens
- Turnips
- Green Bell Peppers (not yellow or red)
- Fish / sushi (not cooked or seared)
- Steak Tartare (not cooked or seared)

More on the Pursuit of Perfection

We all like to eat. The time of the day when you eat matters as much as what you eat. Family dinners and restaurants are the result of the socialization of man. However, eating at night is a sure way to add weight to your frame. If you only ate fresh fruit and or vegetables after 4:00 P.M. you would soon see the scale registering a smaller you.

Successfully modifying the above paragraph would include eating only one type of vegetable or fruit after 4:00 P.M. This approach takes the stress off the digestive tract. In other words, you can sit down and eat all grapes for instance, but nothing else (not including water).

You can have melons if that is all you are having. Do not eat bananas at night as they are too heavy and can add bulk. Do consume: Strawberries, Grapes, Melons, Apples, Oranges, Tangerines, Tangelos, Guavas, Lemons, Cherries, Gooseberries, Mangos, Papayas, Pineapples, Tamarind, Kiwi fruit, Loquats, Passion fruit, Persimmons, Pomegranate and Tamarillo.

Something to Consider Regarding Raw Food

In the last one hundred years, there have been many movements regarding eating. Fad diets come and go with very little actual clinical study behind them. That is completely untrue when it comes to the eating of raw food.

Between the years of 1932 and 1942, Dr. Francis Marion Pottenger, Jr. of Monrovia, California (author of "Pottenger's Cats") conducted experiments on cats to determine the potency of standardized biological extracts. Because there were no extant chemical procedures for standardizing biological solutions, manufacturers of such derivatives had to use animals to determine their effectiveness.

He studied the adrenal glands removed from the cats, as they would harbor the remnants of the extracts being assayed. The decade long cat study demonstrated something odd and very alarming. The rate of mortality for cats receiving adrenalectomies (adrenal gland removal and dissection) was staggering. Clearly there was a relationship to diet and mortality.

To ensure the best possible health of his test cats, Pottenger fed them a diet of market grade raw milk: cod liver oil and cooked meat scraps from the sanitarium. These scraps included the liver, tripe, sweetbreads, brains, heart and muscle. This diet was considered to be rich in all the important nutritive substances by the experts of the day, and the surgical technique used for the adrenalectomies was the most exacting known. Yet, these cats were undergoing severe biological changes.

Why were these cats such poor patients? Why were they dying from procedures that should not have been fatal? In seeking an explanation, he began noticing that his cat specimens were showing signs of deficiency. All showed a decrease in their reproductive capacity and many of the kittens born in the laboratory had skeletal deformities and organ malfunctions.

As he added more and more cats to his experiments, eventually his supply of cooked meat scraps exceeded demand and he was forced to start using raw meat from a local meat packing company in Monrovia. These raw meat scraps were fed to a segregated group of cats each day.

The raw meat fed to the cats was composed of the viscera (1: an internal organ of the body; especially: one (as the heart, liver, or intestine) located in the great cavity of the trunk proper. 2 plural: HEART), muscle and bone.

Within a few months, Dr. Pottenger started to notice that the raw meat group appeared in better health than the animals being fed cooked meat scraps. Their kittens appeared more vigorous, and most interestingly, their operative mortality decreased markedly.

In contrast, the health of the cats fed cooked meat kept declining. The comparison was startling, yet they were polar opposites. The cats were beginning to reverse. It prompted Pottenger to undertake a controlled experiment to observe exactly what was happening. He wanted to find answers to such questions as: Why did the cats eating raw meat survive their operations more readily than those eating cooked meat? Why did the kittens of the raw meat fed cats appear more vigorous?

Why did a diet based on cooked meat scraps apparently fail to provide the necessary nutritional elements for good health? He felt the findings of a controlled feeding experiment might illuminate new facts concerning optimal human nutrition.

After extensive study, Dr. Pottenger proved that when cats were fed a cooked food diet, the prodigy and their parents would have numerous health problems. As generations of cats were born, the problems kept increasing.

These defects include:

- Gum disease
- Heart disease
- Personality problems
- Insomnia
- Liver problems
- Tooth decay
- Miscarriages
- Deformity

Various chronic diseases of the organs were so rampant that Pottenger started a separate study to compare humans to similar stressors.

He noticed the same kind of startling differences while studying twins and siblings reared in different environments.

The same exact health disruptions that plagued his cats were being reproduced in the human study. The results repeated themselves again and again among the twins. Whenever and wherever the diet was changed, the maladies followed. The findings from his human / cat study are often quoted. Pottenger's human study was conducted between 1932 and 1956.

Nothing has been added or subtracted from his findings, and the observations are valid. A careful study of the Pottenger study will reveal irrefutable evidence of disease and deficiency caused through diet. Feel free to look up Pottenger's work on the net; you will be amazed and shocked when you read the full extent of his work.

The above was not the only work done on the subject of what society and cooked food does to a body.

Dr. Weston A. Price (author, Nutrition and Physical Degeneration) was doing a similar study on humans in 1938 - 1939. As a dentist, his focus was strictly on the mouth and gums. He was trying to understand why advanced civilizations had more dental problems than 3rd world countries.

The siblings that retained their more nature based diets enjoyed good health; the more civilized diet recipients became worse with each generation.

A summarization of Price's findings, for those now living a civilized / rural life style, gives us much data. Just as in Pottenger's cat study, the offspring were tracked as well as the health and disposition of the transplant.

to the city

The transplanted or rural relocated sibling reflected:

1. Rampant tooth decay.
2. Tooth placement now incorrect requiring braces.
3. Short stature with brittle bones.
4. Gingivitis common.
5. Narrowing of thighbones.
6. Cancer and malignant tumors.
7. Narrowing of skulls.
8. Deformities of the limbs.
9. Deformities of the skull.
10. Anemia
11. Nervousness

It is interesting that much of our even more damaging processed food had not been invented yet. In 1938 and 1939 the diet included white bread and sugars or candy that was not available in the native home or villages of the transplants.

Therefore, it is not a stretch to conclude that the above problems as well as today's problems (disease) are the result of our diet. The thought that man can safely adapt or adjust to our present (junk food diet) lifestyle is optimistic and idealistic.

Sugar Love It or Flee From It.

42 Salt / Sodium Difference

Note: Humans are the only animals on the planet that add salt to their food beyond what occurs naturally in their diet.

Note: If not for salt's food preservation properties, the America's may never have been discovered, as food storage would never have lasted the entire voyage.

A Brief History of Salt

Should you have visited a museum and gazed at an Egyptian mummy, you have looked at history preserved by use of salt. Remnants of the vast Nigerian and Mali salt mines are still found on the African continent. Salt has held a much-exalted place in man's history.

Salt is obtained either from shallow mines or distilled from soil.

Marco Polo (Italian Traveler and Explorer, 1254 - 1324, Venice, Italy) used salt as currency during some of his travels. For a time salt was as valuable as gold and even traded ounce for ounce. Polo was clearly fascinated by the profitable salt business as he watched it conducted all over China. He followed early Chinese junks as they traveled up and down the Yangtze River (it stretches from the interior of China to the coast). Merchants would conduct their salt business from ship to shore, as people would gather in great numbers to get this valuable element.

Early China was built on salt.

Marco Polo is also believed responsible for introducing the west to the great Kublai Khan. Through Khan (the then ruler of China) we first see the Peng-Tao (or Tzao)-Kan-Mu (the first known pharmacology work), circa 2700 B.C.

One portion of the text documented nearly 50 varieties of salt previously unknown to the ancient world. The Chinese had been extracting salt (almost 5000 years ago) and processing it for consumption via methods similar to those practiced by industry today. Salt can be found almost everywhere from West Africa to China, from the American North and South to Germany. In Medieval times, he who controlled salt production or stores controlled the politics and thus had the power. Our language is still sprinkled with the power of salt.

Salt was a currency and Roman soldiers were paid in the valuable white granules.

Salary: Salary (Roman payment), this word is derived from Latin salarium argentums or salt money, which eventually became the word salary. When salt became easier to mine and was therefore more common, its value declined and it ended up on our dinner tables.

Still sprinkling our language:

- Not worth / worth his weight in salt
- He is the salt of the earth
- Salting away
- With a grain of salt
- Back to the salt mines
- Below the salt (meaning common or ordinary)

Salt is sodium chloride. About 40 percent of salt is sodium and 60 percent is chlorine. Sodium is a life vital element found in fruit, vegetables, meats and legumes (nuts).

Salt is well documented in its ability to preserve everything from mummies to beef from decaying.

By the early 1800s salt was the number one preservative in the Americas. Food preservation was among the biggest problems of the day. The use of salt ensured an adequate supply of meats and grains for the upcoming winter and early spring.

Other than for industrial needs, modern man's need for salt has greatly diminished. Refrigeration has eliminated the need for preserving food to survive the harshness of the seasons. Therefore, all the salt we need for a healthy body is derived from our diet, if we eat a truly balanced diet. Since WWII salt has caused more problems than it has solved as a supplement.

Why Should We Eliminate Salt

Although a small amount of sodium (about 500mg) is essential to normal body functions, it is estimated that the average person consumes 4000 to 5000 mg a day. It is widely understood even by medical science that large amounts of dietary sodium result in high blood pressure (also called hypertension) and may lead to heart attacks, strokes and kidney failure. Man is no longer salt deficient, which is why health care professionals are advising us to eat far less added salt.

Healthy foods do not come in cans. Canned food is loaded with salt / sodium. Look at canned food sometime and you will be aghast at the sodium content. These so called foods are all worthless.

Do not eat anything pickled. Avoid foods such as sauerkraut, olives, relishes, dills and gherkins. They are all packed in vinegar and/or brine (heavily salted water), making them exceptionally high in sodium.

Cheeses contain salt for preserving as well as for flavor. Smoked or canned meat and fish products such as tuna, ham, bacon, cold cuts, corned beef and sausage are well seasoned with salt. Deli roast beef and turkey breast are often cooked with salt.

Beware Of Seasoning

Sodium is a part of many other ingredients added to prepare foods that often have no salty taste. Some are used in amounts that add a significant quantity of sodium to the final product.

Monosodium glutamate (MSG), a flavor enhancer
Baking soda (sodium bicarbonate), used to make quick breads and cakes rise
Sodium nitrate, a curing agent for meat
Sodium saccharin, an artificial sweetener
Sodium propionate, a mold inhibitor found in baked foods
Sodium citrate, an acidity controller found in soft drinks, fruit drinks, jams and jellies
Sodium, when consumed will, by its presence, throw off the functions of your body.

Think of sodium as a random renegade program that is fed into your computer (the computer is your body). This element feeds your computer wayward commands such as to store, delete, purge, format, copy, remove, etc. regardless of what the body needs to do. Sodium does not think it is just reactive.

Other renegade chemicals that corrupt your body's hard drive are sugar, caffeine and all drugs. Life is hard enough without making it harder by poisoning yourself.

What about Over-The-Counter Medications?

Medications can be another unexpected source of sodium in the diet. Over the counter products such as antacids, laxatives, bicarbonate of soda, pain relievers and other preparations often contain large amounts of sodium.

What Do Food Labels Tell About Sodium Content? If a nutrition label is not available, you can check the ingredient statement for the presence of salt or other sodium compounds. Ingredients are listed in descending order by weight, but since the specific weights aren't listed, it only gives you a rough idea of the amount of sodium.

Your best bet would be to never purchase anything that lists more than 120 mgs sodium per ample serving.

—-Consider the following; your FDA is lying right to your face—-

> **The Food and Drug Administration has also established the following guidelines for sodium claims:**
>
> **Sodium Free:** food contains less than 5mg sodium per serving. (No kidding 5mg. really?)
>
> **Very Low Sodium:** food contains 35 mg sodium or less per serving. (Very low sodium...?)
>
> **Low Sodium:** food contains 140 mg sodium or less per serving. (So, this is low sodium!)
>
> **Light in Sodium:** food has 50% less sodium that original item. (What does that mean?)
>
> **Reduced Sodium:** food contains 25% less sodium than the original item. (Does this mean..?)
>
> **Unsalted, No Salt Added or Without Added:** Salt is used only if no salt is added to a food that is normally processed with salt, which means it could still be loaded with sodium. These strategies show just how dangerous government guidelines actually are.

The above points are the equivalent of our government issuing a proclamation:

> 'We recognize that Russian roulette could be dangerous"
>
> "We recommend that it should be played with care."
>
> "Ideally with a 12 chambered pistol rather than the usual 6 chambers"

Why do you think that these salt / sodium guidelines exist? The answers are money and addiction. Foods containing added salt and sodium are addicting and this equals money in the pockets of those using it. If you also suspected that some of that money would end up being paid as kickbacks to the FDA or other agencies, remember I never said that. That was your idea.

Forgive me, but a LITTLE poison is still poison.

If this book has taught you nothing, except never eat anything containing sodium, salt or sugar, then I have done my job. Making these changes would dramatically alter the quality of your life. You would be on the road to the fountain of health and youth. You would actually start to appear younger. This happens every day. Do you deserve that?

You are surrounded by sodium, unless you give it up. This is a losing battle unless you decide not to fight it by not engaging in it in the first place.

Remember, it is best to never eat sodium.

The following foods are ridiculously high in sodium.

- Anchovies
- Bacon
- Baking Soda
- Bouillon Cubes
- Canned Soups
- Canned Tuna
- Canned Vegetables
- Cheese
- Cold Cuts
- Condiments
- Cooking Sauces
- Cottage Cheese
- Croutons
- Diet Soda
- Fried Chicken
- Gravy
- Ham
- Hot Dogs
- Olives
- Pickles
- Salad Dressings*
- Salsa
- Sausage
- Sea Salt
- Soy Sauce
- Spaghetti Sauce
- Tomato Juice
- Vegetable Juice
- Ketchup
- Mustard

* If the worst thing you ate was a little salad dressing that had some sodium in it, so be it. At the same time, if you are sensitive to it, drop it out as well. If you eliminate them from your life, except what naturally occurs in food, you will be lean and healthier.

I encourage you to do this. If you work hard at it, you will notice the difference.

How to Start to Ease into Being Healthy

Starting on this journey may not be easy as it is not what you are comfortable with. But unless you start, your body will eventually get very uncomfortable with waste your body cannot process. The first thing to do is, go to the grocery store and pretend you are shopping for food you would be eating based on this book. Walk down the aisles and notice what you would be eating and not eating.

Then, start over again, this time focusing just on what you would be eating. Walk around the market again. Take these same steps until you feel comfortable with the idea of what you are going to be purchasing.

Pick up the actual items you will be eating, hold them, look at them and get used to them.

Again, when you are comfortable with all of this you can go shopping. This may seem simple but it will prepare you for what is coming by allowing you to wrap your mind around the subject matter.

What Actually Happens When You Gain Weight

The human body is a carbon-burning, oxygen-breathing machine that expends energy based on its activity level. Putting on weight requires one or more of the following:

- Added muscle mass
- Slowed metabolism
- Decreased activity level
- Increased food intake
- Water retention
- Pregnancy

All six points above force the body to adjust its activities to accommodate the changes. The wildcard elements that cause the body to put on weight are:

Sodium: Which causes the kidneys to go "off line" and retain water, not utilizing it.

Salt: Which causes the kidneys to go "off line" and retain water, not utilizing it.

Sugar: Which causes the kidneys to go "off line" and retain water, not utilizing it. Sugar scrambles all of the commands that the body is trying to execute. Initially sugar causes a release of urine as the body goes into cathartic shock. It then commands the body to retain water.

Too much protein: Causes kidneys overwhelm / poisoning. They go off line and the body starts retaining water as it tries to dilute the excess protein. Protein also interrupts sexual function in both sexes.

Drugs: Do all of the above while poisoning the body.

Alcohol: Scrambles all of the systems of the body and is a poison.

Waste that should be broken down isn't and the body can't utilize the fluid present to break down new waste. Interference with the kidneys always leads to disruption of the liver, heart, lungs, muscles, joints, pancreas, sex drive, etc.

On a digestive level, production of hydrochloric acid in the stomach comes to a halt as fluid is being diverted for other purposes. Therefore the food in your stomach is not being digested and is now a compost bin releasing foul gases.

Consequently, you develop varying degrees of indigestion, experience flatulence and begin belching as the food in your stomach rots and turns into putrid mulch. In the morning you have gained 1-7 pounds.

What caused this?

The body's inability to flush itself of toxic waste is the source of weight gain.

That is what goes on in your body.

43 Killer Caffeine

There is nothing like starting your morning with a good hot steaming cup of coffee.

I have never even tasted coffee and I know the above statement is true. How did a little insignificant bean from economically depressed countries take over the planet? Marketing! Repetition is the key and saturation is the result. Good marketing sticks to you like a long sleeve shirt in Florida at a mid August baseball game. There just is no way to peel it off.

Consider this. In the 1960's kids wanted to grow up to be an Oscar Meyer Wiener: "Oh, I wish I was an Oscar Meyer Wiener, that is what I truly want to be-ee-ee, 'cause if I was an Oscar Meyer Wiener, everyone would be in love with me."

What happened to Sara Lee? You might remember, "No-body doesn't like Sara Leeeee." When it comes to addictions, coffee has woven itself into the fabric of our very being.

Consider coffee houses

Coffee cake

Coffee breaks

Toffee candy

In the end nothing compares to coffee. Because coffee said there was nothing that compares to it. Coffee is practically a religion. If some clever pastor, rabbi, father, minister, monk, or other religious leader linked up with Starbucks . . . hmmmmm. Imagine the attendance!

Prior to 1985, coffee was an adult drink. Now, thanks to years of aggressive marketing, yearly coffee sales exceed water.

It is second only to sugar as the most addicting substance on the planet. Shocking, you say? How many people do you know that are addicted to caffeine? Know anyone addicted to sugar? How about to heroin? Can you count those who are entrenched with cocaine? Sugar wins hands down.

Sugar is an ingredient in practically everything, even coffee and cigarettes.

If auto parts makers could perfect a way to coat parts with it, *everyone* would be a mechanic.

Repairs would be ragged, but done in half the time. Men would meet in the auto parts houses not to talk as "gear heads" do, no; they would be sucking on break shoes and spark plugs. What about new innovations in cars, who cares!! Where are the fuel injectors?

Coffee and hot beverages are a real treat no doubt. But no one seems to care what caffeine is doing to the body. Caffeine is a common chemical found in natural sources, such as tealeaves, coffee beans, cocoa beans, cola nuts and carob beans. In the human body caffeine acts as an intense stimulant with such power, many people think they can't start their day without a little.

Caffeine causes your breath to quicken, heart to pump faster and blood pressure to rise (all of this is due to an intense attack on the kidneys). The kidneys under heavy duress start to release fluid (a diuretic response).

This completely upsets the balance of the human body as the caffeine has "reprogrammed the body."

This robs the system of fluid it needs to run on. But you feel great! Soon you stand in the rest-room evacuating your bladder while starting to feel tired. Oh so very, very tired. As the kidneys spasm, blood pressure rapidly rises.

Suddenly you are jumpy, your low back hurts, you are nervous with shaky hands, which you think means that you need more caffeine. This is akin to shooting yourself in the foot and concluding that if you shoot yourself twice you will feel better.

Caffeine Comparison

Drink/Food - Amount of Drink/Food - Amount of Caffeine in mgs.

- Mountain Dew, 12 ounces, 55.0mg
- Coca-Cola, 12 ounces, 34.0mg
- Diet Coke, 12 ounces, and 45.0mg
- Pepsi, 12 ounces, 38.0mg
- 7-Up, 12 ounces, 0 mg
- Brewed coffee (drip method), 5 ounces, 115mg
- Iced tea, 12 ounces, 70mg
- Dark chocolate, 1 ounce, 20mg
- Milk chocolate, 1 ounce, 6mg
- Cocoa beverage, 5 ounces, 4mg
- Chocolate milk beverage, 8 ounces, 5mg
- Cold relief medication, 1 tablet, 30mg

Source: U.S. food and Drug Administration and National Soft Drink Association.

According to the National Soft Drink Association, the following is the caffeine content in mg per 12 oz can of soda:
Product, Caffeine Content

Shasta Cola, 44.4mg
Jolt, 71.2mg
Mr. Pibb, 40.8mg
Sugar-Free Mr. Pibb, 8.8mg
Mountain Dew, 55.0 mg
Dr. Pepper, 39.6mg
Mello Yellow, 52.8mg
Pepsi Cola, 37.2mg
Tab, 46.8mg
Diet Pepsi, 35.4mg
Coca-Cola, 45.6mg
RC Cola, 36.0mg
Diet Cola, 45.6mg
Canada Dry Cola, 30.0mg

By means of comparison, a 7 oz. cup of coffee has the following caffeine (mg) amounts, according to Bunker and McWilliams in J. Am. Diet. 74:28-32, 1979:
Product - Caffeine Content mgs.

Drip, 115-175mg
Espresso, 100mg - 1 serving (1.5-2oz)
Brewed, 80-135mg
Instant, 65-100mg
Decaf, brewed, 3-4mg
Decaf, instant, 2-3mg
Tea, iced (12 oz), 70mg
Tea, brewed, imported, 60mg
Tea, brewed, U.S., 40mg
Tea, instant, 30mg

Energy drinks for kids are now out of control and are being consumed by even preschoolers. "Young people are taking caffeine to stay awake, or perhaps to get high, and many of them are ending up in the emergency department", said Dr. Danielle McCarthy of Northwestern University.

Dr. McCarthy conducted an extensive study in 2006 for the Chicago poison control center. Her findings were not surprising.

"Caffeine is a drug and should be treated with caution, as any drug is." - Dr. Danielle McCarthy

Anheuser-Busch and Miller Brewing Company now produce several "energy beers." This is a mix of beer and caffeine. A favorite is Red Bull and vodka. Bartenders often mix these two and call it a 'Friday Flattener' or a 'Dirty Pompadour.' Concoctions like this have been popular for a more than ten years.

In 2006, more than 500 new energy drinks launched worldwide. No doubt coffee fans are probably too old to understand why. We are building chemically dependent addicted kids almost as fast as they can be conceived.

The following list is taken from the "Caffeine Database." The caffeine content of the newest energy drinks aimed at kids is astounding. The following numbers are based on a per serving measure. Some of these beverages have more than one serving per can.

180, 90mg
Airforce Nutrisoda Energizer, 50mg
Ale 8 1, 37mg
Ammo, 171mg
Ammo, 75mg
Amp, 75mg
Amp Overdrive, 141mg
Arizona Extreme Energy Shot, 100mg
Arizona Green Tea Energy, 200mg
Battery, 106mg
Bawls, 66.7mg
Bazza High Energy Tea, 150mg
Beaver Buzz, 110mg
Blow Energy Drink Mix, 240mg
Bomba Energy, 75mg
Boo-Koo Energy, 360mg
Brawndo, 200mg
Burn, 118mg
Burn (UK), 45mg
Burn2, 199mg
Buzz Water, 200mg
Celsius, 200mg
Chic, 150mg
Cocaine Energy Drink, 280mg
Crunk, 100mg
Dare Devil, 240mg
Diablo, 95mg
Dopamine Energy Drink 120mg
Fixx, 500mg
Fritz Kola, 83.3mg
Fuel Cell, 180mg
Full Throttle, 144mg
H2O Blast, 100mg
High Ball Energy, 75mg
Hogan Energy, 160mg
Howling Monkey, 160mg
Hy Drive, 121mg
Hype, 80mg
Joker, 150mg
Jones Energy, 100mg
Kaboom Infinite Energy, 95mg
MDX, 82.25mg
Monster, 160mg
Morning Spark, 170mg
Mother, 106mg
No Name Energy Drink, 280mg
NOS, 250mg
Nuclear Water Antidote, 180mg
Pimp Juice, 81mg
Power Edge, 80mg
Power Horse, 80mg
Power Shot, 100mg
Rage, 200mg
Red Jak, 164mg
Red Line RTD, 250mg
Relentless, 160mg
Rip It Energy Fuel, 100mg
Rock Star, 160mg
Rock Star Juiced, 160mg
Rock Star Roasted, 225mg
Rock Star Zero Carb, 240mg
Rumba Energy Juice, 170mg
Sobe No Fear, 174mg.
Sobe No Fear Gold, 174mg
Socko, 160mg
Socko Slim, 160mg
Spark, 120mg
Spike Shooter, 300mg
Superfly, 150mg
Upshot, 200mg
V, 109mg
Vamp, 240mg
Viso Energy Vigor 300mg
Von Dutch, 160mg
Who's Your Daddy, 200mg
Wired X344, 344mg

It should not be surprising that at bedtime you and your kids can't sleep. The caffeine you had

earlier that day is still upsetting your liver and kidneys! It also accumulates in yo
sleeping? Your sleeping pills contain you guessed it caffeine.

Does this make any sense?

But you say coffee helps me go #2 (bowel movement).

FACT: Ingesting ANY hot liquid instantly registers "sick" to the body. Why? The body is programmed to fight invaders by raising its temperature. The result is the body will rid waste from the heated area. In the case of the colon, you have an evacuation (bowel movement).

Temperature elevation = immune system response to bacteria, virus or irritant.

Every morning, as a result of boiling your intestinal tract, your body thinks it is sick. "Every morning it thinks it is sick." Is there any question why you are looking old prematurely? Do you wonder why your body hurts?

The byproduct of breaking caffeine is uric acid. When caffeine is present we not only have a superheated body, we have a chemically heated body. Uric acid, a harsh irritant, raises body temperature by .5 -1.5 degrees. This uric acid also stimulates the body to release. In other words, we have just thrown the body into spasm due to excess stimuli (uric acid and a hot beverage). Remember "Toeville"?

Throwing the body into panic mode is never, never, never a good idea. Caffeine causes the body to reject the normal biological processes that it should be running. Whatever the body was trying to do is shut down for hours.

The natural response to reading this chapter is to switch to decaffeinated coffee.

Unfortunately, decaffeinated coffee can be worse than caffeinated coffee. The decaffeination process leaves 6-20% of the caffeine behind. Yes, decaf coffee still has an appreciable amount of caffeine present in the final product. Therefore you are not free from caffeine, you are merely ingesting less. Caffeine is so potent a toxin that even a 1% residue is very damaging to the body. The decaffeination process is often worse than caffeine due to the extraction process. The solvents that can be used to extract caffeine are formaldehyde (embalming solution), methylene chloride (known to cause cancer) and other solvents. There is no safe coffee of any type. Small quantities of poison are still destructive to the body. Caffeine free is safe, reduced caffeine or decaffeinated is not. Do yourself a favor and do not consume this destructive chemical or chemically laced morning cocktail.

If you are not clear about how dangerous caffeine really is, the next few paragraphs will make this very apparent. This information is available at doctoryourself.com.

Roger Bezanis

The articles cited at doctoryouself.com incorrectly attribute emotional function to brain function. Therefore I will not print them in their entirety here. I have chosen to remove the brain references and focus on the 'outcomes' from exposure to caffeine.

So-called allergies to caffeine are being widely diagnosed. Caffeine allergy is a laughable term and can be compared to an allergic reaction to bullet wounds. There is no such thing as an allergy to poison unless we are brainwashed to believe that poison is essential to life.

The work on caffeine / allergy / toxicity is correct when directing the attack at the liver. The liver must be allowed to wash the body free of waste. Caffeine completely disables the liver and is attributed to causing the mania listed below. When the body is 'locked up' and retaining water it is at a toxic standstill and will behave in the following manner.

- Psychotic states
- Nervous breakdowns
- Irrational behavior
- Poor attention span
- Poor comprehension
- Mood changes
- Loss of organizational skills
- Delusions
- Hallucinations
- Paranoia
- Panic attacks
- Anxiety
- Toxic dementia
- Memory impairment
- Social anxiety
- Strained personal relations
- Inability to process information
- Brain damage (actually all organs are damaged by caffeine use)
- Vision impairment
- Loss of verbal skills

Caffeine related disorders were noted as early as 1936.

The general facts indicate that caffeine is the biggest contributor to mental health disorders on the planet today. The 'beans' addictive qualities, prevalence, legal status, and rampant regular use, guarantee that these numbers will continue to escalate to epidemic levels. When society fully grasps the dangers of caffeine, it may be too late.

You now have the truth. Caffeine purveyors hate me. Therefore, if I suddenly disappear from the face of the earth, remember to look for me in or under the cornerstone of your corner coffee shop.

44 Hot / Cold Factor

When the body gets hot or cold for whatever reason, be it environmental or chemical, it does two things:

- **It tries to cool itself / it tries to heat itself**
- **It alters its function in response to the stimuli**

This is why we vomit and get diarrhea when we are sick. This is all an attempt to right the system. Just as sneezing is an attempt to clear the nose. Diarrhea is the colons attempt to sneeze.

Ancient medicine taught us that to break up constipation, a hot compress should be applied directly to the abdomen. This works the same way as consuming boiling liquid. The heat transfers to the bowel and this stimulates elimination. Again, the heat fools the body into a cathartic spasm as part of an immune response and the body evacuates.

Ergo, the body acts as if it were sick.

Consider this, when you eat hot food (as most people do), the body perceives the heat and wrongly perceives it as fever. It then starts to fight a nonexistent infection. Since survival is paramount, the body pulls resources from digestion and begins trying to fix something that isn't broken.

Now imagine that the body is constantly getting hot food. Having imagined that, imagine what happens to your body when digestion is not important and infection fighting is. If you think that the result would be that you would put on fat, you are right.

What about spicy food?

What happens when you ingest hot spicy food? Does it heat the body too?

Exactly right.

No doubt you have seen someone eating hot spicy food and sweating. Their brow is wet and beading with more sweat. To the body, hot is hot regardless of its source. Spicy food is like eating boiling food that does not cool. This is why after a meal of spicy food, the next evacuation or two will burn as the acids are still very potent even on the way out of the body.

When the body gets hot does it want to cool itself? Correct again. The fire-eater reaches for cold water to dilute the heat. Again the body does not differentiate between hot from spice or hot from heating. Hot is hot.

The chemical reaction causes an immune system response as the body tries to cool. Colon formulas are often loaded with hot peppers to cause the colon to heat and then evacuate. When you see African Bird Peppers in the ingredient list of a colon formula, heat is the purpose. The result is a hot rapid evacuation.

The temperature of the body elevates with any potent spice. The tongue is also on fire signaling that the liver is heating as a direct result. To prove this, take your temperature prior to eating spicy food. You will notice that prior to the meal your temperature is around 98.6. After your meal begins, you will feel hotter as your temperature has raised a few tenths of a degree or more.

The body attempts to reject anything hot either by vomiting, or eventually via a loose stool or diarrhea.

What about cold food?

One of the main reasons people tend to be heavier in very cold environments is a response to keeping warm. Fat is an insulator just like fiber insulation is in your attic and walls. Researchers have submitted work proving that the epicanthal "eyelid fold" (found in Asia) is a direct result of thousands of years of frigid climate conditions. In a cold climate the body must keep all vital components as warm as possible. This is the purpose of these folds that make Asians look like Asians.

As the peoples of the earth keep moving to warmer climates, these folds may eventually disappear.

What happens to the person who intentionally freezes or deeply chills some part of their body from the inside out? Eating bone-chilling food (like ice cream) slows the metabolism as the body is pooling its resources to stay warm. Eating ice cream or chewing on ice confuses the body and to some degree fat is the result.

Another interesting response that most of us have experienced is the cold drink / ice cream headache. This is simply the body locking-up and turning on the afterburners to fight off the intense sudden attack of cold on the system. Your headache is due to shock. The body goes into overdrive to heat itself. All systems are put on hold as you are temporarily freezing to death.

In a frigid environment the body needs fat for survival, as food is often scarce in such a locality. To support your body's needs you are forced to eat more and more to stay warm. Arctic conditions require the body to store fat for food and warmth. What kind of environment do you live in? Can you stay warm without fat? This is called hypothyroidism and is a western medical name for "The kidneys need help."

If not, improve your kidney and liver function. You will notice the difference.

What about Hypothermia?

Hypothermia is a slow or sudden drop in body temperature from 98.6 to as low as 86.6 where organ shutdown occurs. Remember the ice cream headache from above? Headache is one of the first symptoms of body temperature dropping.

The body contains 5 liters of blood. Should the body become extremely cold, it is vital to warm the body via the kidneys as 100% of our blood is circulated through them every 1-3 minutes. Therefore, warming the lower back (site of the kidneys) is paramount in cases of hypothermia.

If you are freezing, you need heat not vitamins. Heat is more important than digestion under cold conditions. Cold is trouble to the body. To conserve energy you will get tired as digestion and the nutrient factory is switched off in an attempt to get the body temperature to rise.

Stage one: Goose bumps and slight shaking

Stage two: Shivering increases and muscle coordination becomes very erratic.

Stage three: Speaking is difficult and thinking is extremely clouded.

Stage four: Speech nearly impossible, body blue and puffy, walking nearly impossible. Organ shutdown eminent, yet brain death may take some time as freezing slows this process.

Summation: If we use common sense regarding what we put in our mouth, and therefore stay away from spicy, hot or freezing cold items, we will eat a far different diet. Most people will read this chapter and decide, nope, that is not for me. It was interesting but not for me. Yet some of you will make changes.

Your body will do its best to deal with whatever cards you give it, but you can stack the deck in your favor by just using universal wisdom about your life and diet.

If you are sure your body is smarter than you, your conclusion is thousands of years old. It is also exactly correct.

45 Importance of H_2O (Water)

Water is one of the basic building blocks of life. Without a steady supply of it all life would eventually perish. There are many theories on water. Such as, you should drink half of your body weight in water every day. Sometime in the past someone said, "The AVERAGE person exhales between 48 to 64 ounces of water a day (about 1 to 1 1/3rd liters) just breathing." These statements are almost wholly inaccurate.

Each individual is different as are his or her needs.

Have you ever exhaled on a mirror and noticed the temporary fog you created? The moisture you saw was the direct result of the millions of tiny droplets of water that are carried out of our lungs in every breath. Earlier chapters in this book make reference to the fact that the body is a machine.

This truth is undeniable as the human body exhibits every trait of being a carbon burning machine, including the production and release of gases. Some gasses are harmful (methane for example) and some harmless (water vapor). The way the body cools itself is via respiration, which is defined as:

> 1: the placing of air or dissolved gases in intimate contact with the circulating medium of a multi cellular organism (as by breathing) b: a single complete act of breathing.
>
> 2: the physical and chemical processes by which an organism supplies its cells and tissues with the oxygen needed for metabolism and relieves them of the carbon dioxide formed in energy-producing reactions.

Result? Every breath we take dehydrates us a little more. That is why you wake in the morning with a pasty mouth (you have been air drying all night long) Sleeping, as far as dehydration goes, is kind of like running a marathon every night. Perhaps you sleep with a jug or glass of water next to the bed to prevent this. In the end we are drying out nonetheless.

The amount of water we will exhale in a day is dependent on a number of factors:

1). Climate (the dryer or hotter, the more water lost).

2). Physical activity (the more active, the more water lost).

3). Diet (processed foods in the diet, the more water needed to digest them).

4). Use of Caffeine or any diuretics (diuretics cause your body to expel water thru urine).

5). Stress (stress causes the liver to work harder. The liver runs on water like a washing machine to cleanse and purify your system).

6). Drugs and other Chemicals ingested (this is such a wild card, that the body is wholly defenseless against these influences)

7). Condition of your kidneys

8). Condition of your liver

There is a patently false "old wives tale" known by many that, for every cup of coffee, you need 3 cups of water or 4 cups of water, or maybe it's 5 cups of water. These computations are flawed and have little practical application. Thoroughly examine the above 8 points and decide for yourself if the "so many cup rule" has any validity at all.

The best cup of coffee / water rule is "NEVER DRINK COFFEE." Well, that was simple.

There are even more factors that influence how much or how little water a person needs. Is someone toxic, i.e. are they carrying an undigested load of material in the body that needs to be flushed out? For 100 percent of us the answer is yes.

How much water do we need?

Let's say that you do not eat processed foods and have no caffeine or diuretics in your life. Let's also postulate that you are NOT THE LEAST BID TOXIC to anything and are otherwise healthy.

Then you can follow your thirst.

Yes, you can follow your thirst. As I have stated again and again throughout this book, the body is constantly talking to you. The question is, are you listening and or do you know how to listen.

If you get an impulse to drink water, drink water not soda, coffee, tea, or some beverage that would increase the load on your system.

Do not feel bad, as this is primordial rocket science. You are learning the basics of your body. The body no one ever told you anything about. There are many experts that indicate we must drink between 80 to 100 ounces of water a day just to get by. That is not true. Yet it is not false either.

Follow your thirst. It will tell you when to drink water and how much. But, if you successfully use the "drinking your body weight in water every day" and it works, keep it up. However be willing to change as your body does. Perhaps you have heard "Drink half your body weight in water every day", same rule. It works and only if it works. Stay in fluid contact with your body (no pun intended) and you will know what you need.

Perhaps you just drink a solid 120 ounces a day and you have been tested again and again for the amount of water you should drink. You know the rule. Rules are only good if they work. In this book, WORK = HEALTH.

Is there a time when you do not want to drink water?

Believe it or not, there is an answer to this question and for good reason. Your body must manufacture Hydrochloric acid to help digest your food. Without it, the food just composts in your stomach and eventually your intestines.

It all starts with the glands of the mouth, where saliva is produced. Saliva contains the enzyme ptyalin. Ptyalin, water and mucus combined with the act of chewing, helps your body to start digesting the food in your mouth.

You have heard "death starts in your colon" well "digestion starts in your mouth."

Next in line are the stomach and its glands, plus the intestines. In the stomach we find hydrochloric acid that helps to soften the food you just swallowed to make it more permeable for digestion. It is because of the mucosal lining of the stomach that the stomach is not destroyed by our Hydrochloric acid.

Once in the small intestines the other enzymes created in the body go to work.

Here are some of the enzymes involved in digestion:

- Amylase: To digest carbohydrates
- Bromelain: To digest proteins
- Cellulase: To digest fiber
- Chymopapain: To digest protein
- Diastase: To digest carbohydrates
- Glucoamylase: To digest carbohydrates
- Hemicellulase: To digest carbohydrates
- Hyaluronidase: To digest, proteins, adhesions & fibrin
- Invertase: To digest carbohydrates
- Lactase: To digest lactose and fats
- Lipases: To digest fats
- Maltase: To digest carbohydrates
- Pancreatin: To digest proteins, fats & carbohydrates
- Papain: To digest proteins, fats & carbohydrates
- Pectinase: To digest carbohydrates
- Pepsin: To digest proteins
- Phytase: To digest carbohydrates
- Protease: To digest protein.
- Rennin: To digest proteins
- Trypsin: To digest proteins

Now imagine there was something you could do at every meal that would slow down or interfere with your digestion. Most people would never dream of doing such a thing. But that is just what we do if we consume water with a meal. If we do ingest water after a meal it should be more than 15 minutes after a meal. If you are parched during the meal, the meal is heavy in salt, sodium, sugar or spice. These elements are to be eliminated or greatly reduced in the diet.

This includes any beverage. Therefore do not consume fluids with your meals, as your digestion will slow to a snail's pace. What should be digested within an hour could take 4 or 5 hours or longer. Watering down or diluting the precious stomach acid that would otherwise start digesting your meal makes your metabolism seem sluggish when in fact the body is working the best it can under very trying conditions.

When we drink water, tea, soda, coffee or juice with a meal we are inadvertently telling the body to gain weight. After your food leaves the stomach, the gall bladder introduces bile or bile salts or bilirubin (terminology for bile) into the intestines to further dissolve fat, act as a stool softener and stimulate the peristalsis (squeezing motion of the digestive tract) of the intestines and the colon.

Food and a watery concoction (all mixed up) slow digestion. Can any of this be good? No. By over irrigating ourselves, especially at mealtime, we are doing a great disservice to our health. To reach a happy medium, sip water, as you need to throughout the day.

Your body will tell you when it is thirsty. Those who told you that when you feel thirsty it is too late, were trying to sell you water. Remember, if your needs change; let your water intake change too. Should you be working out, you will of course need more water. These silly tables indicating you need so much water based on your body mass are just a bunch of flotsam and jetsam and completely worthless.

Water is the oil of the body. Without it we put on weight, grow old faster, have poor skin, poor energy, poor hair, etc.

Don't ignore water but don't drown in it either.

46 Disease Labels and Who Owns Them

Imagine you did not have a name. Now imagine no one on the planet had names. Personal identification would be extremely difficult. The purpose of advertising is to separate, validate and inculcate (impress via repetition).

Your name achieves all three of those objectives when it is mentioned to someone you know. That is the purpose of advertising and of course labels. Labels convey a message and a reputation. Nothing without a name or a label is worth very much. Have you ever paid very much for anything that you could not identify or explain? The answer is of course no.

In the world of Allopathic medicine EVERY perceived malady must have its own special name or designation. Human frailties without names are not problems and NOT worth worrying about.

In the world of misguided and mistaken medicine, the word disease has lost its meaning and now means drugs and surgery. Earlier in this book I wrote that the true meaning of disease means DIS - EASE.

So-called diseases such as cancer and aids will never be cured until research stops looking for the magic bullet virus / cell / gene / fill in the blank. There is no such thing as a sickness gene.

There are chemicals that build up in the system / human body that eventually shut down the immune system. Who put those chemicals there? You did by choice or by lack of choice such as not moving your family away when the chemical plant was built a block away.

This is a hard pill to swallow. You are above the average man and can swallow it because you understand it. You reading this book now know it is true.

The word disease is a gold mine. Say the word and the eyes get wide and people go white with fear. Do not be controlled by fear. Consider the fear created and money made by the following list:

- AIDS
- Cancer
- Diabetes
- Legionnaire disease
- Parkinson's disease
- Hepatitis A-B and C
- Erosive Acid Reflux disease
- IBS (Irritable Bowel Syndrome)
- Crones Disease
- Alcoholism (now commonly called a disease?)
- PAD (Peripheral Artery Disease, it has no symptoms? Wow!)
- Restless Leg Syndrome (fidgety legs, hmmmmm?)

Again diseases make money. Clearly in the world of medicine, the name is everything. The above LABELS get your attention. There is little difference in the name West Nile Virus and Stuffed Crust Pizza. Both get your attention. In my opinion, disease is one of the most EVIL words in the English language. That is quite a statement. Why would I say such a profound or provocative thing?

As stated much earlier, disease means you are no longer responsible for your condition. Why? Your life has been stolen away by an invisible monster that attacked you as you slept in your bed. It is literally the plot line to the film "Invasion of the Body Snatchers." Disease means that something out of your control or influence GOT YOU and you now can do nothing about it.

Disease = VICTIM. Your American Medical Association is frothing at the mouth over the word disease.

Disease and your agreement that there are such things, is how they support themselves and in turn the Food and Drug Administration.

The AMA names all disease and recommends the surgery to correct them. In turn, the FDA creates or hosts competition to create the drugs to treat the disease. Your American Medical Association owns the word disease. No natural health healer, practitioner (Chiropractor, etc.) or natural health company can legally name or even breathe the word disease (much less treat it).

A natural health healer would never name a disease as he or she thinks in simple terms. He thinks in terms of basic organ function and corrects that. The word disease by its very nature is meant to be confusing and mysterious. The mere mention of the word disease leaves the listener in distress trying to understand what it is. No disease or label for a disease can be treated, but organs can.

Weak kidneys: Can be assisted, But Diabetes (a kidney condition, cannot). Diabetes can be helped! The remedy requires awareness, responsibility and a little work. Call kidney exsurpo (exact source of the pain) swollen irritated kidneys.

Slow or poor immune system function: Can be helped and or improved, But AIDS cannot. AIDS (Acquired Immune Deficiency Syndrome) is gradual immune system slow down. When you know the component parts of the immune system (as laid out in this book) you can heal. All of this is really exsurpo liver, kidney overwhelm.

Slow or poor liver function: Can be improved, But Hepatitis, high liver enzymes and or cirrhosis of the liver cannot. Again, these issues are exsurpo liver overwhelm.

To be sick, one MUST PARTICIPATE in their demise. No cure causes new symptoms. No natural therapies cause death unlike drugs and surgery can.
The body will not get sick without your help. If you fall out of a tree and break your arm, who was the person that fell? Who climbed the tree? Again whose arm is broken? Who climbed the tree? Was it the tree's fault? Was the branch weak? Who climbed the tree? Who chose to climb the tree?

You get it.

All organs and systems of the body can be helped if you know who did it, and then name the exsurpo, which leads to the changes you will make.

All liver problems can heal if given the chance. Getting sick is not a signal to call the mortuary; it is a signal to DO SOMETHING ELSE. Because what you have been doing has not worked.

HIV is a harmless virus, which sits quietly inactive in the human body. It causes no known problems. But, since it can be found in a large number of people with weakened immune system function it has been assigned the label "Precursor of AIDS." This is all hogwash.

The reason the above three problems are out of reach for a cure is because the names, which say nothing about the source of the problem, keep them hidden. Since the problem (or disease) is not a thing, but a lifestyle (full of chemicals, preservatives, colorings, sodium, sugar, etc.), the cure is never even suspected.

To summarize:
All so-called diseases, such as AIDS (an immune system weakness) require you to confront the problem without panic and then fight to improve the weakened function. Sitting in fear and waiting for the latest drug to come out is slow suicide. Name the exsurpo (exact source of the pain) and take action.

Actively working to improve your system with diet, herbs and exercise is the right answer. You have never been "gotten" by a disease (label). You had to work hard to earn the condition. When you lift weights, the expected outcome is larger muscles and increased strength.

When you eat junk food, use chemicals, etc. you can expect the body to eventually become sick.

Not a popular point of view, but recognizing that you are actually the source of your problems never is. You are responsible for your condition. You can do something about it. If you chose to climb a poison tree and then fall out with a sickness of some sort, just remember you chose to climb the tree. It is also your choice to FIX YOUR condition.

Choose to run your life or someone else will.

47 Microbiology vs. the Sales Pitch

"Tell a lie loud enough, and long enough, and the masses will believe it" - Adolph Hitler

Question: What is the difference between?

- Cancer
- Gonorrhea
- Syphilis
- AIDS
- Diabetes
- Chlamydia
- Herpes
- Polio
- Meningitis
- Tuberculosis
- HIV

Answer: Gonorrhea, Syphilis, Chlamydia, Herpes, HIV, Polio, Meningitis and Tuberculosis can all be *isolated and seen under a microscope.*

Answer: *Cancer, AIDS and Diabetes cannot be isolated and studied with a microscope.*

Question: What else do the items on the list above have in common?

Answer: Every item on the record above that can be isolated under a microscope has been controlled. These substances include Gonorrhea, Syphilis, Chlamydia, Herpes, HIV, Polio, Meningitis and Tuberculosis. These entities are no longer mysteries and therefore do not receive hundreds of millions in grant money donated for research.

Answer: Every item on the list above that CANNOT be isolated and seen under a microscope are massive sinkholes for millions of dollars in wasted grant money. The items that are lucrative to research include Diabetes, Cancer and AIDS.

Conclusion: Cancer, Diabetes and AIDS will never be isolated under a microscope, as they do not exist as germs or parasites. They are conditions, brought on by an overwhelmed and toxic immune system. They are enigmas that capture our imagination.

—-Cancer, Diabetes and AIDS are conditions brought on by an overwhelmed and toxic immune system —-

Those seeking lifetime job security could do little better than to pursue shadows, witches, warlocks, AIDS, ghosts, fairies, evil spirits, Cancer, werewolves or Diabetes. These nebulous shadowy entities rivet our attention. These are the nefarious "monsters in the closet" of our youth.

Remember what Greek philosopher Plato said, "Everything that deceives may be said to enchant."

We are enchanted with danger, mystery and superhuman evils.

Humans love imagining monsters hiding under the bed. We are enthralled with Stephen King, Jason, Freddy Kruger, Dracula and Chucky the killer doll.

Sequestering imagination from the equation, police work requires good evidence, not rumor, not hearsay. "Modern Medicine" is desperately trying to put the smoking gun into the hands of a killer that does not exist.

Rabid medicos are on a modern day "Witch Hunt" with the requisite ad hoc crazed mobs screaming with blood lust!

Wanted posters are posted everywhere. The hounds are frantically hunting for a trail to follow. Yet every trail keeps leading back to their masters. Unrelenting, the news warns us of terror lurking in every shadow. They tell us there is a monster out to kill us as we sleep! Every moment his relentless stalking brings him one step closer to sinking his teeth into our jugular vein to satiating his terrible thirst.

Few suspect it is actually slow death via poisoning by our own hand. You cannot arrest your murderer, if the murderer is you. Suicide is not glamorous. But invisible monsters are. Until you realize that you invented and fed the invisible fiend, it will never stop

–DISEASE BACTERIUM / PARASITES unseen by a microscope do not exist–

Yet drugs are produced for so-called diseases that cannot be isolated? How can we compose a therapy such as AZT, Radiation or Chemotherapy without knowledge of what we are trying to kill? These drugs and "treatments" are accepted deadly poisons. They work on the premise of differential toxicity.

The concept in "differential toxicity" is that the cure is deadlier than the so-called disease. Ergo, the doctors *hope* that the cure does not kill you. But if it does, your death is blamed on the so-called disease, never the treatment.

Does this make any sense? No!

How anyone can be administered these horrendous poisons and then recover, is a testament to our monumental infinite power to heal.

South African deaths attributed to AIDS are factually malnutrition, which facilitates the collapse of the immune system. Not surprising to find malnutrition in the backwoods of a third world country. *Every* South African so-called AIDS case that received proper nourishment recovered.

The United States Government does not allocate funds to countries with deaths occurring due to malnourishment. AIDS diagnoses receive sympathy and American cash. Therefore, it behooves third world countries to report AIDS deaths in volume.

Whenever there is a national disaster anywhere in the world, the news media immediately jumps in and electrifies us with death. They pad the body count by attributing all deaths that occur during the calamity to the event, regardless of the actual cause. Fear sells newspapers. Deaths assigned to AIDS sell condoms and furthers the public terror of an invisible enemy.

Because of that, whenever AIDS research asks for money, it gets it.

Is there a conspiracy? Do men in black sneak around abducting citizens, then poisoning / infecting them with dirty injections or viruses? No.

These so-called diseases are actually conditions and all brought on and made worse by:

Sugar
Salt
Sodium
Drugs (over the counter)
Drugs (illegal)
Alcohol
Hormones (supplemented or added to the food supply)
Pesticides
And a junk food diet

We are poisoning ourselves every day. AIDS, Diabetes and Cancer are getting a mega boost by "Big Fast Food."

What about the dangerous virus, HIV?
Everyone knows that HIV is the precursor to AIDS!

False, completely false! There are thousands of people who are diagnosed with the HIV virus, yet those same people do not develop AIDS. HIV is a dormant actor in the human body. Like the appendix, there is no information on what it actually does. It does not spread, it does not mutate. It is a zero in the human body.

What about how AIDS is spread?
Again, *everyone knows* that sharing needles, anal sex, vaginal sex and blood transfusions spreads AIDS.

Blood Connection

Sharing needles: Those who share needles have compromised immune systems as they are using drugs. Shooting heroin is deadly and destroys the immune system.

Anal Sex: This group (homosexuals) in the past used Amyl Nitrate as a recreational drug as well as many others. Previous drug use in this group is clear and not up for debate. All recreational drug use is well known to attack the heart, liver and kidneys. Therefore, anal sex has little or nothing to do with contamination and passage of this so-called disease. Use of cocaine, heroin, barbiturates and alcohol all tear down the system of anyone, regardless of sexual preference.

Vaginal Sex: It is believed that women can pass AIDS via vaginal sex to their boyfriends and husbands, not by kissing or any other method, strictly via intercourse. It is further believed that men can pass AIDS to their girl friends and wives via the same method.

Given that AIDS is supposed to be passed via direct blood to blood contact, are we to believe that there really are men and women having sex while simultaneously bleeding from wounds on their genitalia?

The answer is emphatically no.

Regarding women, the vaginal cavity and uterus is very tough and some of the strongest most durable membrane (skin) in the human body. So durable are these area of the body, it actively hosts new life, while withstanding baby kicks, twins, triplets etc. Clearly the theories on AIDS are full of battleship size holes.

The conclusion is clear. We are being sold condoms, drugs, surgery and fear. Fear makes money. We have not a clue that we are the sole cause of our health conditions, good or bad.

Coincidence vs. Good Fortune

What form of contraception was almost out of business until so-called AIDS made it mandatory? That would be the condom. Do you think the boys at Trojan might have a hand in keeping the public fixated on an incurable non-existent disease? Do you think that maybe there is a division over there pushing AIDS stories into the news?

Fear not only sells newspapers, it sells condoms.

If we continue to ignore the affects of our diet and chemical lifestyles, we will all be victims.

In the gay community, it is far more infrequent to hear about deaths caused by so-called AIDS. Why? The gay community, as a group righted itself and made a conscious effort to be healthier. Drug use has dwindled while consumption of health food and regular ingestion of supplements has skyrocketed.

If we feed ourselves correctly, use supplements and detox our bodies, we can heal anything and stop chasing witches and warlocks.

We are standing at the precipice with a .44 Magnum clenched between our teeth. Do not pull the trigger. Put the weapon down and get busy improving your health.

Do not be fooled by the fear mongers telling you that little green men are hijacking your health. You control your health.

AMA / APA / FDA Drug Company Think

- You are a commodity of infinite value
- Your health is worthless
- Your sickness is a priceless gold mine
- Your insurance is a treasure chest to be dug up and plundered
- Your free will and ability to think is to be controlled

Drug companies sell drugs via fear, while insurance companies sell fear and surgery. These two nefarious entities (drugs and insurance) want you to believe that every issue of life has a drug answer or a surgery solution. Once you have accepted this kind of sales pitch, you have given your power away.

Only you can guarantee your future health.

48 The Flu the SUPER GERM

Flu by all accounts, is one of the most controversial maladies that man has ever known. It is now widely accepted that the "flu" is the result of a 40 million dollar a year media campaign. We are asked to believe that germs follow a season. Like clockwork, they arrive twice a year in October and March. Between these times they mutate for no apparent reason.

It is the contention of many researchers that the "flu phenomena" is a conglomeration of scare tactics, real pneumonia and stress factors that aid the body in breaking down.

According to the CDC (Center for Disease Control):
The flu constantly changes; it can either mutate and "Antigenic Drift" or "Antigenic Shift" as much as twice a year.

Antigenic shift indicates the flu abruptly changes without notice.
Antigenic drift indicates the flu gradually changes.

To understand more about this medical enigma, read what is posted on the (Swiss pharmaceutical giant) Roche-Tamiflu website (below):

Introduced in 1999, Tamiflu is one of the only medicines proven in clinical trials to reduce the duration and severity of avian flu (bird flu) if taken within 48 hours of infection. It can also be used as a vaccine. Currently, the U.S. will have enough doses for 2 percent of the population by 2006. Many European countries have ordered enough to treat 20 percent to 40 percent of their populations. Currently, President Bush is meeting with vaccine manufacturers.

Read that last line again.

Currently, President Bush is meeting with vaccine manufacturers.

Aside from the clear political overtones of the above statement, the CDC indicates that Tamiflu would be obsolete in *"one season."* Yet Tamiflu sells billions in product every year.

Why would the US government get involved with business in the private sector? Why would a sitting president interest himself in the worldwide sales of vaccines? Could it be that vaccine sales support and line the pockets of government officials? Could our government be involved with helping to place lucrative manufacturing contracts into the hands of a favorite few friends and supporters? Finally, is the US government profiteering from flu?

Conspiracy minded individuals would champion the truth of the above paragraph. If you think it is true, you are not alone. But sane individuals like me know that this sort of behavior would NEVER HAPPEN IN WASHINGTON.

George Bush is not getting kickbacks and lining the pockets of friends or supporters with profiteered cash. That would be illegal. No Democrat or Republican president, congressman, governor or mayor would ever do such a thing. Accept tainted money? Bite your tongue. Next you will be insisting that we are in the Middle East solely for oil. That is ridiculous; fighting a covert war for oil? Who would believe such a thing?

FDA Patent Connection

There is tremendous confusion surrounding who and what the FDA is. The Food and Drug Administration is part of "The US Department of Health and Human Services." To be clear, the FDA is a government agency.

All drugs that are sold in the United States regardless of country of origin must receive an FDA approval patent. This patent insures 7 years of zero competitor competition (no generic knock offs) and allows the paying "customer" an exclusive market. Market protection is vital so that the paying company can recoup its investment.

The FDA 7 year patent costs 800 million dollars and must be paid prior to release of the new drug. In the United States today, even a marginally profitable drug can make over one billion dollars a year in sales. Patents are only granted to formulas derived via rigid laboratory process. The approved formula must remain unchanged for the entire 7-year period otherwise the patent is invalid.

The following is a paragraph from FDA NEWS *(http://WWW.FDA.gov/BBS/topics/NEWS/2006/NEW01423.HTML)*

This season's approved formulation for the U.S. vaccine is identical to that recommended by both the World Health Organization and FDA's Advisory Committee. The formulation includes one strain that was used in last year's vaccine and two new strains. ***Seasonal flu vaccines do not protect against avian flu, which is caused by a different viral strain (bird flu).***

Notice that last line again: ***Seasonal flu vaccines do not protect against avian flu, which is caused by a different viral strain (bird flu).***

Did you notice while reading earlier, that Roche-Tamiflu is the ONLY drug approved for AVIAN flu (bird flu) and was supported by the Bush administration?

CDC WARNING - Avian Flu - Bird Flu -

The most common type of flu is avian influenza virus. Viruses found chiefly *in birds*, but rarely infectious to humans. The risks are generally low to most people, because the viruses do not usually survive human contact.

Tamiflu is only made for the avian flu and is a patented non-changing formula.
Bird flu is practically unheard of in humans. Why then is Tamiflu #1 produced, and #2 sold the world over?

The 1999 flu season (October - January) marked the arrival of the avian bird flu. Remarkably this event just "happened" to coincide with the October 27th, 1999 release of Tamiflu specifically for, YOU GUESSED IT **avian bird flu.**

Was the avian flu warning for 1999 leaked to Roche in 1997? Was the avian flu on the FDA / AMA calendar in 1997 for announcement in July 1999? Do the AMA / FDA produce a schedule of upcoming flu's? Many do believe that this schedule does exist and was given to Roche.

Otherwise what kind of business acumen would it require to purchase an 800 million dollar patent for possibly only one year of sales? Tamiflu, based on CDC data, clearly indicates that Tamiflus' bird flu formula is practically useless.

Tamiflu should have been completely obsolete by January 1st, 2000 (four months after it was first marketed). Was the US Government helping Roche? Could we as consumers be brainwashed, uninformed, in fear and blind not to know this?

Again, Roche released its Tamiflu in October 1999, the same month that avian flu arrived.

Regarding the so-called ever-changing face of the flu, how could independent labs create vaccines completely in the dark without a blueprint or a little help? If avian flu is so rare and it shifts or drifts EVERY YEAR, THEN WHAT TAMIFLU IS SELLING IS A WORTHLESS FRAUD.

Keep Selling

The opportunity to make over a billion dollars a year in sales is what keeps Tamiflu on the market.

The business of making flu shots is the fine art of predicting the future or being handed a memo from the AMA / FDA hinting at what to manufacture next. Step two would be producing a non-offensive vaccine that does not poison the end user while making huge profits.

FDA PROTECTION

While under protection of the FDA, complaints are listened to, considered and for all intent and purposes ignored. The FDA "investigates" complaints until the 7-year patent protection phase has passed.

GLOVES OFF AS THE PATIENT EXPIRES

This explains why suddenly (November 27th, 2007) news started leaking out concerning rising deaths (300) while recently using Tamiflu in Japan.

Pay close attention to the dates in the next paragraph, i.e. (October 27th 1999 - November 13th 2006 = 7 years)

On November 13, 2006, the FDA alerted doctors and parents to watch for signs of bizarre behavior in children treated with Tamiflu. This warning was based upon federal health officials noticing an increasing number of such cases from overseas. Tamiflu (generic: oseltamivir phosphate) is prescribed to treat the flu is manufactured by Roche Laboratories, Inc. and was approved for use by the FDA on October 27, 1999.

However, analysts at Morgan Stanley Equity Research have said that Tamiflu is recognized as causing psychological disturbance, and apparent suicidal behavior.

The FDA said the 12 deaths it was reviewing included one suicide, four cases of sudden death and four cases of cardiac arrest. There also were single cases of pneumonia, asphyxiation and acute pancreatitis.

The 7-year patent has expired on Tamiflu. Therefore, pay attention as the heat on Tamiflu increases as the FDA's former customer" starts defending its interests. The FDA will now direct all inquires and law suits directly to Roche.

The flu is an amazing mix of history, media hype and lack of personal responsibility for our own wellbeing.

GOVERNMENT CONSPIRACY?

Is the US government behind the flu? Some think that our government is secretly helping to manufacture flu virus and then spreading it around the planet. Is our government behind this? Does the FDA / AMA or some other government agencies have a hand in poisoning the people of earth?

As exciting and Earth shattering as such a conspiracy of this magnitude would be, it is simply not the case. The FDA / AMA and our government do not need such a plan. The necessary factors that make bi-yearly sickness possible are already in place without any covert government help.

FLU GROUND ZERO

To understand the flu you must appreciate its roots. Flu is an astounding story full of mystery and intrigue. How a so called and 'imaginary" SUPER GERM would take over the world is fascinating reading.

Influenza, or the Flu, was first noted March 20th, 1918 in the latter part of World War I.

Morning sick call at Camp Funston in Fort Riley, Kansas, was uneventful until soldier Albert Mitchell reported under the weather. By day's end, almost 100 young men had reported sick. Our newly trained "doughboys" were about to ship off for England and an uncertain fate.

IMPORTANT NOTE: Prior to their infirmary, soldiers at Fort Riley were VACCINATED with a cocktail of bacteria to protect them against the dangers of Europe. Injections were administered two days before the men became ill, exactly one week before they shipped out. Not surprisingly, vaccinations were never suspected as a venomous contributor to our so-called 1918 flu epidemic.

STRESS CONNECTION

Stress has been accepted as the leading cause of all sickness for the last 40 plus years. Why would these soldiers about to leave for war get sick? Imagine that you were about to go into a conflict that could cost you your life. Would you get sick? Would this be stressful to you? This postulation would mean that stress could make someone unwell regardless of his or her present health.

In 1918, stress was not a consideration in sickness. Today the world of health is a much different and forward thinking place. From MedicineNet.com

David Krantz PhD.
Chairman of the Department of Medical Sciences at the University Bethesda, Maryland

"The link between stress and heart-related problems has been widely studied, and researchers say that mental stress increases the body's demand for oxygen by raising

blood pressure and heart rate. For people who already suffer from heart disease, this additional burden can increase the risk of heart attack, stroke, and even death. Stress can also act as a trigger for heart attack or stroke in people with undiagnosed heart disease."

Suzanne Segerstrom, PhD,
Assistant Professor at the University of Kentucky

"What happens is that certain components of the immune system become less effective at fighting off illness, especially those caused by viruses, when exposed to stress over days or weeks. Attitude plays a critical role in tempering that reaction."

"The main principle is that the effect on the immune system is not a factor of what's happening in the environment, but it's an effect of your perception of it. To the degree that you feel threatened or overwhelmed, the immune system will be affected more."

Dr. Segerstrom is saying that the actual threat is not as important as the perceived threat or YOUR reaction to either one. This explains how a whole family can get sick for no reason yet one or two family members are left untouched. The threat of loss or danger due to the "believed threat" of "catching" another's germs is more important than the germ.

To handle stress better, read about the LIVER in chapters 9,34,35,36,37,38,39 & 40.

Half of the Americans deaths in WW I are blamed on the flu

WW I lasted from 1914-1918. War claimed 20 - 40 million lives. Yet most flu deaths circa 1.5 million occurred at the end of the war 1918 -1919. Why would the there be so many deaths associated with flu occurring at the end of the conflict? Is there another smoking gun other than flu? Was something else contributing to these sudden deaths?

POISON GAS THREAT OVERLOOKED

American soldiers arriving in Europe were blamed for spreading flu. Little noted (at the time) was the escalating use of caustic poison gases. Even without poison gases, the stresses of war cannot be denied. The 1000-yard stare of soldiers who have been on the front lines too long is one example. Unmanaged stress makes any man sick.

Soldiers on both sides were terrified of the life stealing gas attacks.

World War I Witch Hunt

In search for an explanation for skyrocketing deaths from pulmonary catharsis, the flu was "invented" as an explanation. No one at the time understood the long term affects of chemical warfare on, the human body. Nor did they comprehend the contaminating affects these poisons would wreak on Earth's ecosystem and our food supplies.

The Germans invented Mustard gas and introduced it on the Eastern Front in 1915. It quickly gained prominence and was in regular use by both sides by late 1917. The three types of gasses used were Mustard Gas, Chlorine gas and Phosgene. Both sides viciously employed poison gas attacks. These attacks were unwieldy and relied on the direction of blowing wind. Meaning if the wind shifted your own gas could kill you. But according to statistics, half the Americans who died in WW I died from the flu, not consistent long-term exposure to poison.

The day-to-day threat of daily gas attacks was far worse than the attack.

Another validation of the so-called flu as the wrong source of death was that men age 20-40 were hardest hit. The ages with the strongest immune systems were hardest hit?

Hardly noticed in clouds of war, was the stark fact that even a non-fatal gas attack weakened the immune system. Soldiers and civilians downwind of the attacks were now open to TB, fevers, pneumonia and other respiratory disorders.

Gas Attack Results:

- Nausea and vomiting
- High Fever
- Diarrhea
- Coughing
- Burning sensation in the eyes
- Watery eyes
- Blurred vision
- Heart failure
- Low blood pressure
- Pulmonary edema (water in the lungs within 2 to 6 hours)
- Coughing up white-pinkish sputum

Notice that the above list matches the accepted model for flu and pneumonia symptoms.

CDC Pneumonia Symptoms

- High fever
- Cough (with white or pinkish sputum)
- Shortness of breath
- Rapid breathing
- Chest pains
- Nausea
- Vomiting
- Headache
- Tiredness
- Muscle aches

Why are these symptoms and chemicals relevant? Because these biohazards, released into the atmosphere lingered for months in our water, livestock, farmland (like DDT) and therefore our food supply.

Caustic agents (or gases) store in fatty human tissue and, like LSD, may be released at a later date causing toxicity or death. Just as hormones are changing humans in the 21-century, poison gasses were clearly mutating man in 1918 - 1919.

Man never wants to blame himself. But our actions clearly caused the so-called flu.

"Flu deaths" were heaviest in the countries where fighting was the most concentrated (the exception is the United States). American cities with high humidity featured the most so-called "flu" deaths. Were these gases traveling in the atmosphere and settling thousands of miles away? We now know that this is exactly what happened.

It has been postulated and then proven that an environment with moist, thick air creates an excellent incubator for reconstituting gasses such as mustard, chlorine and phosgene.

Interestingly, the death rate for 15 to 34-year-olds of influenza and pneumonia were 20 times higher in 1918 than in previous years.

Various physicians noted in their writings that patients with seemingly ordinary influenza (then considered "cold like" symptoms) would rapidly "develop the most viscous type of pneumonia that has ever been seen" and "it is simply a struggle for air until they suffocate" Another physician wrote that the influenza patients "died struggling to clear their airways of a blood-tinged froth that sometimes gushed from their nose and mouth."

Again notice chemical symptoms are consistent with so-called flu symptoms and mimics pneumonia. Was this early 1918 flu really flu, or a combination of gas attacks and pneumonia?

Needless to say, war is an aggressive act. The victor always spells out the terms of surrender. These terms become a further punishment and are often extremely harsh. World War I was no exception as surrender terms would be stern with no quarter given.

The Treaty of Versailles imposed tremendous such hardship on Germany, that she hedged in signing it. The British naval blockade of Germany was not lifted until the treaty was signed at the end of 1919. One result was that many German children starved to death. Reparation payments were very steep; the German government was literally broke. The Treaty of Versailles was so harsh; it was blamed as the major reason that Germany started WW II.

ON THE MOVE Refugees and Victims of War

Homeland exodus was rampant during 1918 – 1919. Homeless Chinese, Irish, Japanese, Scotsmen, Australians, Indians, Poles, etc. fled and headed to America.

Stress on the Move

Cramped boats, humidity and a lack of sanitation make for a stressful trip regardless of the final destination. Fearful of these "invaders" the United States "welcomed" these travelers by quarantining them, often without proper medical care. Consequently, many immigrants died before they even left their vessels.

From 1918 through 1945 immigrants looking for streets paved in gold were crowded into little villages in big cities. This is where the term "Little Italy", "China Town" etc., derived from.

Immigrants were blamed with causing the stock market crash, escalating crime, the blurring of American values and the weakening of the American social structure. Mass hysteria over the "unknown" is a flaw that can unhinge any civilization. How does this lead to today's mass hysteria over the flu?

1957 - The Hunt for the Smoking Gun.

In 1957 NBC news broke the terrifying story that the Spanish Flu had returned from the dead. It was back from its long 1918 - 1919 hibernation. If you carefully cull through the facts, you too will see there is always an event leading to flu claims. There is always a catastrophic event that leads to stress, which facilitates immune system weakness. What could have happened in 1957 to stress the American public?

Understanding What Led to the 1957 "Boogey Man Flu"

In 1953 the precursor of the IRS (the then Bureau of Internal Revenue) was under attack. Evidence of gross irregularities had surfaced and was front-page news and scandalous. Overwhelmed, the agency teetered on the brink of demise. Sweeping reorganization took place as the TAX MEN hired more agents, were given wide and comprehensive authority and thus became more antagonistic.

The agency renamed itself the **Internal Revenue Service** (IRS).

IRS in Action

TREASURY DIRECTIVE 15-42, of 1956, allowed the IRS via an audit to "collect" up to $500,000.00 in property, business, farms, stocks, paychecks and automobiles while seizing bank accounts and bonds, should the public be found cheating on their taxes.

The IRS Finally had Teeth!

The American public was of course terrified of the new money-eating monster, the IRS. Remember the threat of danger causes the immune system to shut down.

A Very Dangerous Environment Leads to Sickness

Abundant sickness was duly noted by an attentive news media. Suddenly, because the news media said so (and they are never wrong), the "Spanish flu" had risen from the grave to bite the American public again. The Spanish Influenza from 1918 was not dead; it was only hibernating.

The Flu phenomenon was front-page news. The public was riveted to their newspapers, TV sets and radios.

The Hunting for "IT"

In a "plot twist" deserving of an Academy Award for "Best Screen Play", a multinational contingency of scientists was dispensed to Spitsbergen Norway. Their assignment was to exhume mummified bodies buried deep in the permafrost. Victims of the 1918 Spanish flu were to be harvested for their tissue. It was hoped that frozen genetic material could be "revived" and used to defeat a flu monster that could wipe man from the face of the Earth. Stephen King would be proud.

Remember, if the news media says it, it must be true. Consider the power of the pen.

"Print is the sharpest and the strongest weapon of our party" - Joseph Stalin

1957 Flu in England

England was reported to have received the Asian flu, while America had the Spanish flu. How odd.

Additional Odd Data on the 1957 British Flu

6,000 Brits lost their lives due to so-called "flu"
0 Brits lost their lives to pneumonia
0 Deaths from the Cumbria, Nuclear reactor graphite core fire (reactor "melt down")

More 1957 British Nuclear Meltdown

Radioactive waste covered the county side, tainting milk supplies, killing cows and chickens, yet no human deaths were reported or ***attributed*** to *radiation*.

Death count oddities

Wherever death associated with influenza (a.k.a. flu) is calculated (68,000 in 1957) the flu death totals are always padded with pneumonia deaths. What is the purpose of linking these two seemingly different maladies?

"The death of one man is a tragedy. The death of millions is a statistic" - Joseph Stalin

To Be Truly Deadly and Threatening, Flu Must Come From Great Distance

Russian flu 1978
Hong Kong flu 1997 (chicken flu)
Spanish flu 1918 and 1957
Asian flu 1957

SWINE FLU 1976 (ORIGINATED AT FORT DIX, KANSAS)

The afternoon of February 5th, 1976, 19-year-old army Private David Lewis of Ashley Falls, Ma, entered the army hospital complaining of fatigue. Within 24 hours he was dead. It was "claimed" that Swine flu killed him. Keep in mind his death somehow became considered an epidemic. Nationwide, private Lewis was the **ONLY DEATH** from swine flu in 1976. Yet **hundreds were reported killed** and seriously injured by **flu inoculations provided by the US government.**

Question: Since more deaths have been caused by adverse vaccine reactions than any other source since 1900, why are we still vaccinating?

Answer: Good question. There are numerous books on the subject, including: *"The Great Bird Flu Hoax: the Truth They Don't Want You to Know about the Next Big Pandemic"* by Joseph Mercola and *"A Shot in the Dark"* by H. Coulter.

Note: The news media supports sponsors who purchase ad time. Like it or not, advertisers influence what we think and do. The public is warned about "The next big THREAT or pandemic." The news, at sponsor request, warns the public that **IF** they are not prepared, they we will suffer grave consequences.

When there is an earthquake the news media does stories on earthquake preparedness. The result is, we PURCHASE bottled water, can goods, flashlights and batteries in large amounts and store them. Grocery stores love the added revenue provided by panic shopping. It is really no different than being warned that Halloween is coming. The difference is that little hungry candy seeking monsters do arrive at your door. Noise of a *possible* flu pandemic is a sales pitch created to instill the most fear possible for the greatest possible capital gain.

We react to what the media says as influenced by its advertisers. When the word "**If**" is heard, we react as if "**If**" meant the world had collapsed. "If" is synonymous with fear.

Remember all sickness requires at least one of the stimuli below:

#1 Stress (as stress will weaken the strongest of immune systems)
#2 Sugars
#3 Salts
#4 Sodium
#5 Drugs (over the counter)
#6 Drugs (illegal)
#7 Drugs (prescription)
#8 Alcohols

Our bodies are loaded with enough bacteria that if our immune system shut down right now, we would be dead in a matter of hours. The "SUPER GERM" theory is ridiculous.

We become ill with the seasons due to stresses brought about by changes to our home life, diet, etc. The idea that any branch of government would or could be ready in advance with their "healing" goodies is optimistic and unrealistic.

The flu is a product of an amazing sales campaign, which has taken almost 100 years to fully implement. The flu concept and its remedies do not follow the natural laws of nature or common sense.

The flu has never been identified under a microscope. If you cannot see it and isolate it, it cannot be tested against antidotes. Pneumonia can be seen but flu remains invisible. Flu is a ghost explanation that makes billions every year.

Lies that are commingled with truth are hard to detect. That is why the flu story is so hard to let go. The flu legend **is** based in history. The flu threat is based on a legend that 1) it exists, and 2) that it mutates twice a year.

Roche – Tamiflu brilliantly capitalized on this empty yet potent legend and is selling strong seven years after it should have been off the market. The flu is one of the best marketing campaigns witnessed less AIDS and cancer.

"Terror marketing" creates petrified automatons that will do whatever they are told. Witness the instant affect of broadcasting the word flu. Suddenly we become hypnotized spending machines grabbing up vaccines in excess of 25 billion dollars a year.

We are allowing our NEWS MEDIA to dictate how we live our lines. We are the victims of a government funded ad machine. Profit based fear spewing marketing is not only affective; it is unstoppable unless we are constantly vigilant against it.

About the flu:

- Marketing—-It is promoted via TV, radio, print media and Internet.
- Marketing—-It arrives in March and stays until April.
- Marketing—-It returns in October and leaves in January.
- Marketing—-Every year it mutates and therefore needs a new vaccine.
- Marketing—-It is always predicted before it arrives.
- Marketing—-Forward thinking scientists somewhere in the world devised a vaccine that will eliminate flu before it exists and ruins our lives.
- Marketing—-The flu vaccine is mass-produced and distributed just in time to ward off the "bug"

October - January

October starts the holiday season, which equals family, shopping frustrations, financial worries, overeating, partying and alcohol. Consider the stress of this bombardment. Is it any wonder why people are sick during the holidays? Halloween = sugar poisoning, Thanksgiving for many, equals family and food stress, Christmas / Hanukah / Kwanzaa, etc., equals financial woes, family woes and general holiday overwhelm. Follow that up with New Years Eve.

March - April

Tax season, which is full of stress over money. We are buried in new tax laws, deadlines, payments, complicated forms and worry. Note April is tax month worldwide.

Worldwide, flu seasons just happen to coincide with the most mentally, physically and financially stressful times of the year.

This is the totality of what flu season is. The CDC keeps stumbling over itself contradicting its own information. Flu vaccines are a joke and potentially dangerous. Stress is the only consistent factor in the so-called flu. If stress is understood and handled, "flu" becomes a non-factor.

Stress is guaranteed to devastate immune function and is underneath all sickness. Notice those around you who never get sick. How is that possible? They will tend to be those who have less stress, handle stress better or take excellent care of themselves or all the above.

Flu is a mindset, not a microbe or virus. Get your stress under control and be healthy. Make your own decisions about your health.

Get active and make sure those around you know what the flu score is. We are up against a multi-billion dollar a year INDUSTRY.

We as a group can fight flu and make the truth known. Only then can the flu myth be eradicated.

If we all work together, it might only take 20 years or so to make "flu season" a memory. Until then our lives are at stake. We have to win this battle. Imagine a future where mention of the flu does not instill fear. Imagine that the word flu makes people laugh at how stupid we were "way back then."

Tell everyone you know what the truth is.

49 What is Fibromyalgia?

Fibromyalgia is another name for a hodgepodge of organ symptoms that have appeared under one umbrella and then called Fibromyalgia.

MedicineNet.com defines it this way:
"Fibromyalgia is a chronic condition causing pain, stiffness and tenderness of the muscles, tendons, and joints. Fibromyalgia is also characterized by restless sleep, awakening feeling tired, fatigue, anxiety, depression and disturbances in bowel function. Fibromyalgia was formerly known as Fibrositis. While Fibromyalgia is one of the most common diseases affecting the muscles, its cause is currently unknown. The painful tissues involved are not accompanied by tissue inflammation. Therefore, despite potentially disabling body pain, patients with Fibromyalgia do not develop body damage or deformity. Fibromyalgia also does not cause damage to internal body organs."

That is a mouthful!

What you have just read is amazingly wrong. Here are the facts. There are two distinctly different forms of Fibromyalgia (both of which are of course not diseases).

- Skin based, where the skin burns, tingles or is numb. This version may be accompanied by restless sleep, awakening feeling tired, fatigue, anxiety, depression, blurry vision, headaches and muscle pain in the right shoulder region.

- Muscle and joint based, where the joints are sore, stiff and tight. The muscles may feel the exact same way. This type of irritation can include left shoulder pain, ankle pain, low back pain and general muscle soreness and stiffness.

These two types of problems, that are now commonly called Fibromyalgia, are actually liver & kidney problems. Yes, you read that right. Fibromyalgia is nothing more than exsurpo liver and kidney overload.

If this so called disease was anything more than a kidney and liver overload, I wouldn't have been able to successfully treat myself twice! Thousands have discovered these simple facts about this oddly named kidney / liver overload problem.

Read over the kidney symptoms & then read over the liver symptoms in the chapter "How to Do Face Reading." As you read it, did you notice that all of the Fibromyalgia symptoms were kidney or liver symptoms?

I have personally experienced both variations of Fibromyalgia; trust me, they are not fun. What I did then was treat myself for liver issues and/or kidney issues and within a week the symptoms were gone.

Mind you, I went hog-wild crazy taking herbs for liver (during one incidence) and kidney herbs another time. I really indulged myself so that if it was possible to beat, I could. I rapidly eliminated these problems both times. Anyone trying to tell you that your symptoms are anything more than kidney and liver symptoms is trying to sell you something.

Don't buy it. You are being lied to. Go out and treat yourself. Please take some time and research herbs for the liver and/or kidney and use them, you will notice a huge difference in a short time if you act vigorously enough.

You can do this; it is very effortless to feel better. Get used to using the word exsurpo to train yourself in finding the real source of all of your problems.

50 Heart Disease and Ear Piercing

The body will try to adapt to any situation. If the left leg is hurt the right leg will bear more weight. When the kidneys are in trouble it is the liver that steps up and takes some of the load and vice versa.

Approximately 5000 years ago the Chinese developed the practice of Acupuncture. The practice has performed miracles for thousands of years. Acupuncture is the practice of using very fine high-grade surgical steel needles to gently pierce and stimulate an energy meridian of the body to bring about a healing.

These pre-sterilized and disposable needles are used 'only once'. Since your body is a dynamic environment of interrelating and interconnecting networks, it is appropriate to address them as needed. Some people will find great benefit from the subtle and broad changes through this practice. Western science has focused its attention on the obvious networks such as the nervous, circulatory, endocrine and lymphatic systems.

On the other hand, when Acupuncture points are stimulated, they cause an increase in the production of endorphins and simultaneously activate the immune and endocrine systems. Acupuncture can relieve pain and has been used for all maladies. Millions of patients have enjoyed the benefits of Acupuncture and Traditional Chinese Medicine. They report the elimination or reduction of pain, and increase in function, and a greater sense of vitality and well-being. As you have read earlier in this book the ear is the domain of the kidneys and the heart. If you have studied traditional Acupuncture you know that there are far more points on the face than those mentioned earlier.

Isn't it nice when different modalities converge and agree? In late 2004, I started wondering if an Acupuncture point could be destroyed or continually stimulated if punctured via piercing. I took this question to several different Oriental Medicine Doctors (OMD's) and they all agreed that not only is that possible it is factual.

On the face reading chart you have learned that the ears are represented on the upper lip, nose and ear lobes. I then asked, since that is true, does that mean that women with pierced ears are more susceptible to heart disease than men? That was also confirmed. I was buried in e-mails when I returned home. I then wondered if piercing is the culprit. If that were the case, then wouldn't it also be true that ear piercing among men would have been on the rise in the early 1980s and then leveling off and declining since. Ear piercing among men was on a steady climb since 1980 and topped out in 1986.

When I looked into this that was exactly what the numbers showed. The numbers in several studies support my conclusion regarding both men and women, see below.

The American Heart Association reported the following regarding women statistics:

- Cardiovascular Disease (CVD) remains the leading killer of women in the U.S. and the world. CVD kills nearly 500,000 U.S. women each year, claiming more lives than the next seven causes of death combined, including cancer.

Consequently, women's awareness of heart disease has been on the rise. The American Heart Association's first national survey in 1997 found that only 30 percent of women spontaneously listed heart disease as women's leading cause of death, a figure that increased to just 34 percent in the 2000 survey.

In 2003 that figure jumped to 46 percent, a significant leap.

From the BBC, regarding men, latest available figures show that in 2001 there were around 79,800 deaths from cancer and around 79,500 deaths from heart disease in the UK. This compares with 10 years ago, when there were 84,250 male deaths from cancer and 100,600 from heart disease.

It is estimated that by 2010, deaths from heart disease in UK men will have fallen to 30,000 while there will be 85,000 men dying from cancer. Perhaps there is another unknown reason for all of this heart disease. In the end, if you can reduce your risk it is far safer and healthier.

Diagnostic Face Reading and Acupuncture both agree that constant meridian point stimulation is not healthy. If this were a healthy activity, Acupuncture would have given us this information

5000 years ago. Also, remember, my research indicates that each impaired ear lobe indicates a 30% increase in heart issue tendencies.

Eyebrow piercing is swelling in popularity. We know that the eyebrow represents the lower part of the bladder; does that mean that bladder issues will mount as eyebrow piercing gains in popularity?

Yes, that is exactly what it means.

Therefore, if you have piercings and continue to put them in, you do this at your own risk.

Eyebrow piercing has become very popular among young woman. Statistics illustrate that there is a direct connection between bladder infections and eyebrow piercings. In the past 10 years bladder infections among women with eyebrow piercings have increase exponentially.

Fact: Eight million women a year visit a doctor for the treatment for a urinary tract / bladder infection. If you compare male and females statistics women suffer these infections four and a half times more often than men.

Fact: Eyebrow piercing is a female dominated phenomenon.

Remember, the bladder meridian (via face reading) intersects across both eyebrows. Does that mean that bladder issues will continue to rise if eyebrow piercings continue to escalate in popularity? Yes, as stated above, that is precisely what it means.

What about nose piercing? Again we are looking at heart disease. How about tongue piercing? There are a number of conflicting ideas about the tongue. Some believe it is the brain that is affected. Others say it is the heart or stomach. In the end it is safe to say that some organ is adversely affected.

You could also conclude that destroying any meridian of the body would lead to health issues. My research never stops and it is clear to me that tongue piercing stimulates stomach issues. I have witnessed more than a dozen tongue piercings lead right to vomiting and mock sickness.

What can we expect long term? We will have to wait and find out. Needless to say, it can't be good. My editor has assured me that brain problems lead to tongue piercing, but I can't prove that.

Pierce at your own risk.

51 Pressure and the Body

Consider that every organ of your body hates pressure. That is a strange statement, is it not? Think about it. What does it take for a bullet to pierce your skin? High velocity = pressure! The body is fairly safe from anything that cannot in some way exert pressure or move rapidly. Do this simple test. With your right hand squeeze your left hand until it hurts. Why did it hurt? Pressure!

Pressure equals pain. Remember in the explanation of Quantum Physics? Energy and mass must be in equal amounts or one is pushing hard on the other. This is pain and this is pressure. Why does a Chiropractic adjustment work? The bone is putting pressure on nerves and surrounding organs. The energy flow is interrupted and we feel pain.

This sounds too simple to be true. But the body in all of its complexity is very simple. Screwing it up requires our participation in misunderstanding its simplicity and trying to make it complex.

Consider this, what is blood pressure? Answer: The pressure needed to move blood from one point to another. When blood pressure is high, it indicates that the kidneys are being pushed "offline." Offline, meaning: not in charge of their own actions or processes. What weakens the kidneys? Pressure they don't create.

One way we pressure-damage our kidneys is by sleeping in the wrong position.

When we sleep flat on our back the pressure of the body is equalized from organ to organ. When you feel full from a meal it is due to the exact same pressure phenomena. This also explains why going to bed on a full stomach is difficult for your body as extra pressure is now being exerted on your vital organs.

Have you ever seen a man lay on a bed of nails? The reason he is not hurt is due to the fact that his weight is distributed evenly over the entire bed of nails not just one.

When we slumber lying down, the more surface area that we can distribute weight over, the more healthfully we will sleep.

When we sleep either on our right or left side, pressure is not equalized

The pressure exerted by the body compressing or squashing down on the side that you are sleeping on (next to your sheets) is excruciating. This can be witnessed via increased blood pressure on the side that is down. Based on hundreds of tests, the side that is down will have blood pressure as much as 70% higher than the side that is up. If you sleep on your left side you are crushing your left kidney and corresponding organs.

To sleep on the other side creates problems for those organs. Better break out your anatomy book to see what you have been doing.

The increase in blood pressure can reach 200 / 155. The side that is not down will have normal blood pressure (120 / 80 or so).

Imagine squeezing your left thumb until it turned blue and went numb. That is what we are doing by Sleeping on one side or the other rather than flat on our back.

How long does it take for blood pressure to rise while sleeping or lying on your side? Answer: 30-60 seconds!

Even the New England Journal of Medicine recognizes that blood pressure should be taken while standing or laying flat. Sorry to scare you but, the above is true. If you sleep on your side for any length of time you are doing damage to the organs on the down side.

This news is a real problem for couples who love to spoon (sleeping on their side while touching front to back). Regardless of age, lifestyle, gender, race or size, the results are always the same.

When your eyes drift shut
Sleep not on your front, left or right
Sleep flat on your back
And deliver your body from its plight.

Sleeping flat on your back is healthy. You can sleep your way back to kidney health!

A special note on flying

As a seasoned traveler I know all about flying. I fly about 150,000 miles a year. I know and appreciate the road bumps of the sky called turbulence and so much more!

Most people have no clue why they feel so bad when they fly. Here is why. Unless you live in Denver, Colorado or Mexico City, you are well adjusted to high altitude. Airline cabins are pressurized to 8000 feet of elevation. Meaning that when you fly, you are experiencing pressure (remember the last section on kidneys and pressure?) 7 to 8 times greater than what you are used to. The results are lack of energy, muscle pain, joint pain, heart arrhythmia, vertigo, frequent urination (or no urination at all) and decreased hearing. What do the airlines feed you? Salty nuts, salty crackers, sweet cookies and alcohol!

Yummy! All poisons at sea level! Ingesting them while flying is like receiving "kidney punches" (punches to the kidneys, also known as "rabbit punches", now illegal in pro boxing). Now you know why you feel so bad on arrival. When you fly, drink lots of water, and if you have to eat, bring fruit (ideally grapes), the body you save will be your own.

When flying, be sure that your liver and kidneys are functioning at optimum capacity. Alcohol may seem like a fun treat or a good way to relax while in the air. The so-called calming benefits of sprits consumed while flying is a false promise. The actual affects of alcohol are even more severe / damaging to your liver and kidneys while airborne. Alcohol is a poison (see the next paragraph). Do not involve yourself with this toxic substance while in the air (or on the ground). If you do, your flight / vacation experience / life can become a disaster.

The Truth About Alcohol

No one disputes that the FDA business model is based on bribes and corruption. Not surprisingly if an honest FDA received a request to approve alcohol for human consumption today, it would be flatly denied.

Known as a light solvent and preservative (similar to formaldehyde), alcohol erodes the stomach lining and destroys delicate tissue on contact. Alcohol infused products would be labeled poisons *for industrial cleaning use only*.

Classifying alcohol as a poison may seem harsh nevertheless it is completely accurate. In the old west it was common to stumble into a tavern in search of a drink after a long and exhausting, dusty ride on a horse. The friendly bartender would welcome you with the words "what is your poison partner"? The frontier mixologist was asking his patron what he wanted to drink while acknowledging the properties of the brew. Now when we leave a bar or pub, we don't climb on a horse and ride away, we get into a 3000-pound car.

Despite the tireless efforts of thousands of advocates, impaired drivers continue to kill someone every 30 minutes, nearly 50 people a day, almost 18,000 citizens a year. These are direct alcohol related deaths.

In the U.S. the annual indirect alcohol related death totals soar above 82,000 people. Indirect causes of death include cirrhosis of the liver, falls, cancer, and stroke. If we included complications of the kidneys and heart due to alcohol, the numbers swell beyond 200,000 deaths per year.

Traffic crashes are the greatest single cause of death for persons aged 6-33. About 45% of these fatalities are in alcohol-related crashes. Underage drinking costs the United States more than $58 billion every year. If this money was used constructively it would purchase every public school student in the U.S. a state-of-the-art computer.

Not surprisingly alcohol is the most commonly used drug among young people (20 years of age and under).

Problem drinkers average four times as many days in the hospital as nondrinkers — mostly because of drinking-related injuries. Alcohol kills 6? times more youth than all other illicit drugs combined. Studies continually indicate that every 30 days, 50% of high school seniors drink while 32% report being drunk at school least once.

Our actions teach the 'social pleasures' of this poison to our children. "Do as I say not as I do" is horrible parenting. The example you set carries weight. You are a leader whether you like it or not.

Consume alcohol at your own risk and the risk of those around you.

Grapes and Your Kidneys

There are foods that are incredibly healing for the body.

One of them is a grape. The organs that love them are your kidneys. That is correct, they LOVE grapes. You can heal more problems of the kidneys by eating grapes than with most supplements.

I have been using grapes this way for everything under the sun in regards to kidney issues including diabetes and high blood pressure with excellent results. For the past 8 years, Grapes have proven themselves as affective as any herb or therapy. The type or color of grape does not seem to matter. A seedless grape versus no seeds does not seem to matter.

Organic versus non-organic may matter but it is not clear. To be safe, eat organic or use a pesticide "removal wash" to clean off any residue. What does matter is that they are eaten often (2-3 4 5 times a day). Since the eating of grapes aids the kidneys in resetting themselves, thus turning off pain and reducing swelling in kidney regulated areas, eat them as needed.

The only type of grape that does not work is any grape that is fermented (wine). Raisins show no benefit at all, as they are not live. If you planted a raisin and tried to grow grapes you would fail. Raisins are dead globs of sugar and for that reason of little use to the body. Go back and study what the kidneys need and you can see what sorts of things that grapes can help.

As stated above, I suggest eating grapes 2 to 5 times a day or as often as you have symptoms. Remember that food is the oldest and safest drug on the planet. Mother Nature made no mistakes and intended for us to utilize it. When we ignore it, we pay in pain and discomfort. Even Vertigo (dizziness) has been aided with use of grapes as the kidneys regulate the ears and the inner ear regulates your balance.

Keeping grapes at your bedside might be more important than water. When you wake up, eat a few grapes and you will be back to sleep in no time.

Another interesting aspect of eating grapes which takes advantage of the "left / right side of the body" (kidney / liver) dominance factor is to chew grapes on the left side of your mouth. Observed hundreds of times, the chewing of grapes on the left side of the mouth activates their action immediately. Grapes are an unparalleled kidney food. Remembering that the left hand is the test plate for kidneys aids in this explanation of what is behind these left vs. right phenomena.

I am sure that all foods that "turn on" the liver or the kidneys can be chewed this way (left or right side of the mouth) to activate and be affective faster, yet I only have data on grapes at this writing.

What Does Fresh Fruit Mean?

Fresh fruit or fresh vegetables are defined as recently picked and alive.

Fresh fruit seeds can be planted and will grow. The enzymes of fresh fruit break down and will cause fruit to rot if not eaten in a timely manner. This is nature cleaning and fertilizing itself, guaranteeing its future.

I am often asked about eating trail mix that has fruit added. The fruit in such a mix is no longer whole and no longer enzymatic or alive. This type of fruit is worthless to the body.

As mentioned before raisins are not alive and if planted would not grow or produce new grapes. Fresh means fresh. Sealed bags of mango are not fresh. Fresh fruit needs air and goes bad in a few days of purchase if not eaten.

Fruit or veggies that are dried pressed or in air tight sealed bags are not fit for consumption. Is this making sense now? If you are going to eat fruit or vegetables, eat them fresh, not out of a can, sealed bag or box.

52 Sexual function

As stated earlier in this book, the kidneys regulate the entire reproductive process, including sexual performance, pleasure and fertility.

One of the many functions of the kidneys and the liver is to break down and then wash excess protein from the system. Both organs swell when too much protein is present. The question is how much protein is too much? When you eat a bite or two of some type of meat or nut protein and notice that you feel low back pain or pain in general, you have just discovered your limit.

If you remember the earlier chapters on kidneys, I wrote that protein poisoning of the kidneys could bring them and the body to a halt. Kidney overwhelms / poisoning is real and happens every day.

How did we become a nation of beef / meat / nut eaters? Like all advancements, it was advertising.

Prior to WWII, meat was more of a luxury. Since 1945, beef and chicken lobbyist have become very aggressive. The result is the public would soon be eating more of their goods. Looking at supporting kidney issues, the result of excess protein in the diet skyrocketed since 1947.

If you are old enough, you remember the 1960s and the 1968 "threatened" beef shortage. People were actually eating canned dog food. The big news from this time period was that "one table spoon full of peanut butter contained more protein than an 8 ounce steak."

Nuts (also known as legumes) are the most concentrated form of protein we can eat. Nuts are the protein equivalent of the atomic bomb. For instant protein, nuts are very potent.

How could this be a problem? How could there be a problem in the fact that there is more protein in a handful of nuts than there is in the equivalent amount of beef, chicken and fish. But there is!

The result was simple. People were living on nuts. They were suddenly eating 400-1000 times more protein than they needed. Beaten up and overwhelmed, weakened kidneys do not run well.

My testing has proven again and again that kidney health can be greatly improved by monitoring protein intake. Today everyone's kidneys are weak and protein is a huge irritant.

The public, not knowing this and hearing the advertising, eat more and more protein. The result is more back pain, frequent urination and all of the other kidney symptoms, plus the new hitherto unseen problem, sexual malfunction.

The kidneys regulate the entire reproductive system of both sexes.

They can't do the job of protecting and cleaning your blood if they are off line. Protein pushes them off line and into slower response time. Thanks to protein, your reproductive organs are taking a massive hit.

Remember this all started in the late 1960s. Then protein heavy weight loss diets became all the rage in the early 1980s. By 1987, Viagra had appeared as a result of "erectile dysfunction," which did not exist in large numbers prior to 1980.

Do you follow what happened?

We poison our kidneys for 6 years

We notice erectile dysfunction

We start taking the NEW drug designed for the problem.

Interestingly, when women are fed a diet high in protein from nuts, they have the same problems men do.

Lack of interest

Lack of lubrication

Lack of orgasm

Like it or not, we have eaten our kidneys right into a corner. In our western pursuit of protein, we eat nuts on top of the meat we eat and add nut butters to that.

Another interesting aspect of any addiction to poison is that we will crave it regardless of the outcome. The human body always craves what it is most toxic to.

Why would your body crave something that is poisoning it? In the case of the kidney, that is very simple. The body does need some protein, but when the kidneys are not operating at capacity, the body keeps asking for protein that cannot be digested. Imagine being thirsty yet only able to splash your face with water. Water would keep being asked for, as your thirst will not quench.

The question becomes: where does protein come from? I will cover this at more length in the section on raw food. All fruit and vegetables have a trace amount of protein in them. To heal the kidneys a protein fast is an excellent idea.

Fad protein rich diets will continue to cause a further rise of erectile dysfunction. Go on the net and you will see for yourself that the fad protein craze matches the rise in products for erectile dysfunction.

Avoid all nuts including:

- Pistachios
- Almonds
- Pine nuts
- Pumpkin Seeds
- Peanuts
- Cashews
- Sunflower seeds
- Sesame seeds
- Brazil nuts
- Walnuts
- Etc.

The type of nut does not matter: raw, roasted, fried or any other variation that you can imagine. Let your body be your guide. Eliminate nuts and you notice the difference.

Find herbs and herbal combinations from the list of herbs for kidney and liver and start testing. You will be pleased with your results. Relax; you will be fine. Just clean up your diet.

53 The Food Combining Myth

At one time or another have read or heard about food combining. Food combining is the concept of consuming foods that mix well in the stomach to improve digestion. Logical and makes sense, isn't that right? As concepts go, this is a good one.

The theory being that indigestion, heartburn, acid reflux, GIRD and weight gain come about due to eating foods that do not combine well and therefore causing some sort of digestive distress. For some, it works well. For others it is just too hard to understand and keep up with. For those people, it is just another diet failure.

For many, food combining equals frustration and failure. The concept of food combining is a good one. By food combining we are theoretically stressing the digestive tract less and absorbing more. Great, fantastic idea, this food-combining thing!

What is behind food combining is the same thing that we see in offices today. Seldom do we see someone who is an accountant, receptionist, salesperson, shipper and vice president. It just does not happen that often.

Why?

Because giving too many jobs to one person invites failure. Simply, if you want production, don't give your assistant six jobs when he or she can only do 3. Food combining wants you to combine fruit with fruit but not fruit with meat. Meat is good with vegetables but not processed carbohydrates.

Nothing is good with processed carbohydrates.

Great big, famous scientists, researchers and nutritionists are behind this. To which I say, so what!

Aside from being far too complex to do (for most), we are still sitting with a compost pile in our gut, fermenting. Because, sure enough, we ate a conflicting meal before the last meal was digested.

There is a far simpler way to eat.

But, it is tough to do. It could be so tough you might not even try it. But, once you read about it, you will see the logic and simplicity of it. The best way to combine foods is to not combine foods at all.

The best way to combine foods is not to combine them at all.

I call this the MONO DIET.

If your health concerns are just not responding to anything else, try going MONO.

What is the mono diet?

Eating a lot of one thing per meal such as oranges, apples, grapes, tomatoes, etc., as this takes all stress off the digestive system.

In food combining you are like a juggler trying to keep 2 and sometimes 3 balls going at once. That is an improvement over trying to keep 6 balls going. Consider how easy it would be to throw one ball up in the air, catch it, toss it again, catch it, etc? Very simple!

This is the totality of the mono diet. It may be boring, yet when you want to detox, there is no better way to go. Imagine eating one thing at a meal, and eating a lot of it. If you want tomatoes, eat 8 or 10 of them. Eating strawberries? Eat your fill.

This does not mean that you should eat a meal of bread. No one should ever eat bread.

Any eating approach that is halfway successful says the same basic things, which are:

Do not eat processed carbohydrates, bread (including whole wheat bread which is not whole), pasta, crackers, cakes, cookies, candy, doughnuts, tortillas, potato chips or chips, etc).

Eat lots of fresh fruit and veggies.

Drink plenty of water.

Do not eat later than 7:00 p.m. (and that can be too late); ideally stop eating by 5:00 p.m.

Get enough rest and, if you can, exercise.

If this sounds boring, trust me, it is. It is not very social, either. Who stops eating at 5:00? You will if you want to lose weight and feel better than you have in years. Imagine how well your digestive tract would run if it only had one thing to digest per meal. That is the simplicity of it all. By giving your digestive tract less to do, your body can spend more time on healing itself and you.

Eating a Mono Meal Diet takes work, and the rewards are there to be had. Try it and you can judge it for yourself.

54 Your Mouth, Your Thighs

No one wants to gain weight. We all hate the idea. Anyone who likes the idea, I am jealous of. We have heard about all the fad diets. In this book I wrote about the Mono Diet in the last chapter. Boring but it works.

This chapter is devoted to explaining all of the things I didn't say in that chapter, or only hinted at.

Definitions:

Calorie: A unit of potential energy. The body can only use a calorie if there is an enzyme present that is inherent to the structure of what you are eating. Enzymes must be alive and viable.

Empty Calorie: A unit of potential energy with no enzyme attached. Empty calories are often stored (fat) as they are unusable to the body.

Enzymes: Catalysts, used by the body to correctly utilize a calorie or unit of potential energy.

Processed Carbohydrate: When wheat, rice, grains or fruit and vegetables are cooked, milled, ground up or made into another form via processing, it is called a processed carbohydrate. The wrong ways of thinking (below) are the reasons why someone will never lose weight.

Wrong Thought or Mind Set in Losing Weight:

I can't lose weight.
I have a genetic predisposition to gain weight.
I have a genetic predisposition to not lose weight.
I gain weight even if I don't eat.
I can't lose weight because I am too nervous.
I can't lose weight because I ________ (you fill in the blank).
I am too busy to eat right.
I can't eat more veggies because I can't eat that much.

Why is this wrong thinking?

You are hindered from reaching your desired result. It separates you from everyone else whether they can lose weight or not.

The first step to losing weight is confronting how much you weigh. You must own a scale and weigh yourself. To not know what you weigh is the equivalent of trying to sail a ship without a rudder. You will go whatever direction the tide and the wind takes you. The next three most important steps to losing weight are:

Wanting to do it
Knowing you can do it
Being determined to do it

The only rules to know about weight:

- You should weigh the same or less tomorrow morning.
- You should not weigh more this morning than yesterday.

If you weigh more today than you did yesterday, you either did something wrong in your diet yesterday or are putting on muscle mass. Gaining weight is not a problem if you are trying to put on muscle mass.

- If you weigh less today than you did yesterday, you did something right yesterday.
- If you weigh the same as you did yesterday, you did something neutral for your metabolism.

You could have also done just enough wrong as opposed to all of the things you did right, therefore, you lost no weight.

Always weigh yourself with no clothes on and the same hour each day. Use your scale right after you get up and use the toilet. Again wear no clothes.

To Lose Weight

You have to understand that most people are actively doing two or three things that are good for them and several (could be 25 to 30) things that are keeping them fat. The bad news is that you may be correctly doing 23 things right, but still accidently doing one thing wrong. This one thing could be to keep your weight from moving.

An example of this is eating late at night. The only thing that is safe late at night is fruit or fresh fruit juices. Avoid bananas at night, as they are too heavy.

If you can stop eating your major meal at no later than 2:00 p.m. and only eat fruit and the occasional salad you cannot help but lose weight. Fresh fruit juices are not off limits. Do your own testing and you will be please and shocked by your results.

55 Digestion and Citrus

There is a lengthy story I like to tell at my lectures which explains this in detail. How I validated the efficacy of citrus on the colon.

Instead, here is the abbreviated "Readers Digest" version.

Several years ago I woke up at midnight with horrible indigestion. After trying everything else I had in my kitchen, I saw, peeled and devoured a Clementine Tangerine and in seconds the indigestion was gone. I was amazed. Over the next several months, I expanded my testing to include thousands of people.

Speaking to friends and doctors, I discovered this was an old home remedy that had fallen into the dust of the old days. Yet it worked like a charm.

To date I have produced a 98% success rate with citrus for indigestion. Citrus works for indigestion and for all digestive disturbances. This old home remedy is safe and painless to use. The fact that it is old is not bad at all as eventually everything becomes an antique.

The active (citrus) component can be found in any type of citrus (oranges, tangerines, lemons and even grapefruit). Clementine Tangerines seem to work best.

The juice does not work at all but the pulp does. The source must be fresh and not packed or processed. In other words, tangerines from a can or packed in a bottle are worthless.

You need fresh fruit for this to be effective.

The uses for citrus include:

- Indigestion
- Bloating
- Acid reflux
- Gas
- Mild constipation
- Abdominal pain

If you find more uses for citrus feel free to write me. Remember, your liver, as it regulates the digestive tract, benefits from citrus as well. Therefore, even right elbow pain and some liver issues are added with citrus.

You may find untold uses for citrus outside of the list above. Feel free to experiment, as this is the way great discoveries are produced.

Occasionally citrus does not work on indigestion. In this case, it is always a bacterial infection in the intestinal tract or colon. This is called H. Pylori and gives all the symptoms of being indigestion or GERD, yet it only responds to improving immune function.

This can be done a number of ways, yet I have found that some of the best herbs for this are natural antibiotics such as Goldenseal or Echinacea.

A Few Words about Organic

We have all at one time or another heard the term organic. Answers.com defines organic this way:

or·gan·ic *adj*. 1. Of, relating to, or derived from living organisms: organic matter. 2. Of, relating to, or affecting a bodily organ: an organic disease.

3. a. Of, marked by, or involving the use of fertilizers or pesticides that are strictly of animal or vegetable origin: organic vegetables; an organic farm. b. Raised or conducted without the use of drugs, hormones, or synthetic chemicals: organic chicken; organic cattle farming. c. Serving organic food: an organic restaurant. d. Simple, healthful, and close to nature: an organic lifestyle.

4. a. Having properties associated with living organisms. b. Resembling a living organism in organization or development; interconnected: society as an organic whole.

The above definitions are correct.

To make it even simpler we would need to add the following.

Grown in pesticide free soil

Grown from seeds that come from pesticide free plants

Fertilized with pesticide and chemical free substances

Watered with chemical free water

In other words, to really be organic, produce must be grown in a completely controlled environment. This can be done and is worth looking for. But how do you know you are getting organic fruit and vegetables at the market or health food store? Surprisingly, few know what you are going to read. It is right on the fruit or vegetable label or sticker.

There is a code there. If the produce is organic it will carry a sticker with a five-digit code starting with 9, such as 94413, which came off the pears I just bought. If the code on your produce starts with a 4, 3 or 2, it does not matter what the grocery store sign says, the produce is of a conventional source.

Just remember, *'Nine is fine! 4, 3 or 2 are not for you'*.

Occasionally, like today, I have found produce either intentionally or unintentionally mismarked. The store had a sign up indicating that the oranges were organic while the fruit sticker starting with a 4 said otherwise. I pointed this out to the produce person who immediately discarded the organic sign.

Be certain that if you are going to spend the money that you get organic.

56 Magnesium

Most of us have heard something about Magnesium. Perhaps it was in combination with calcium. Perhaps you have taken or remember Milk of Magnesia. You may have taken magnesium in many forms but it is what it does that is important.

When people hear the term Osteoporosis they think of bones breaking due to lack of calcium.

This is again all thanks to advertising. Could the "powers that be" want you needing hip surgery by giving you bad advice? Did you know that using calcium by itself does just that, make bones brittle?

Perhaps they think of an old man hobbling around on a cane and falling and breaking his hip. Either way, the pictures that come up are not attractive. How would you feel if your house burned down after you had spent most of the day fighting the fire?

You fought the blaze with every bit of courage and determination you had. You stood there staring down flames that nipped at your ankles but nothing you did worked. You even used a heavy-duty fire hose and yet at the end of the afternoon your house was reduced to ash. So what exactly happened?

As mentioned above, bones are like the ashes of your house and the calcium is like the gasoline you were pouring on the fire that you thought was water.

Yes, it turned out you were using a hose that was pumping only gasoline.

You were trying to put out a fire with gasoline! You were pouring explosive fuel on your fire and expecting to put it out.

This sounds ludicrous, does it not? Consuming gasoline instead of water? The terrible, sad & tragic thing about this made up story is that it happens every day. Calcium when consumed alone destroys bone. People try to keep their bones from deteriorating but what they are using is causing more damage.

As a public, Americans are preached to on a daily basis. It is now accepted that TV has a hypnotic affect on humans. You are being brainwashed every night and do not notice. We are told to take calcium supplements to prevent bone loss.

If you don't take magnesium with calcium in a ratio of 1 to 1, the body will use its own magnesium to break down the calcium.

Yes, magnesium is the tool or the element / mineral that breaks down calcium.

<u>Where do you think that magnesium is stored in the body?</u>

Is it in the: A) Liver? B) Bones? C) Kidneys? D) Brain? E) Muscle?

Did you say B, the bones?

If you did, you are right. When magnesium is leached from the bones for any reason, the bones become brittle and are prone to breakage at any age. Magnesium is the answer to brittle bones. Again, your bones become weak and brittle when you take calcium because the body now must use its own magnesium to break down this rogue calcium.

Therefore, supplementing calcium without equal amounts of magnesium is dangerous and at the least not healthy.

On the other hand, magnesium is vital at any age. After oxygen and water, magnesium is clearly the most important element to the body other than food. Magnesium is involved in close to 400 different body processes. When magnesium is eroded away, or leached from the body, the body starts weakening in the following areas:

- Energy
- Digestion
- Muscle function
- Bone formation
- Cell health
- Heart function
- Kidney function
- Adrenal function
- Brain function
- Immune function
- Bladder function
- Nervous system

The following substances rob the body of magnesium, some of which will not surprise you, as I have been preaching their evils throughout this book.

They are:

- Sugar
- Salt (added to food)
- Drugs
- Tobacco
- Distilled water
- Caffeine
- Diuretics
- Sodium
- Fast foods
- High calcium
- Antacids
- Alcohol

The elements listed here are just deadly to the body. Research indicates that 95 % of the American public is deficient in magnesium. To be sure your magnesium is being assimilated; use a form that dissolves in water. If you take magnesium tablets, you are now dependant on systems of the body that may be weak. To ensure absorption use a mix that dissolves in water.

I could list all of the problems that are improved when magnesium is used correctly. If I did, I would fill the next 3 pages. It would be hard to come up with a single body process that is not enhanced by use of magnesium.

Please look magnesium up on the web. Go to your favorite search engine and type in magnesium and read a few pages on it. Magnesium is remarkably well documented again and again. You will be shocked and wonder why I didn't include more of it here.

Be smart and use magnesium correctly and never, ever use calcium by itself.

57 Sports Injuries

Watching sporting events has been one of man's favorite pastimes since he invented competitive trials thousands of years ago. Injuries are par for the course as bodies smashing into bodies do break.

Yet there is something very interesting in the injuries we have today as opposed to 50 years ago. In one study it was reported that injuries in pro sport increased by 33% between 1991 and 1999.

Aberration: Professional baseball has more hamstring and knee injuries than football, soccer, hockey or basketball. At a much slower pace and as a non-contact sport, how can such data be true? Yet it is without reservation clearly the case.

Football features lethal career-ending injuries such as shattered bones, the never-ending concussion, patella tendon blowouts, medial collateral ligament (MCL) and the anterior cruciate ligament (ACL) ruptures.

Yet knee, leg and joint injuries are most common in the comparatively docile sport of baseball. No other sport creates the nagging injuries of baseball.

Basketball, by the numbers, is a safer sport than baseball yet far more violent. Football is off the scale with brutal collisions. Yes football players do play with incredible pain, but they stop when they cannot walk. Why then are football players somehow immune to baseball like injuries?

What is at work here?

Is it diet related? Is it lack of conditioning? In comparison to basketball the frequency of baseball injuries is shocking. The game of hoops involves constant movement and pounding yet muscle pulls / injuries do not occur nearly as frequently. Why then are there so many hamstring injuries in baseball?

The answer seems to be one of bad habits. Certain activities separate a large percentage of baseball players from players in other sports.

The terrible trio is chewing tobacco, sunflower seeds and Gatorade.

Before you bust a gut laughing yourself to death, consider this. All muscles need fluid in continual circulation to run properly. Pain equals the absence of circulation, oxygen and energy.

What does salt, sodium, sugar, excess protein and Nicotine all do? They shut down the kidneys. They also shut down the body's washing machine the liver. When waste is not moved, it becomes solid and causes havoc. Suddenly knee cartilage shreds. Muscles tear or are pulled and damaged. Scenarios like this are common where fluid is not free to wash the system free of waste.

The cocktail of the above items is a promise of disaster.

Gatorade's own website spells out their formula for doom: water, **sucrose syrup, glucose-fructose syrup,** citric acid, natural and artificial flavors, **salt, sodium citrate,** monopotassium phosphate, ester gum, **sucrose acetate isobutyrate,** red 40, blue 1). This yummy concoction is practically a 100% guarantee of KIDNEY and LIVER TROUBLE.

What sport features all of these irritants being ingested during the playing of that sport?

Baseball and baseball alone, is the sole owner of these insults to kidney and liver health.

Toxic kidneys cannot wash the system free of lactic acid and uric acid, the byproducts of physical activity. You already know that the kidneys monitor your joints, tendons and ligaments. Weak kidneys equal weak muscles equal appalling injuries.

A toxic liver cannot wash the waste accumulating via the kidneys and remains stagnant preventing any inner-body cleansing at all.

Pro basketball, football, soccer or hockey players, using chewing tobacco, chewing seeds and guzzling sports drinks during a game, unheard of.

Yet Gatorade is part of other sports too. I am certain that if those "sports drinks" were replaced with water, we would reduce injuries across the boards.

Chewing tobacco is an aberration all to itself found almost entirely in baseball. Considering the earlier segments of this chapter, it is no stretch at all to conclude that what goes in the mouth is more involved in physical performance than anyone ever dreamed of possible.

Remember, pain is the precursor to damage, and is caused by the interruption of oxygen, energy and circulation to any part of the body. Electrical impulses cannot move through a massy or junked up joint or muscle.

Nicotine, sugar, sodium, salt and excess protein are all factors weakening the kidneys and therefore weaken strength, endurance and recovery time.

Pain is the absence of circulation, oxygen and energy. Do not interrupt it or you will feel the pain.

58 Detoxing The Body

Every company that makes supplements is always working on detoxing the body. Company "A" focuses on liver cleansing, while company "B" focuses on colon cleansing. We are always talking about detoxing some organ somewhere.

Detoxifying of the body simply means: mobilizing waste and then rendering it inert by processing or excretion via liver, kidney, lung, lymphatic, skin or colon. Waste can be removed by urination, exhalation or excretion. The excretory system consists of the bowel, skin, liver, kidney and lymphatic system. In a healthy body these processes occur thousands of times a day and for the most part go completely unnoticed by the host. The body has a program that runs twenty-four hours a day if it is not interfered with.

The following is what is wrong with these "IDEAS." Yes, ideas! Detoxing the body is the concept that we are smarter about the body than it is about itself. In other words, we are taught to believe that it (the body) is stupid.

The Body is Not Stupid

Actually it is far smarter than we are, but we do not speak the same language. Stated yet again, the body is a machine that has exact programming that it is running. This programming is to run 24 hours a day Monday to Monday, including holidays.

IF YOU GET NOTHING OUT OF THIS BOOK THAN WHAT I WRITE IN THE NEXT PARAGRAPH, THEN THIS BOOK IS WORTH MILLIONS TO YOU AND YOUR HEALTH.

The only organs that can be cleaned or detoxed are the colon, skin and the respiratory system consisting of the lungs, sinuses, and nose.

These are the only organs that actually accumulate waste that can be directly assisted in flushing out. All other organs process waste. The fatty tissue holds waste as does muscle tissue, tendons and ligaments.

We can flush out only:

- Colon
- Skin
- Lungs
- Sinuses
- Nose

Yes, all other toxins are housed in the fatty tissue, muscle tissue and connective tissue of your body. They are warehoused and held there until such time that your filtering organs can process this refuse.

It is a common practice to "cleanse the digestive tract or colon and intestines." This is an excellent thing to do. But, to do it alone, while being beneficial, is akin to cleaning the sewage system of your house or just the bathroom as opposed to cleaning the entire structure.

Since the colon is a hollow organ it can be made to "sneeze." The sinuses can drain and the lungs can release their waste in the same fashion. This explains sneezing and coughing.

The bladder and kidney do not harbor toxins; they process and excrete them. You may want to argue "what about kidney stones"? These "stones" are just common masses that are moving, albeit slowly through the kidneys. I am correctly stating that kidney stones are extremely common. Yet, 99.9 percent of them will never be noticed, as they are broken-down and excreted by the body.

Kidney stones are just small masses of minerals that form and dissolve constantly.

What detoxing herbs and foods are doing, is giving the body food to turn itself back on.

Toxicity (unresolved waste) overwhelms the body's filters and begins to slowly collect throughout the system. When the backup is too immense, we begin to feel terrible or sick. Too great a toxic build up facilitated by liver and kidney overwhelm, guarantees feeling and looking toxic.

Any good formula or herb for liver or kidneys only helps to reset the organ. The liver and kidney are not too sick to work if we let them. They are very able to protect us if we allow them to do their job without our interference.

If your liver is slightly off, you will feel all manner of symptoms. The same is true with the kidneys. If they are not running at full capacity, the body will not be either. Therefore, detox is all about giving your body the food or fuel it needs so that it can do its job.

Your body knows when your blood pressure should go up and when you need fluid in one part of the body or the other. It knows when to raise or lower your respiration. It knows itself far better than you ever will. Please, please, please take the phrase "_______ (<<<insert organ name) Cleanse" out of your vocabulary, unless you are talking about the colon, intestines or respiratory system.

Beware of any company that does not understand this as they do not understand the subject of detox at all. Even though the term "liver cleanse" is bandied around like a tennis ball, no one has ever done a liver detox. The liver is a clean lab that harbors nothing but the materials it needs to do its job. Again the liver harbors no toxins. It is the washing machine of the body and must be kept active running at full capacity.

What about gallstones? Again these, under the right conditions, are dissolved and passed. The only reasons people get their gallbladder taken out are:

- They are unformed on how to fix their diet to dissolve gallstones naturally.
- Prefer to have surgery versus another method (caused by medical brainwashing).
- Their surgeon needs a new boat, a new house or braces for his or her kids and has sold surgery as the only alternative to the gallstone induced pain.

The healthy approach to gallstones is #1: Realize they did not happen by themselves. In other words they are caused by diet. #2: Make it our job to learn what the offenders are and eliminate them from our diet; #3: Find products and foods that aid in softening them and getting them to dissolve.

It is that effortless. Yet it is also that hard. It is a good idea to become an expert on gallstones, and then assign yourself a course of action that you can follow. Then you can pass them naturally.

Ideally, a correct diet will prevent them from ever forming.

The oldest form of detox is fasting, as it forces the body to release waste from the cells (cellular toxicity), including muscles, tendons and ligaments. Fasting is perhaps the hardest form of waste removal as the waste is removed due to necessity.

During a fast, we obviously are not consuming food. Thus, the only form of sustenance that the body has to utilize is to cannibalize its fatty tissue reserves. Fat can be broken down via diet or exercise. Remember, the fat is marbled with toxins being stored for disposal at a later date. Fat, if and when it is clean, is a ready source of tremendous energy.

But the body will not release this fat because it is commingled with toxins. Consequently, a fast of any type forces the body to release these reserves (toxins and all) into the system. Often, we reabsorb this waste and feel like we are sick.

During a fast we may feel or experience fever, lethargy, soreness all over, headaches, migraines, bloated, irritable, insomnia, wired, rapid heartbeat, hot, cold, moody, depressed, burning eyes, constipated and or itchy skin.

The reason why is that we are forcing the body to release its toxic waste dumps to survive. Once those poisons hit your system, you will often feel it and feel it hard.

Simply put, a fast forces us into a bath of impure matter. This huge vat of gunk is corrosive and harmful. But as the body being a self-perpetuating organism, it quickly weighs the options, death by starvation or longer life with poisons. The body chooses longer life every time. Presented with the same dilemma, you would make an identical choice to live longer or survive.

Now the question becomes: do you ever fast? The answer is, fully know what a fast is. In other words, read about it in detail. Then when you start, support the process with herbs, vitamins and juices, if allowed. At the very least you need something to keep your colon moving or you will feel the wrath of your toxic load.

Rather than risk the discomfort and loss of production, start it on a Friday. By Monday you may feel good enough so that work and or family time is not destroyed. Remember it is better to aid your body with the right herbs that reset the liver, kidneys and colon, than to ignore them.

Fasting or not, always think in terms of resting and resetting your body's filters and in the end you will be far better off.

A polluted system promises:

- Faster aging
- Aches, pains
- Trips to the doctor
- Drugs
- Surgery
- Insomnia
- Loss of basic control of your body

When you really get that the idea that you are running your body based on its needs and wants, it is then no accident that you are in the condition you are in, good or bad. Whether you blame your good health (or lack of it) on healthy living / poor living, blind luck or no luck at all, you are the source of your health, no one else.

59 Clear-Cut Answers

This chapter is devoted to a collection of data that has much use but is not dense enough to warrant its own chapter. Year after year I am asked the same questions again and again. Here is the data you will be asking for.

Stated much earlier, the body signals you as to what it wants and needs. Every pain or signal is a request for action. You job is to identify the exsurpo and aid your body correctly.

What you do with those signals will absolutely determine how well you live and enjoy your life.

F.A.Q.s

Right Elbow Pain

Your right elbow and upper right forearm indicate the health of only one part of the body. These symptoms are indicators of one organ or an entire system interruption. It is also very reliable.

Right elbow pain, stiffness or right elbow joint crepitus (crunchy joints) indicate:

- Digestive disturbance
- Stomach issues
- Colon issues
- Intestinal issues
- Liver issues (this is the exsurpo = exact-source-of pain)

This can be further defined as acid reflux, indigestion, heartburn, acid indigestion, ulcers, parasites, stomach irritation and bloating.

The above problem(s) will lead to the symptoms:

Symptom: The right elbow will hurt, in unison with other symptoms.

Symptom: You may occasionally feel pain directly in the stomach.

Symptom: You may feel no symptoms in the stomach and only feel irritation in the elbow. When you correctly treat your digestive system, pain localized in the elbow decreases.

When you feel these symptoms, address them by treating your stomach with citrus or an herbal. Your stomach will immediately show change unless the disturbance is caused by H. Pylori. If it is H. Pylori, Goldenseal or Echinacea will make an immediate change.

Itchy Face or Dry Face

An itch or dry patch on the face corresponds to the organ associated with that region of the face. As the face is dominated by the liver or the kidneys, these factors are also either liver or kidney issues.

The next time you have an itch, try drinking some water or take an herb or formula that you know (via your own testing) is fantastic for the function of the organ asking for help. You will be amazed at what happens. This is not a cute parlor trick or hocus-pocus. It is simply the direct response to a direct communication, directly from your body to you, and the correct response back to it. Remember finding the exsurpo is the key.

•• Every itch, from your neck down (not including your face) is your LIVER asking for help.

•• Every itch of your scalp is your BLADDER / KIDNEYS asking for help.

Treat the direct organ along with the liver or kidney for best results.

Supplement Use and Label Recommendations

Supplement bottles do not think. The clock does not think. Your body computes how to improve your health 24 hours a day.

Maybe you have found and herbal supplement that really works. Many produce excellent balancing in the body.

Question: The bottle says take ______ 3 times a day. Is there a better way to take my supplements?

Answer: Take your supplements based on your body's symptoms. Your body tells you what it wants when it wants it. You would never spend all day Monday scratching an itch that you were not going to have until Tuesday. You would of course scratch your itch when you had it.

Taking supplements is no different. When you take supplements for an ache or pain and the pain goes away, you have done something right.

Now wait for your ache or pain to come back and then take your supplements again. Yes this may mean that on some days you take them six times. But on other days you may not take them at all. Let your body tell you when to take your herbals.

Finally, you will also learn what is making you feel so bad that causes you to need your supplements. How? Because pains and aches always follow the absorption of a stimulant that caused it. Such as, eating a Snickers bar (or whatever) that "turned on" the pain. Pain never occurs without a cause,

All Low Back Pain

This is solely and only a kidney irritation (may be modified by the transverse colon). Drink water, eat grapes and or take a supplement to turn back on your kidneys as they are slightly off. Remember, addressing the transverse colon with citrus or a gentle colon formula can modify low back pain.

Spasms / Pain Or Cramps Above The Right Hip

This is the location of the ileocecal valve. It is the valve that opens and closes, letting matter move from the intestines to the ascending colon. Sugars, parasites, breads, processed foods, alcohol, processed oils, caffeine and heavy protein can block it, causing irritations. When very severe pain is present (in this area) accompanying a very high fever, suspect that the appendix is at issue. When this occurs, seek medical attention immediately. If the appendix ruptures and goes untreated, death can result in 24 to 72 hours.

Right Shoulder Pain / Fuzzy Vision / Irritated eyes / Bad Mood

This is solely and only a liver issue (may be modified by the transverse colon). Drink water, eat citrus and or take a supplement to turn back on your liver as it is slightly off.

Ketones and Protein Intake

Ketones are waste particles derived from fat / protein and are irritants to your kidneys. When the body is fed more protein than it can use, it signals that it is overwhelmed. We may see floaters: clear shapes passing through our vision (undigested protein). Men may notice very foamy urine (as it hits the toilet water) first thing in the morning. The foam will break-up very slowly like soap foam. I believe most people consume seventy five percent more protein than we need on a weekly basis. Most Americans could cut back their protein intake to two times a week, as protein cannot be stored in the body. Ketones build up in excess and can poison and even kill cells of the body. Too much protein or more protein than the kidneys can synthesize can lead to calcium loss via the urine and lead to bone loss (sometimes called osteoporosis).

An over abundance of protein can also rob us of our vitamin B6, as it is required to break down protein.

Kidney Details

The kidneys hold 20-25% of the total volume of blood in your body. They are very delicate.

They must filter:

- Uric acid, which builds up in your joints
- Lactic acid from your muscles
- Wastewater from the liver

It is again left to the kidneys to handle the burden, which causes much weakness and actual pain.

Vaccines

It is becoming clearer that vaccines are extremely dangerous and over the last 100+ years have cost millions their lives. Why would this be the case? Vaccinations use a microscopic amount of dead bacteria as a catalyst to get the body to react. A dead bacterium isn't harmless or it wouldn't cause the body to react.

Using poisons to treat the body is clearly not a good idea and uses the principal of differential toxicity (the hope that the poison is more poisonous to the bacteria than it is to you).

Allopathy commonly uses such an approach (such as with the FLU), but it should be avoided. If you shift your focus away from individual hairs that turn grey and instead address the organ regulating the hair, which is the kidneys, you can achieve great results.

Acne is not just a skin condition; it is an accurate reflection of how well the organs connected to that part of the face are running. The skin anywhere else on your body reflects only the liver, but on the face we have subdivisions.

When you identify the correct organ at the bottom of a symptom, you can even identify what caused the problem in the first place. Treat the body as a whole and remember that what you do to one part of the body affects all of it.

Trouble Eating Wheat or Gluten

Commonly called Celiac disease, Sprue or "Celiac Sprue," it is a permanent adverse reaction to gluten (a byproduct of wheat).

Gluten is a composite of the proteins gliadin and glutenin. These exist, conjoined with starch, in the endosperms of some grass-related grains, notably wheat, rye and barley. Gliadin and glutenin comprise about 80% of the protein contained in wheat seed. You are already aware of the body's aversion to excess protein; here is another indicator of this condition.

What is so unusual about this 'reaction' is that it is common among the entire population. Why are there those who do not notice it? Because some people are so toxic they cannot perceive the reaction, or do not connect their discomfort with this aversion.

No one should ever eat bread of any type.

What Kind of Meat or Heavy Protein Can Be Ingested?

This is a tricky question to answer as some people like me need very little or even none. If you must have meat protein, try sushi (raw fish), steak tartare (thinly sliced raw steak) or even a raw egg in a smoothie. If you do eat raw nuts, a little goes a long way. Eating 5-10 nuts a day for many will suffice.

Why cooked protein is so dangerous is because cooked protein is foreign to the body. The enzymes that made it digestible are now gone or destroyed. Placing a piece of raw steak on a plate and leaving it there undisturbed for six months will produce dust, as the steak enzymes consumed the meat.

Cooked steak left alone for six months will produce a hard piece of leather, as the self-digesting enzymes are dead from cooking. Cooking results in indigestible substances that compost in the gut.

Should I Add Enzymes To My Diet?

The answer is flatly no. Enzymes, to be viable, must be found in their whole natural uncooked source. The reason enzymes are destroyed is due to cooking. Enzyme supplements must be cooked or processed to extract the enzyme residue and then encapsulate them. Enzyme supplements are just another sales pitch and sinkhole for money.

Whole foods are the answer to correcting your health as they are self digesting. The lack of effort / energy used by the body in the digestive process, means that, energy is now available to *heal the body.*

60 Parasites in Your Dinner!

Truth: All parasites live on and are enhanced by receiving sugar. The type of sugar to avoid is white table sugar or added sugar. Sugar that occurs naturally in fresh fruit or vegetables is not a problem.

No one likes the idea of being taken advantage. Some of us may like watching the 3 Stooges but no one wants to be a stooge.

Stooge: *noun; the partner in a comedy team who feeds lines to the other comedian; a straight man. One who allows oneself to be used for another's profit or advantage; a puppet: Slang: A stool pigeon.*

No one likes being the victim of someone or something that is taking advantage of his or her kindness, thoughtfulness or hospitality. Have you ever had a houseguest who decided to stay a while? Remember how that made you feel?

Do you remember how frustrated you felt when you saw an individual taking advantage of someone you cared about? Remember how hard it was to keep your mouth shut and let them find out for themselves? Or perhaps you risked your friendship and took the role of protector by alerting your friend to the danger they were in. If you did, then you know how difficult it was to get your point across.

On the other hand, how could your friend have been so blind? What if the stooge was you? What if it was happening right now? Read on. If you are a radical like me, you say that 100% of the public has parasites. The conservative right says it is only 90 %. As you can see, there is not much difference between the left and the right.

Parasites are blamed for every malady / disease and ache or pain known to man. They may very well cause most, if not all diseases. I am of the attitude that we all have parasites and in a strong body (one that is healthy) the parasites do not get a good foothold and your body can defend itself. My belief is not a common one but when did adversity ever stop me? It is clear to me that if our bodies are weakened through diet and lifestyle, we can fall victim to such attack.

In a weak enough state, even a cold can be fatal. Regardless of what side of the fence you are on, it is safe to say that parasites are the opposite of money. You don't want more now. You always want less. You don't want more at a later date. You want none. And when faced with the option of not having them, you don't want them ever.

Par·a·site: noun 1. Biology, an organism that grows, feeds, and is sheltered on or in a different organism while contributing nothing to the survival of its host.

Parasites have caused the greatest loss of life in history. The black plague, Yersinia Pestis, a species of rod shaped bacterium, ravaged Europe from 1347 to 1352. Unless treated immediately it is nearly always fatal.

It first appeared in recorded history in Athens in 430 B.C. and appeared again in 532 A.D. in Europe. But in 1347, the epidemic started in Asia and killed countless numbers before the oriental rat flea, a common pest among rats, hitched a ride to Italy during trade with the Far East.

Once a person was infected symptoms began showing up in 1-7 days. Death could come in 24 hours. Yersinia Pestis developed into 3 forms of plague, bubonic (death rate about 75%), pneumonic plague (death rate almost 100%), and septicemic plague (death rate not charted). All forms have been responsible for enormous mortality in many fearsome epidemics throughout Mankind's history.

Yesinia Pestis was identified and named during another outbreak in Asia in 1894 by Swiss-French bacteriologist Alexandre Yersin. Thanks to the ferocity of these breakouts, we are left with something else rather haunting.

A nursery rhyme you have known about and probably sang to yourself since childhood.

Ring around the Rosy

Ring around the rosy
Pocket full of posies
Ashes, ashes
All fall down

What the Rhyme really meant

Ring around the rosy
This was the mark of the plague on the skin (the rosy) a red or black circle.

Pocket full of posies
It was believed that posies could ward off the plague.

Ashes, ashes
There is much conjecture as to what Ashes, Ashes meant. Most agree it referred to the burning of the dead. Yet there is another variation, 'a tissue-a tissue' (indicating a runny nose). There is also the variant "ahchoo ahchoo" for sneezing or Ashen, Ashen, referring to the grey pall of the dying.

All fall down
We all die.

Suddenly that rhyme means a whole lot more. Parasites can come to us from hundred of locations.

Common Ways To Get Parasites

- The ocean
- A river
- A stream
- A lake
- A pond
- Your cat
- Your cat box
- Your dog
- Your bird
- Other animal
- Salad Bar
- Sushi Bar
- Raw pork
- Raw fish
- Raw beef
- Raw chicken
- Mosquito bites
- Oral sex
- Cockroaches
- Ants
- Kissing/Mononucleosis
- Flies
- All bugs
- Tap water
- Buffets
- 3rd world travel
- Hose water
- Animal Pet Kisses
- Pets Sleeping in your bed
- Eating food after it has been on the ground

Parasitic forms often have quite complicated life cycles, moving between several different hosts or locations in the host's body. Infection occurs variously by eating uncooked meat with larvae in it, by entrance into unprotected cuts or directly through the skin, by transfer via blood-sucking insects, and so forth.

As I said earlier, parasites are common. The question is, 'are they making you sick'? Here are the common parasites.

Hookworm

The hookworm is the diarrhea and cramp causing intestinal parasite. Heavy infestation with hookworm can be serious. Hookworm infections occur mainly in tropical and subtropical climates and affect about 1 billion people – about one-fifth of the world's population. One of the most common species of hookworm, Ancylostoma Duodenale, is found in southern Europe, northern Africa, northern Asia, and parts of South America.

Hookworms have a complex life cycle that begins and ends in the small intestine. Hookworm eggs require warm, moist, shaded soil to hatch into larvae. These barely visible larvae penetrate the skin (often through bare feet), are carried to the lungs, go through the respiratory tract to the mouth, are swallowed, and eventually reach the small intestine.

This journey takes about a week. In the small intestine, the larvae develop into half-inch-long worms, attach themselves to the intestinal wall, and individually consume small amounts of blood. When there is an infestation, the small amount of blood consumed becomes quite large and can lead to anemia. The adult worms produce thousands of eggs. These eggs are passed in the feces (stool). If the eggs contaminate soil and conditions are right, they will hatch, molt, and develop into infective larvae again after 5 to 10 days.

Hookworm infection is contracted from contact with soil contaminated by hookworm, by walking barefoot or accidentally swallowing contaminated soil. Children, because they often play in dirt and go barefoot, are at high risk. Since transmission of hookworm infection requires development of the larvae in soil, hookworm cannot be spread person to person.

Chronic heavy hookworm infection can damage the growth and development of children. The loss of iron and protein retards growth and mental development, sometimes irreversibly. The first signs of hookworm infection are itching and a rash at the site where the larvae penetrate the skin. These signs may be followed by abdominal pain, diarrhea, anemia, loss of appetite and weight loss.

One further symptom, though not common in Hookworm infections, is anal itching. As their waste is produced, it can cause irritation of the anus. Hookworms can also cause difficulty breathing, enlargement of the heart, as well as an irregular heartbeat. When Hookworm infections go unchecked, the symptoms can be very severe and, in infants, may even lead to death.

Pinworm

Pin·worm: Any of various small worms that is parasitic on or in cattle, horses, rabbits, and other mammals. Pinworms (Enterobius Vermicularis) are a species that infests the human intestines and rectum. A common variation of the name pinworms is threadworm and is the same thing. The pinworm is about the length of a common staple and lives for the most part within the rectum of humans. While an infected person is asleep, female pinworms leave the intestines through the anus and deposit eggs on the skin around the anus.

The symptoms of a pinworm infection are caused by the female pinworm laying her eggs. Most symptoms of pinworm infection are mild, and many infected people have no symptoms or, at most, some itching around the anus, disturbed sleep, and irritability. Should pinworm infestation be heavy, your symptoms may be more severe and also include loss of appetite, restlessness, and insomnia. As infections get worse, so will your symptoms, such as, insomnia, voracious non-stop itching, loss of concentration, mood swings, loss of productivity (as all you can think about is the itch that you can't scratch in public).

Within days of infection, Pinworms begin attacking the liver directly and indirectly via the byproducts (waste) left in the blood due to their presence. Liver issues can be very severe during Pinworm infestations. If this is not clear to you, review the symptoms of liver weakness in the chapter on the liver. Pinworms are the most common parasitic worms in the United States among school age children. Infection or contamination of preschoolers runs a close second with day care centers coming in at third. Adults are not immune to pinworms but are not as likely to have pinworm infestations, unless the worms were acquired from their infected children.

If you thought the movie Alien was scary, consider this: pinworm eggs can survive up to 2 weeks on clothing, bedding, or other objects. Infection is acquired when these eggs are accidentally swallowed. Also consider this, within a few hours of being deposited on the skin around the anus, pinworm eggs become infective (capable of infecting another person). At night, the adult worms can sometimes be seen directly in bedclothes or around the anal area. In hotels the comforters are cleaned only twice a year, unless severely soiled. Therefore it's a good idea to have the comforters removed by the housekeeping staff upon your arrival.

When pinworms are suspected as a problem, your doctor can order a microbiology test to verify his suspicions one way or the other. Be aware that these tests can take 3-5 weeks to receive after testing.

The tests involve acquiring a smear or sample of the debris around the anus using transparent tape or a pinworm paddle. The eggs adhere to the sticky tape or paddle and are identified by examination under a microscope. The test needs to be done in the morning prior to showering and prior to bowel movements as washing and wiping will remove the eggs. Fingernail samples also may produce eggs for examination. Pinworm infestation can be treated with herbal formulas or with over the counter products.

Treating pinworms correctly can take up to 3 months. Always consult your health care provider before treating a suspected case of pinworm.

Always consider treating the entire family if a member is infected. Beware that infected playmates, schoolmates and close contacts can bring about a re-infection.

Tapeworm

They live in the intestinal tract, attached with a rounded head equipped with hook-like structures that attach to the intestinal wall. Once secured to the wall, the worms begin feeding. The host unwittingly feeds the visitors, as the tapeworm has no digestive tract. The tapeworm is also called a flat worm and is shaped like a hollow strip. The worm is made up of proglottids (worm segments), starting below the neck. An adult worm can reach a length of 15 or 20 ft. As a segment dies off it separates and is removed in the bowel movement of the host.

A tapeworm is a true hermaphrodite, having both male and female reproductive organs. Self-fertilization does take place but it is more common that a second worm will be necessary. Human tapeworm infestations are most common in regions where there is fecal contamination of soil and water. Tapeworm incidence will be higher where light cooking or raw meat consumption is most common. The beef tapeworm is the most prevalent tapeworm in the United States. This happens when a host cow becomes infected while drinking or grazing.

The round-bodied embryos, equipped with sharp hooks, hatch and bore through the cow's intestinal wall into the bloodstream, where they are carried to the muscles. Here each embryo encloses itself in a cyst, or bladder; at this stage it is called a bladder worm. During the bladder worm stage, the embryo develops a miniature head. It remains encysted until the primary host eats the muscle. If the head has not been killed by sufficient cooking of the meat, it sheds its covering and attaches to the intestinal wall, of the human host, where it begins growing.

Intestinal tapeworm infestation frequently occurs without symptoms; occasionally there is abdominal discomfort, diarrhea, constipation, or weight loss. The most serious tapeworm infestation in humans is caused by the ingestion of T. Solanum eggs through fecal contamination. The embryos migrate throughout the body, producing serious illness. Interestingly, the dog tapeworm embryo encysts in various internal organs of humans, most commonly in the liver.

The cysts produced by these embryos are called hydatid cysts, and the infestation of the liver is called hydatid disease.

Heartworm

Heartworms are found primarily in dogs but can be passed to humans via mosquitoes. They can be hard to eliminate and can be fatal. Heartworm symptoms usually can't be detected until advanced stages. Symptoms are similar to congestive heart failure and include coughing, difficulty breathing, lack of energy, etc.

Adult heartworms live in the heart and pulmonary arteries of infected dogs. And as mentioned above, rarely in humans, but they can be affected. They have been found in other areas of the body, but this is unusual. Heartworms survive up to 5 years and, during this time; the female produces millions of offspring. These offspring live in the bloodstream, mainly in the small blood vessels. 30 different species of mosquitoes can transmit heartworms. The female mosquito bites the infected dog and ingests the blood borne offspring during a blood meal. From there mosquitoes can pass the parasite young to unsuspecting hosts.

When fully developed, the infective larvae enter the bloodstream and move to the heart and adjacent vessels, where they grow to maturity in 2 to 3 months and start reproducing, thereby completing the full life cycle.

Roundworm

The roundworm is the most prolific internal pest known to man. There are more than 20,000 species documented at present. They are often passed from dogs to humans through accidental ingestion of eggs. They can be found throughout the world and even in Antarctica and oceanic trenches. There are more species of roundworms than species of man and animal combined. They possess a complete digestive system with a mouth that attaches to the intestines with sharp projectiles. They are thin, round voracious little feeders. The skin of the roundworm secretes fluid made of keratin that protects the body from drying out due to digestive juices. Roundworms have a simple nervous system, with a main nerve cord running along the ventral side. Simple or not, they are very debilitating to the host.

Protozoa

(Greek protos = first and zoon = animal) are single-celled creatures with nuclei that show some characteristics usually associated with animals, most notably humans. The most common protozoa variants are; Flagellates, Amoeboids, Sporozoans, Apicomplexa, Myxozoa, Microsporidia and Ciliates.

Most protozoans are too small to be seen with the naked eye, being around 0.01-0.05 mm. To detect protozoa you need a microscope. The common symptoms of protozoa are anemia, back and muscle pain and occasional diarrhea. The organ that is most often attacked by protozoa is the kidney.

Amoeba

Genus of protozoa that moves by means of temporary projections called pseudo pods, and is well known as a representative single cellular organism. They are found in sluggish waters all over the world, both fresh and salt, as well as in soils and as parasites. The Amoeba itself is found in freshwater, typically on decaying vegetation from streams, but is not especially common in nature.

However, because of the ease that they may be obtained, they can cause havoc with humans. The most well known species is A. Proteus. Each has a single nucleus. The name "amibe" was given to it by Berry St. Vincent, from the Greek amoibe, meaning change.

Giardia

A genus of Protozoa that is parasitic in the intestines of vertebrates including humans and most domestic animals. Giardia reproduces and lives in the intestines and may produce minor symptoms include diarrhea, abdominal cramps and nausea, flatulence and/or weight loss. It is passed via unwashed hands of an infected person, or by drinking groundwater polluted by the feces of infected animals such as dogs and beavers (hence the nickname "beaver fever"). Once it migrates to the small intestine it multiplies quickly.

Symptoms, when present, occur one to three days after infection. In some cases the infection becomes chronic. Giardia is common in tropical climates and can hold aggressively in developed countries. Interestingly, men and very young children in close contact with each other are most susceptible. Anywhere where hand washing is not common or not mastered, Giardia can be found. Microscopic stool analysis or testing for antibodies to the parasite is the best way to detect them. In most cases, if the body is healthy and strong, no treatment is necessary.

Toxoplasmosis

Toxoplasmosis is an infection caused by a single-celled parasite named Toxoplasma Gondii. It is found throughout the world and infects more than 60 million people in the United States. Infestation with the Toxoplasma parasite may carry very few symptoms because the immune system usually keeps the parasite from causing illness.

How can humans get Toxoplasmosis?

1). Touching your hands to your mouth after gardening, cleaning a cat's litter box, or anything that came into contact with cat feces.
2). Eating raw or partly cooked meat, especially pork, lamb, or deer.
3). Touching your hands to your mouth after contact with raw or undercooked meat.
4). Organ transplantation or transfusion, although this is rare.

If a woman is pregnant when she is infected with Toxoplasmosis, the infection can be transmitted from her to the baby with catastrophic consequences.

What are the usual symptoms of toxoplasmosis?

Flu like symptoms
Swollen lymph glands

Muscle aches and pains that can last several weeks. If anyone develops more severe symptoms it is because their immune system is weak or they are actively weakening it with use of sugar and drugs, including OTC (over the counter drugs). If you have any of the symptoms mentioned in this chapter and you suspect that you may have parasites, see your health care practitioner and be fully examined. It is important in any treatment for parasites that the therapy (whatever it is) is administered long enough, usually 3 months.

NOTE for whole chapter

Vermox is often given by the medical profession for parasites and is a one-dose treatment. I have seen this approach fail again and again.

I will leave this up to you whether you think a one-dose treatment of anything can be successful. Always follow your doctor's protocols and recommendations. Should you decide to add something else to your treatment of your own design, or that is purchased somewhere else, always let your doctors know, as the two approaches may not work successfully.

61 The People At Q-Link Will Hate Me But...

I only bring you information that I have personally tested and the Q-Link is no different.

A Q-link is a super high tech (health enhancing) necklace made of quality-molded materials. Flipping it over reveals a clear resin window, this presents an inner ring of copper coil. This coil has been scientifically treated to produce something that Q-Link calls Sympathetic Resonance Technology (SRT3). This SRT balances the body and its energy.

Over the years the look of Q-link has evolved. They will continue to do so, but as of this writing, that is what they look like. The Q- Link folks also make a flexible bracelet that does not feature the computer chip, but is elegant and made of body friendly metals.

They also offer bracelets and earrings that do the same thing.

Athletes and those in touch with their bodies and performance often wear Q-Links. The big question is what exactly does a Q-Link do? Some say it is all frou-frou, smoke and mirrors or suggestibility.

The above is patently false. Q-Links actually do something. What they do is quite special. When presented with the above question, the good folks at Q-Link would say, "What don't they do"?

Based on tests the Q-Link improves the function of the body so that it runs better. Literally, the body runs better with a Q-Link.

Think of a Q-Link as a tune up for your body. The Q Link Company recommends the device be worn 24 hours a day, day in and day out.

I have tested the Q-Link several times over the years using Electro Dermal Screening (EDS). For 10 years I have witnessed reproducible phenomena using these devices.

What EDS demonstrates is the energy flow of the body available in our vital organs. According to

traditional Chinese medicine, a form of bodily energy called chi is generated in internal organs and circulates throughout the body. Forming paths near the surface of the skin called meridians; this whole-body energy-grid-network is called the meridian system.

Q-Links have been proven to increase energy flow through these meridians.

Our entire system should be receiving energy. Where it doesn't, "breakdown" occurs. That is what EDS validates via computer program. This registers the general health of the tested organs. An organ with a low number indicates that the organ needs help. An extremely high number indicates the same problem, just at the other end of the scale.

You know as I do that BALANCE IS WHAT KEEPS US HEALTHY.

The Q-Link accelerates the energy of the body. This is needed when the body is sick but not needed when the body is balanced.

That is where the problem lies. As you know from reading this book, anything used to excess is damaging. This includes the Q-Link.

While a raincoat has a use in the rain, it would have little use while bathing or showering. You would not run your car through the car wash or have it tuned up every day. It would be a waste of money.

I wore mine all the time for years. When I tested my numbers they were all out of balance (extremely high). Then one day (while testing), I took off it off. Immediately the "redline" numbers went right back to normal (every time). I have witnessed these same responses with dozens of others for almost 6 years now. All manner of testing produced the same response every time.

Is Q-Link bad?
No. Based on results, everyone should have one.

The Q-Link offers amazing results when one is sick, as it will bring up lowered energy levels and help heal the body. When the body is balanced take it off. Use it when sick and then take it off.

You would not continue drinking water past the point of thirst being quenched. You would not keep scratching an itch that has long since been relieved. The Q-Link is no different.

Use it and take it off.

TAKE OFF YOUR Q-LINK, if you are not sick.

Band Aids are useful but not without cuts.

Again, take off your Q-Link and put it away until you need it.

62 A Morning Ritual Flaw

Ever hear or read that breakfast is the most important meal of the day? That statement is completely not true, but it is not a lie either. Confused? Read on.

What is your morning routine? Is it something like this?

1. Turn off the alarm
2. Use the toilet.
3. Shower / brush your teeth / do your hair / do your makeup.
4. Eat breakfast
5. Get dressed
6. Go to work.

Perhaps that is not your routine, but for most, it comes close. The routine has a glaring flaw in it, a flaw that completely throws our body off center every morning.

What is it?

You breakfast. You read correctly. You ate breakfast. If you have read the chapter on water you know that the body burns water all day and all night. You know that the body's need for water is greatest in the morning since you have been dehydrating all night and every organ of your body is parched. Your digestive tract (which is trying to catch up from the night before) has the contents of dried oatmeal.

Therefore, the need for fluid is greatest in the morning. The morning needs to start this way:

1. Turn off the alarm
2. Use the toilet.

2b. Drink 6-8 oz. of water or fresh squeezed juice

3. Shower / brush your teeth / do your hair / do your makeup.

3b. Drink 8-10 oz. of water or fresh squeezed juice

4. Eat breakfast (fruit, salad or more juice)

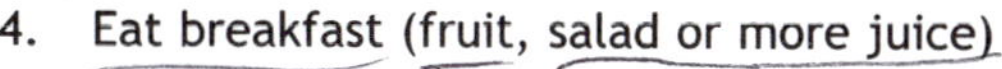

5. Get dressed
6. Go to work.

A ban on solid food breakfast appears to fly in the face of the old statement that "Breakfast is the most important meal of the day!" It does not. Breakfast **is** the most important meal of the day.

Breakfast is the most important meal of the day to not eat anything solid.

What people miss is that we live in an entirely different age than when that statement was made. We don't live on 100 to 1000 acre ranches. There is no need to get up before dawn, chow down on a huge breakfast, ride old Ben (the horse) for 45 minutes to the north 140, where you had to mend the fence and tend to the herd, and arrive all before the sun is coming up.

In those days, come noon you were stuck where you were. You didn't have the option to go to a fast food place or a restaurant. You didn't have the time to ride an hour and a half one way back to the house for lunch. When noon came you were stuck with whatever you could carry on your horse.

Therefore, if you didn't eat a huge breakfast, you were "plum outta' luck." There you sat, hungrier than a glutton at a buffet after not eating for five straight days. For you, no soup, tuna, egg rolls, pasta, salad, desert or seconds. You are sitting there looking at beef jerky, hard tack and coffee, if you're lucky.

What you have with you right now must last you until supper. Your next meal is 5 hours away, cowboy. Did you eat a big enough meal to hold you over? Are you going to pass out from hunger about 3:30 pm?

Will you lose your mind?

Life was tough for a rancher 150 years ago. For the rancher on a horse, breakfast was the most important meal of the day. Because, that was all you would eat until after a long evening ride home.

But you don't ride a horse. You can get food anytime you want. So what is the problem? You have too much choice and the "breakfast food" companies keep trying to improve your life via better meals.

Today you can have 50 kinds of sugar and 15 different kinds of dairy products all before 8:00 am.

What your body really needs is something liquid which is not coffee and not hot or boiled.

Today, the trick is to give your body what it needs in the AM. That thing is water. Perhaps it's time to review the body clock chart in the chapter, The Body's Built in Clock, and you tell me what the body is doing in the AM. Unless this is the only chapter in this book you have read, you know what to do.

If not, or if you are a bit sketchy on it, re-read the chapter called "The over importance of H_2O."

Some people will not eat solid food until they have their first elimination (or bowel movement) of the day. Not a bad idea. Whether you take a train, ride a horse, take a bus, catch a trolley, hail a cab or power walk to work, drink your water. And when you start your day, remember to stop and quench your body's thirst.

63 How Can You Change?

I grew up playing sports. I played football, baseball and was a shot putter. I was completely out of control in football and played the roving linebacker position of Monster Back. I was just as intense in baseball. If I could have tackled a pitcher I would have.

I was remarkably fast but it was not always this way.

In elementary school I was the fattest, slowest running kid in the school. I was not really that fat, I was in a school that was in good shape. Nevertheless, when on the grounds many of the other children playing called me "Fatty!"

In the 6th grade we had a national physical fitness test. Part of that test was to run 3 laps around a 600-foot track (100 yards). I could not stop running. I was hypnotized looking at those dashed lines disappearing under my feet. I ran (fully clothed) 25 laps until I was made to stop.

For at least two hours I was drenched in sweat.

The next day I was playing sock ball (like baseball) and I hit a ball to the shortstop. The kid I hit it to was much faster than me, yet I beat him to first base (much to my surprise), then to second base, on to third and then home plate. All the while the boy was yelling "Fatty slow down, slow down fatty."

Something dramatic had happened!!

I was remarkably fast the rest of the day. I had gone from being the slowest runner in school to really fast overnight. The next day I sought out Roger Lane, the acknowledged fastest kid in the school.

When we raced, we were dead even. Wow! How remarkable. Can you expect this? Anything is possible.

At age 34, I decided to rebuild my softball career. I was out of shape and overweight, but that did not stop me. Two left knee surgeries when I was 24 did not stop me. What stopped me was my right leg. One afternoon I had just lined a clean single to right center and was racing to first base when my right upper leg (the rectus femoris muscle) decided that my day was done.

I was suddenly in great pain and nothing I did relieved it. I was yet again knocked out of action. I suddenly had a fist-sized knot in my upper leg. No massage or treatment (less surgery) would relieve the knot or the pain. I again hung up my bat and glove.

For the next 10 years I did not play again.

Three years ago (age 44); I took up softball again (after I had lost 63 pounds). There was no reason to believe that I could still play. I had blown out my knee twice playing softball when I was 24 years old. Now at 44 I was going to play softball again?

That is just what I did.

Yes, fast-forward ten years (44 years old). The fist size knot was still in my upper right leg but I decided to celebrate my 44th birthday at the batting cage. For three straight days and about 3 ? hours, I swung away. My right leg was sore but I pushed through it. The sports bug had hit me again and I decided to take up organized softball yet again. I had just lost the 63 pounds I mentioned at the beginning of this story and I felt good.

Amazingly, the knot in my leg was almost completely gone!!! Did years of herbs, weight loss and 3 ? hours of the batting cage change me again?

The following Monday I was walking in and out of my office and as I was walking up the steps, my leg hurt like it hadn't in ten years. When I sat down to massage my right upper leg something happened. The knot was now gone!! This is no exaggeration. The knot was gone.

I have been playing off and on ever since and I have recaptured my speed that I earned that day in elementary school.

Nothing should have fixed my leg, but something did. To be very fair, here is what the influential factors were:

a). I had switched to a completely raw diet 3 months earlier.

b). I had been taking herbs for kidney (sometimes 7 times a day) for three weeks. Remember, the kidneys regulate all muscles, tendons and ligaments.

c). I was exercising intensely (batting cage).

d). I had decided to not be stopped by my leg.

Any one of these factors or a combination of all of them could have played a role in this major change. In the end, something changed, and without figuring it out further, it would be accurate to write that I changed and my body changed with me. Remember, ten years without playing and at the age of 45 years old, I am again playing like a high school kid.

I have since been relaying this story to numbers of doctors. Most do not understand the relationship of intention over the physical world and have attributed this change to the use of the herbs and diet.

In retrospect it is clear to me that weak kidneys led to my leg and knee problems years earlier. It is also clear that circulation was the key to all of these problems. If there is no circulation or energy flow there is not life.

I have said it again and again, when there is reduced circulation oxygen or energy flow there is reduced life / energy / strength.

All of this leads to injury.

64 Power of Intention

What we believe becomes law. You may have heard it or just always believed it. Regardless of how you came by it, it is very true. Here is a story that illustrates this simple point, I have at least 20 of these stories, but this is one of my favorites.

In the early 1990s, I was on my way to Anaheim, California, for a convention I was going to be working at. On the way I either ate something or was exposed to something that swelled my left eye. It was puffy and red and it hurt like hell. I looked like I was drugged or something. It was terrible. Since I had never missed a day of work in my life (now there is a story of intention right there) I was not about to be stopped by a red throbbing eye.

At the time, I had not developed any formulas for eyes so I was stumped. I tried things to get the red out and nothing worked. I looked like a reject from Animal House, not a lecturer or expert on anything. Something had to be done. So I used my cell phone and called anyone with a clue. Nothing seemed to work. I was destined to look like a red-eyed freak. I had to come up with a solution. I bought a pair of cool looking shades and attempted to look ultra cool (by hiding my eyes).

As I left my hotel room in my suit and cool sun glasses, feeling self conscious like a man with a third eye that throbbed, I had visions of people pointing and gawking at my eye. I realized I would get nothing done unless this eye thing went away and I mean soon. Walking onto the convention floor no one even noticed me. Everyone was looking cool; half of them had sunglasses on. It was going to work out!

But I still had this sinking feeling of not trusting people in sunglasses. Therefore, I didn't trust myself behind sunglasses either. If I didn't trust me, who would? In about 10 minutes of working something happened. My eye swelling and pain went completely away. I was cured and just in time. When the day was over, I walked back to my hotel room and, as I walked, my eye started throbbing again and it was starting to swell again. This was not good at all. It was also very odd.

What was going on here? My eye allowed me to work but not relax. The next morning the exact same thing happened:

Dark shades
Short walk
A few minutes of work
No swelling or redness
Day over

Short walk
Big swelling
Lots of pain
No rest
Repeat

This continued until the end of the weekend when I was driving home and all the pain and swelling went away. My only thought was that nothing was going to stop me from working. My intention to make things work was senior to the physical problem.

We might all have these stories. If you do, champion them. You are a powerful human being. The fact is we all are. Part of being able or powerful is deciding to be powerful and able.

If you have no reality on this, that is okay. Perhaps one day you will. The fact is that nothing ever changes until someone has identified a problem and decided to change the condition. You are this powerful and can do things like this, but you have to decide to effect change in your own life and not be a victim.

You make a difference. Make it a point to get this book into the hands of people who need it and want to read it. Do not forget how important our kids are. They are the future of our planet; they need this information and instantly 'get it.'

Help me heal this planet. It is all of our responsibility.

The choice is yours how you will help.

65 Shopping for Supplements

How fun is it to shop? Some of us live for it. Some of us can't stand it. Others just don't care one way or the other. If you have ever had the experience of standing in the supplement aisle of your health food store and staring at the bewildering wall of bottles confronting you, you will love what comes next.

I have been preaching, "Your Body is Smarter then you are" I am going to reinforce this in this short chapter.

The intelligence in your body that you are not fully aware of is always active. This is a simple little trick that you can use again and again.

Stand in the aisle looking at the wall of supplements and see what bottle you are drawn to. Walk over to it and pick it up. Then, find the nearest herb book, usually in the aisle for easy access, and read what it says about that herb. Compare what is known about that herb to what you know about your symptoms.

Did this bottle of herbs match your symptoms? Do not be surprised how often what you are drawn to is just what you need. If every bottle is emanating some sort of energy, and your body is energy, being drawn to a bottle makes sense.

Do not be afraid of using this. No one will know what you are doing. You also can do several dry runs to test yourself.

Do not expect to only be drawn to herbs you know. You will be picking up all sorts of odd combinations and herbs. This is because your body knows more about itself than you will ever know.

You are employing the body's innate intelligence. It is just your body trying to help you. You may initially find that you are not very good with this technique. If that is true, your ability to use it will increase, as your system gets healthier. Stick with it. If after a few months you still can't use this little trick, figure you are in the 3-5% range of those who cannot do this.

There is another group of people (that I am not a part of) who can detect energy of organic objects. They can pick something up and feel whether something is good or bad for them. I don't have a clue how to train someone how to do this, as I don't have the ability. If you do, my hat is off to you. If you want to test it for yourself, pick up a bottle of supplements or 5 or 6 and see if you feel anything.

Regardless of what approach you take, best of luck and be healthy. Choose to be healthy.

Roger Bezanis

66 Those Who Want Help

Try as you might, some people, regardless of what they say, do not want help. There are people who will buy this book and never open it. They will just add it to their collection. Some people will read some of this book and tell everyone how good or bad it is as if they are an authority. But when you analyze them, you see a wreck that is not applying anything they've "learned" about health.

Some people will ask you for advice or, if you are a practitioner, come in and ask for help. They will not have any intention of following anything you have said. The best way to handle anyone asking for advice is not to give it to him or her. People can't ignore advice fast enough. Just look at all the advices you have given out to people who didn't follow them. How many times have you said or thought, "I told you so."

If someone comes to you with a question answered in this book, hand them the book and have them read the chapter concerning it. You will have done more good than you know in more ways than one. Pain is a fantastic motivator when it comes to health. If someone is in enough pain, they will seek help. They will listen to you or someone. Their pain is more persuasive than their pride or anything else that would prohibit them from seeking help.

But even in the case above it would be vital that they read the sections or section in this book that pertains to them. Why? This book is authoritative and is not you. You could be saying the exact same thing this book has said. You may be parroting entire sections. But because you are saying my words they may not have as much impact. When this happens and you are not reaching your patient, hand them my book. The written word is king. Use it. This book is your friend and as such, it will never abandon you. The impact of these pages is without out boundaries don't forget that. This book is your tool as the words in it spell something.

What does this all spell? T-R-U-S-T. It is shocking to think that your husband or wife would listen to a stranger and not to you, but those are the facts. If you have been with this person long enough, you have seen it again and again.

I was once talking to a CA (Chiropractic Assistant) and she was telling me how constipated she was. She would have eliminations once a week at best unless she used an herbal formula to help move her colon. Keep in mind that constipation is defined as having less than one-elimination per meal eaten. In questioning her about it, she indicated that she drank 2 to 3 pots of coffee a day and hated water and refused to drink it. But she also did not want to be constipated and also did not want to take her herbal laxative.

Her conversation with me was like someone talking to me while hitting themselves over the head with a cast iron frying pan. What they are saying is, "Gee whiz, my head hurts, can you make it stop?" bang, bang, bang, "This is a headache right?" bang, bang, bang, "I don't know why my head hurts!" bang, bang, bang, "But I sure wish it would stop", bang, bang, bang.

Get the picture? This was absolute insanity. How could someone complain about knife wounds while cutting their arm with a knife? But there she was. When I explained the relationship of diuretics and elimination, she seemed to understand. When I told her she would have to give up her coffee or forever be constipated, she told me "I would rather die first."

Hearing that kind of statement was like being kicked in the head. I was stunned. So I tried to reason with her, I said, "If you were on your death bed, and you hated corn on the cob, to you it was the most vile thing on the planet, and the doctor told you that if you just eat a stalk, you would live, but if you don't, you will be dead within 24 hours, what would you do"?

She said, "I would die." I said okay.

That was the end of that. You can't help everyone.

Concentrate on those that want help and save your grey hair.

Do not risk disaster by commingling with people who don't want you to succeed. Some people believe that if you succeed, they fail. To them, all success of any type means failure to them. They want you to stay fat and unhappy, sick and tired, or frazzled and weak. Just imagine if you got healthy. Minimally, they would have no one to compare stories with. You do not have to help everyone.

You may meet someone who absorbs all your free time and energy in an attempt to get them feeling better, but they never get better.

I have met many people who love the attention from being sick. They are thrilled to know that you are up all night worried about them.

Cut them loose. They are poison to your practice, Mr. or Ms. Practitioner. If you are focusing 60 percent of your ability and attention on only 3 of your patients, set them free.

They just want attention with no intent of ever getting better.

My Mother's Story

This next story makes it clear that only those who want help can be helped. Notice that until my mother wanted help she was just a sinkhole for attention.

My mother's name was Mozelle. She was a little feisty woman who taught me to work hard and be a good listener.

Some of my first memories of her were of her complaining how sick she was. Oh was my mother sick. She was always complaining of this and that. Eventually I learned to ignore her. She did not want help, just someone to listen to her.

I constantly heard how sick she was. She would call me, drop by, write me, flag me down on the street and block intersections just to gloat about how sick she was.

Then one day she had a battery of tests done on her medicine ball sized abdomen. These tests confirmed that she had cancer. Cancer that, if she knew was there would cause her to fold up like a tent.

Good for her, she could not stand / hated her doctor. She disliked him so much; she refused to speak to him. Under the circumstances the doctor asked me if I would pass on the bad news. They thought she might only have six months to live.

She never spoke to him again.

I conveniently (for my mom), neglected to tell her what the doctor told me. Good thing too, because she would have just folded up like a tent.

A day or two later she asked me if I could help make her feel better. Honored, I agreed and then proceeded to give her various vitamins, magnesium, grape juice, other herbs and fresh juices. This went on for 3 months. Her abdomen reduced to a normal size and she felt great. She lived another 20 years before she succumbed to Alzheimer's disease in 2002.

But cancer was not listed as her cause of death.

The point of all this is, help those who really want to be helped.
Share this book with you friend or spouse. That is the least you can do. Better than that, become the best you can be and set the example.

It is our choice to change our conditions in life.

We can change the world we live in.

Choose to be healthy; it is well worth the work.

67 Tobacco vs. The World

There is a huge ground swell out there that tobacco is bad, has been bad and will always be bad. It had been easy to trash smokers almost as easy as it is to trash those people who talk on cell phones while driving. Tobacco is an easy target, as even smokers take shots at themselves, and when did anyone, smoker of not, recommend it. Tobacco has come a long way since it was endorsed by our government and given freely to the GIs of World War II.

Over the years, you have seen marches on Washington protesting this or that. You have witnessed the Million Man March, and it is commonly accepted that such activities don't work. We as a public often feel powerless to do much of anything to change the way big business operates. As we know, they are not listening so we take to grumbling in pubs, car pools, chat rooms / the internet.

Attention All of You Grumblers

All of us who have picked on and yelled about tobacco companies have made a difference. Please look up (on the net) the largest tobacco company on the planet, Phillip Morris. They have been attacked and lost in our state and federal courts numerous times.

Smoking is dangerous, causes birth defects, cancer and more. We all know that. Lawyers know that too, and Phillip Morris is well aware of it.

Tobacco has a target on its back the size of New Jersey. Though, in the last couple years, they have taken to advertising that they are the leaders in getting young kids not to pick up the habit.

WHAT?

These folks are the devil incarnate; they can't tell people not to smoke! What kind of mind game, reverse psychology bologna is this? This has to be a public relations move. This is some calculated legal move to avoid lawsuits. Maybe it is, but it is clearly something else when you consider other factors. Philip Morris' stock fell 43 percent in the past year (2005) and is falling further now. The smoking-related legal challenges are still snow balling.

This explains why Philip Morris has been actively merging with or purchasing food companies.

These mergers create a gigantic food company that combines such dominant brands as Oreo cookies, Ritz crackers, Planters nuts and Life Savers candies with the Philip Morris brands of

Kraft, Jell-O, Maxwell House and Oscar Mayer. More than 90 percent of Nabisco's U.S. brands are leaders in their respective categories, according to the company.

The acquisition makes Nabisco, which once was part of the large tobacco company RJR Nabisco Holdings Corp., again part of a large tobacco company, at least for now. Analysts said they expect Nabisco might someday be spun off again. Last year RJR Nabisco Holdings Corp. created Nabisco Group Holdings when it split up its food and tobacco units. RJR sold its international tobacco business and spun off its domestic tobacco company as R.J. Reynolds Tobacco Holdings, Inc.

What does this all mean? Phillip Morris has started to diversify, so that when the day comes when smoking is banned or is so unpopular that it is no longer economically viable, they have an out.

IN OTHER WORDS, THE PUBLIC IS WINNING!

Does anyone remember the last time this happened? This is important news. Yes, it has taken 20 years or so but it has worked and is working. You are making a difference! Remember, in the world of advertising America, one letter represents 10,000 people.

Your voice matters so speak up.

68 Extremism and Extremists

Extremism is an interesting subject for this book. Yet it has a direct correlation between your humble author (yes, I am an extremist) and you the reader. Extremism is not so unusual; it is actually revered and held as normal when lives are not at stake. Extreme devotion to the eating of chocolate would not be healthy. Yet extreme devotion to saving lives such as in a trauma emergency room would be a healthy and applauded lifestyle.

It is safe to say, we all have some extreme tendencies or habits from time to time. Here are a few:

- Crossword puzzles
- Playstation or X-Box
- Cleaning
- Shopping
- Organization
- Collecting
- Knitting
- Surfing the Internet
- Magic
- Exercising
- Eating
- Traveling

Habits that are part of a balanced life that include, proper finances, health, family, friends and work are considered normal and social. When habits require secrecy to be carried out, then it becomes correctly labeled harmful.

A good rule of thumb to determine if an activity is social or harmful is to ask this question:

"Would I feel embarrassed to carry this activity out while being seen on my roof"?

If the answer is yes, then you should examine the activity. Perhaps it is not the kind of activity that includes you in the race of men but excludes you from all men. Heavy statement, I know. But remember any man who profoundly isolates himself is slowly dying, be it obvious or not. Humans, craving only solitude and isolated from his fellows, is on a spiraling road to blackness.

Mixing social activities and living alone is not a crime, it happens every day. Keep in mind that isolation is not the goal in this scenario. Man is looking for companionship.

Extreme extroversion and a need for the company of hundreds 24 hours a day is also a dilemma. Therefore a happy medium between these two opposites would be called normal and healthy.

On a professional level being an extremist is by all means not an awful, terrible thing. Living in the midst of extremists has brought us much social and economic change. If it were not for Edison's extreme fascination with the light bulb and all things new you would be reading this book by candlelight.

Famous extremists in history (good and bad)

- Alexander the Great
- Hippocrates
- Harriet Tubman
- Henry Ford
- The Wright Brothers
- Adolph Hitler (made the list for obvious yet not wholesome reasons)
- Albert Einstein
- Christopher Columbus
- Kobe Bryant
- Harry Houdini
- Napoleon Bonaparte
- Michael Jordon
- Tiger Woods
- Louis Pasteur
- Jacques Cousteau
- General George S. Patton
- Stephen Hawking
- Booker T. Washington
- Benjamin Franklin
- Oprah Winfrey
- Roger Bezanis (I've always wanted to see my name on a list with Oprah & Kobe Bryant)

As you can see from the above list (which is very short and could go on for pages) extremism, at its best solves global / social issues. At its worst causes death and destruction. Therefore it we can say that the intent of the extremist activity will establish its social or humanitarian value.

Extremism is only considered ghastly when it obsessively endangers the life of the participant or that of others he or she is contacting (See Adolf Hitler).

Extremism that saves lives is always welcome. A thrill seeker who chooses the life of a fireman or the life of a Navy Seal or Special Operations tactician is a welcome extremist. If focused or channeled, extreme behavior can be very powerful and useful to society.

All of this talk about extremism is very interesting and has a direct relationship to the next section of this book on addictions and eating disorders. These problems all revolve around out-of-control extremism.

69 Eating Disorders and Addictions

An addiction is an overwhelming urge to repeat some activity or habit over and over again. An addiction may involve a certain time of day or a certain type of stress or environment. The longer any habit is practiced, the more it ingrains itself into the fabric of the individual. Due to this imprinting, and its repetitious nature, it can be hard (yet not impossible) to re-pattern the body to a new condition or state of better health.

There are five classes of substances (all manmade) that are extremely toxic to the body. The five toxic classes are:

Manmade sugary substances (acid)
Manmade salty substances (alkaline)
Manmade chemicals that create sedation
Manmade chemicals that create stimulation
Manmade chemicals that create hallucination

When consuming a toxic substance, the body will crave the exact same material 24 hours after its first ingestion. This has been proven 1000s of times on test. If you look in your own experience you will also find that your more negative cravings follow a schedule.

Yes, if you ingest xyz toxin today at 5:00 pm, you will crave the exact same xyz substance tomorrow at 5:00 pm. This speaks to the 24-hour clock that the body runs on.

Seeing that the body is attempting to create balance, toxic substances confuse the body and trick it into making the toxin part of its daily program. This is why an addiction is so hard to beat. The toxin may mimic hormones or amino acids and or vitamins that the body desperately needs.

Psychiatry does not understand these phenomena and believe that an addiction is a brain problem. It is strictly a toxic body problem manifested and or made worse via an overwhelmed liver. Bulimics do not binge on oranges or fresh fruit to latter vomit. No addiction is impossible to defeat as it is modified by the individuals personal will power, which is infinite.

Again, all craving rules hold true for bulimia, which involves a habit and a toxin. There is no urge to vomit up food taken directly from nature such as oranges, apples, grapes, melons, etc. Only artificial foods / junk / manmade / man processed foods become toxic to the body.

The above paragraph gives the clue to beating the habit / addiction.

What you are about to read for some may be the most important part of this book. Over the next several pages I am going to investigate, answer and offer solutions to Bulimia / Rumination and Anorexia.

The solutions I give can be used for any addiction. Later you will read the chapter Control = Cause, in it you will discover how I handled my stuttering. Out of control habits only remain so because no one is controlling them. When the source realizes that he or she is the source of their affliction, healing can take place.

The practice of bulimia and bulimics are fascinating. They are the equivalent of the modern day vampire. They are the un-healthy immortals of the food / nutrition world.

70 What are Bulimia and Rumination?

Definition: Bulimia (*pronounced— BAH-LEE-ME-AH*) is the secret (hidden from others) practice of eating, usually to excess and then either vomiting or taking bowel purging substances to ensure evacuation the next day or sooner. Bulimics tend to believe "they are alone and the only one" which leads to isolation in order to continue their self-abuse.

The bulimic may have a treasure chest of supplements that they take on a daily basis. They may be "health nuts" and know the fat, sugar, salt content and calories in an amazing amount of foods.

They may be voracious pill poppers and use all manner of vitamins and or supplements. Often experts on metabolism and digestion and disorders of the gut, they are a virtual resource book of health related information.

Some bulimics take supplements to support their habit upwards of 10 times a day.
All of us live by or with life's consequences and rules. Bulimics have found a way to bend those rules.

The rules of healthy eating are:

- Eat in excess = get fat
- Eat just enough = maintain weight

- Eat small amounts = weight loss
- Eat too little to sustain life = death

The formula / existence of a bulimic runs as follows:

- Eat a lot = Vomit or laxative = No weight gain = Hide the habit = Repeat
- Eat a lot = Vomit or laxative = No weight gain = Hide the habit = Repeat
- Eat a lot = Vomit or laxative = No weight gain = Hide the habit = Repeat

The literary world says that vampires are never satiated. They are dead and yet have to rely on the blood of other living beings. Likewise, the Bulimic is never really satisfied, as the urge to eat is never fully satiated. Both are stuck in a repetitive cycle of eat and hide, eat and hide.

- **Bulimics and anorexics are extremists / perfectionists.**
- **Bulimics and anorexics do not want to be the way that they are.**
- **Bulimics and anorexics are terrified of what will become of their bodies if they stop their practice.**
- **Bulimics and anorexics seek total (or close) control of themselves and their surroundings to feel safe and happy.**
- **Bulimics and anorexics feel it is almost (but not quite) out of their control to discontinue their habit.**
- **Bulimics do not actually expel all the contents of their stomachs as some food always gets through. This is proven as the body still produces stools. It is further demonstrated as the bulimic does not wither away to skin and bones, unless there is another factor missed such as parasites / cancer, extreme laxatives, etc.**
- **Bulimics believe they are too smart to ever be caught. Bulimics are the chameleons of the nutrition world, as they appear to be like all of us, but in fact are very different.**
- **Bulimics tend to gulp their food taking large bites in a frenzied struggle to hurry ingestion so that it can be removed before it does damage and digestion occurs.**
- **Bulimics and Anorexics need isolation to carry out their starving, binging and purging, as it is not a socially acceptable activity.**

What makes these conditions or states tenable are man's free will, worries, stresses, misunderstandings of nutrition, micro awareness of self, desire for perfection and wholesale choices in getting and ingesting sustenance.

Man (and to a slight extent the ape / monkey) is the only species on the planet that eats for pleasure. This is where free choice comes into play. A rattlesnake never turns down a mouse meal unless he has just fed and can take any more.

can't

Conversely, when it comes to a meal, man wants the first and second course, two helpings of desert and then a snack before bedtime.

Some might argue that "but my cat (or dog) puts his nose up at food he doesn't like". That is learned behavior. In the wild, food is food for a hungry animal period.

Elephants do not seem to be concerned about how much weight they are gaining. Lions and tigers are not trying to look better than the alpha male or matriarch of the pack.

Man is. Man desperately wants to fit in and be young forever.

Rumination / Bulimia

There is an additional level of bulimia seldom noted called rumination.

Definition: Rumination is derived from the Latin word ruminare, which means to chew the cud. It is the voluntary or involuntary regurgitation and re-chewing of partially digested food that is either re-swallowed or spit out.

This type of regurgitation is effortless and is similar to belching. Rumination does not involve nausea or gagging.

I am an expert on this subject as I have had this ability since I was a small child.

Since so little is known about this ability / phenomena, that for the next several paragraphs, I am going to spell it out very clearly.

Rumination Factors:

- **Food is swallowed and then returned to the mouth for more chewing. It is considered a pleasurable activity to re-taste food no longer available for tasting.**
- **The larger the piece of food, the easier it is to ruminate.**
- **Food can be returned to the mouth prior to reaching the stomach. This indicates that esophageal control is also a factor.**
- **Flexing the stomach muscles and pushing the content up to the mouth achieves rumination. The esophageal sphincter is a valve that is meant to remain closed after food passes into the stomach. In rumination the esophageal sphincter is flexed open and allows food to pass back up the esophagus and to the mouth. There is no pain or discomfort. It is simply the flexing of a muscle.**
- **Some rumination is performed before the food gets to the stomach as it is flexed back**

up the throat before it passes the esophageal sphincter.

- **The esophagus and esophageal sphincter is so sensitive it is possible to correctly identify what kind of food particles are being returned to the mouth to be re-chewed.**
- **The food is not bitter or acidy until after about 35 minutes in the stomach left undisturbed as digestive acid takes over.**
- **Dairy products such as milk become acidy faster than other more dense foods. This means they increase the speed of the digestive process.**
- **Yeast bearing foods such as bread, crackers pastry, cereals, cake, cookies etc. foods also become acidy quickly in the stomach and are then more difficult to extract.**
- **When a ruminator is sick and the body needs to or is trying to vomit, the ruminator resists vomiting. When sick, the body is actively rejecting something. This reaction seizes control of the stomach and esophagus and to a great extent renders the free will of the ruminator a non-factor.**
- **Rumination may be achieved by flexing the diaphragm (that sits under the stomach) to push up from below the stomach, thus pushing the stomach content up the esophagus.**
- **It is believed that infants involuntary ruminate. There is no way to validate this postulation, because infants do not explain their actions. Clearly rumination is not involuntary later in life. It is clearly a voluntary action.**
- **Watery fluids are the most difficult to ruminated.**
- **Thick fluids can easily be ruminated.**
- **Once food is mixed with water it is much harder to ruminate.**
- **Food mixed with water has very little appeal to the ruminator as the water has diluted the taste of what they have eaten.**
- **Tomato based products quickly become acidy in the stomach.**
- **Mixing different food types slow digestion and makes rumination possible for 2-3 hours after digestion.**

If monsters are scary, as we do not know much about them, rumination is the stuff of nightmares.

Until this reading you, like most of the planet, had never heard of it or knew it had a name.

The ruminator is not a monster. Yet, the ruminator feels like an outcast. Other than instilling a personal feeling of being a pariah-like recluse, rumination serves no real purpose to humans.

With the exception of extracting poison or drugs given in a hostage or terrorism situation, rumination serves no valuable human purpose. Most of us will never be poisoned or in captivity and therefore rumination serves no utility.

Most bulimics, who have this ability to regurgitate by just flexing their gut, secretly think they are sideshow freaks.

Since our thoughts become laws, for all intents and purposes, until the habit is controlled and stopped, this is true. To be fully vested in society one must not hide in closet practicing habits that they are embarrassed about.

Again, mankind is not meant to be isolated; any activity that by its nature must be practiced in secret or private is damaging to the individual and needs to be discontinued. Rumination just like its sister bulimia, is socially unacceptable.

Steve Starr "The Human Regurgitator" is not a ruminator. He is a performer doing a feat of entertainment. Any real ruminator can spot this, as the esophagus never flexes.

You might ask how I, your humble author Roger Bezanis, so intimately know so much about bulimia and rumination. The raison d'être that I am so versed is because I was bulimic for two years and before that anorexic. I am an authority as I have actually lived these two amazing (and life threatening) habits / lifestyles. I am also and always will be a skilled ruminator though I do not practice it.

I know / understand the motivations / psyche or emotions that comingle to create this aberration in humanity that exist in no other species on earth. Man has free will and that is good. It is in a toxic environment that our best intentions can go askew.

When I was in my late teens and early 20s, I was anorexic and bulimic. I dropped from 175 lbs to 125 lbs in a month and a week (anorexia). I became anorexic as I went off to college. I was wired on vitamins and orange flavored Jolly Rancher candy. Dropping weight, I looked like a sick 40-year-old man.

The final week of my anorexia involved not sleeping for a week. I couldn't sleep as my body was wired like a bomb. After 5 days of 24 hour a day consciousness, I finally fell asleep for 16 hours. When I awoke, it was time to finally eat. As mentioned before, I had dropped from 175 lbs down to 125 lbs.

Roughly two weeks later, I discovered bulimia. Bulimia is simply the expelling or purging of food matter after eating.

What I did was not at all healthy. I could have done a controlled fast or adapted another healthy diet but without knowledge I starved myself.

A short time after giving up bulimia, I went from the frying pan to the fire so to speak.

Within one year of giving up anorexia, I became bulimic. Very soon, I was spending ridiculous amounts of money vomiting up food that I had just swallowed. I might as well have been flushing $20.00 bills down the toilet.

Just like I mentioned before, I felt I was:

Worthless

A leper, pariah, outsider or stranger to mankind

Cheating the food I was eating

Hiding

An idiot

Cheating life as I was changing the rules

I was flushing my self-respect right down the toilet

Food was controlling me versus the other way around

The signs and symptoms of Bulimia:

- **Closet eating, seldom eating in public**
- **Hiding food**
- **In the office, hiding food in a desk drawer**
- **Late night grocery shopping sprees**
- **Poor teeth (as stomach acid wears away at the enamel)**
- **Large amounts of money spent on dental work and caps**
- **Quick trips to the toilet immediately after eating**
- **Rinsing ones mouth after use of the restroom (rinsing acid from the mouth)**
- **Excessive spending on food**
- **Obsession about weight**
- **Obsessive eating of junk food (or any food) but not gaining weight**
- **Undigested food (chewed) particles in the toilet after the suspected bulimics use**
- **Strange splattering on the walls of the bathroom the Bulimic frequent most often (food splatters)**
- **Eating for comfort when stress arises**
- **A bulimic may also be overly health conscious. Not necessarily in the business of health but practically an expert on the subject.**
- **They may also be obsessed with caloric intake and food content (sodium, salt sugar etc).**
- **Most bulimics are careful to clean the toilet after every use but occasionally make a mistake and leave food matter behind.**

- **In general bulimics tend to be perfectionists (this is not always true but it is very common).**
- **They tend to be very controlling individuals, as control equals safety. A bulimic must control everything they can so that they are in charge and can keep their secret, secret.**

Be aware that anyone who is thrust into a job, which is dependent on looking good, may be stressed to extremes. Those that are affected most with bulimia and anorexia are actors, strippers, food servers and models. Yet anyone can be a bulimic. Keeping the secret is an all or nothing venture. They tend to believe that their habit is all that helps them hold onto their sanity.

Bulimics are not necessarily lean yet they usually are not terribly overweight. It is very hard for even the most skilled bulimic to fully empty their stomach. Otherwise they would not still have bowel movements and they do.

Yet the strain from constant vomiting can damage the esophagus, stomach, lungs and more. What is always ignored is that once the body receives food, it goes into digestion mode and starts producing all the material needs for the task.

This includes bile (from the gallbladder), which is vital to proper digestion. Some bulimics will vomit 8 to 10 times a day, although the average is closer to 4-5 times a day.

One of the main things keeping the bulimic in check is the cost of the habit. It is not cheap to always be hungry and constantly purchasing food. Just like cocaine it is not cheap to have this habit.

The dollar cost of being a bulimic is staggering; depending on how extravagant one's taste happens to be for this kind of gratification. Imagine flushing 25-70 dollars down the toilet every day. The 25-70 dollars does not include the food that the bulimic intends to "keep" and not vomit up. Bulimia is not as expensive as a cocaine habit but just as addicting.

Bulimia, like any addiction, requires the addict to believe he is helpless to do anything about their condition without the use of drugs or confinement / hospitalization. This is patently false.

This kind of frantic attitude toward food is accompanied by the belief that they are victims of something outside their control.

Gorging oneself to the point of physical illness is not a new problem. A popular belief was that all of Rome (circa 1800 A.D.) was using vomitoriums to expel unwanted ingested food for the sole purpose of ingesting more food, thus being more social.

This is a slight misunderstanding mixed with some truth.

The vomitorium was actually an access tunnel used at a stadium or theater for public or performer access during or after a show. In most theatres, these passageways are restricted to actors for entrance or egress from the stage. Some live theatres still have vomitoriums. Nonetheless, these passages are meant for ambulation, not in any way for human waste of any type.

As for the factual part of this misunderstanding, some Romans of the aristocracy were practicing upchucking of their meals on occasion. The practice appears to not be widespread but did occur. It was certainly not an accepted and or common practice among the Roman commoners.

Eating enough to get sick is clearly not a new problem. It has existed as long as man has been eating.

For early man, Mother Nature was the wild card affecting survival. Monsoon, drought, snow etc of course plays havoc on the food supply, creating major shortages. When food is scant the initial reaction is to gorge oneself when it is found. This over reaction can cause digestive upset and induce vomiting on contact. Too much sustenance introduced too quickly can even cause death depending on how emaciated the hungry man was.

Food must be introduced slowly to the starving individual.

Other factors that can influence how humans view food are:

Fear of mortality

Fear of hunger or no more food

Peer pressure to fit in and look a certain way (be skinny)

Fear of loss of control of one's body (getting fat)

Obsessive desire for unlimited pleasure

Distorted view on oneself (always think they are fat)

Fear of disease

Fear of bowel movements

Education or lack of it in the area of nutrition

Other

The purging of food from the body can be accomplished a number of ways.

Shoving a finger (or something) down the throat creating a gag reflex
Voluntary regurgitation (up chucking on command)
Laxatives used at extreme strength

The way I finally beat Bulimia

Breaking any habit, from biting ones nails to shooting heroin, starts with a personal choice. Sure a solution can be forced on someone, but unless "The Someone" decides to be the author of the choice, the change will not stick. Witness the revolving door of celebrities forced into rehab that revert to their pervious patterns.

When I decided that, once and for all, any food entering my mouth had to stay there, I was able to allow myself to reenter society. I knew I had to do something or I was going to die a lonely man with rotting teeth.

In order to kick this problem, I knew I had to tell someone (a large group) of people that I was bulimic.

I attended a weekend retreat called the Wall offered on the San Juan Islands off the coast of Washington State. This event was a combination of intense activity and deep discussion. We did Tai Chi, ran walked two miles a day and ate a Spartan diet of rice with some protein.

This retreat was like a sort of boot camp yet had nothing to do with addictions or diseases. It was strictly for discovering what ones mental and physical limits were. Men and women had separate sleeping quarters in a military barracks like environment.

The weekend was all about completion. One did not have to run the two miles; they could walk it but had to complete it. Personal introspection was encouraged and no personal comments or self-realizations were ridiculed. Being so isolated and in such a safe environment made my decision to go public with my weakness easier, yet it was not easy at all.

Attendee after attendee stood to up to blather on about something or the other. I not only could not hear a word they were saying, my heart was beating over one hundred times a minute. I was terrified to stand out and spill my guts.

The after dinner sharing session droned on and on. Then I took center stage and through my fear, shame and embarrassment, I told the whole room of 45 people my dirty little secret. I was bulimic! I was finally honest about who I was. I felt so free and relieved; far more than I ever had before.

I explained in detail how I did what I did. I promised the group for myself that I would never upchuck again.

It was alternately one of the most difficult and most rewarding things I had ever done. I was no longer a space alien. I had again re-entered the land of the living. I was no longer in a world of light and shadow. I was alive again. This was in February, 1982 I was 21 years old.

The rest of my quest was to recondition myself into new healthy habits. I recognized that as a bulimic I wanted to eat everything. But now to avoid being a bloated sick version of myself, I had to make adjustments or that would be my fate.

One enjoyable way I discovered that I could eat was to go to a restaurant and order 5-8 items on the menu and have a bite or two of each. I never allowed myself to take home leftovers, as that would be giving food power over me. Since I paid for the meal, it was mine to do whatever I wanted with it.

I taught myself to always leave food on my plate. I also made it a regular habit to never overeat during the holidays. My target was to lose a pound or two during every holiday seasons. This is a challenge, yet lots of fun.

The key to handling Bulimia:

- The Bulimic is not a social active person, as his habit must stay hidden.
- Understand that no bulimic really wants to be a bulimic.
- He or she feels alone and isolated and hungers to be normal.
- Every bulimic loves the taste of the food.
- Every bulimic feels ashamed and or embarrassed, while flushing their self-respect down the toilet.
- Do not make the bulimic wrong. No one can ever make the bulimic more wrong than he or she is making himself. Instead encourage him to look at his behavior to evaluate its survival versus contra survival potential.
- Support them in regaining their self-respect via education of nutrition and love.
- Help the bulimic get honest with society by announcing publicly to as many people as possible who and what he was. This may involve writing a letter but should be done in person as much as possible. The world is rooting for the bulimic to regain control of his or her life. The world loves a good success story.
- If necessary, give the bulimic a safe place to break their habit. A quiet place may mean a house or cottage to rest sleep and focus on who they were and who they are becoming. Encourage him or her to document in written form what their life has been like. These writings may one day help someone just like them.
- Follow these steps and the later points on the steps to beating addiction and you can help anyone.

Conquering / Controlling Bulimia

- Never grocery shop alone. This is another step to keeping honest about what you are eating. After a few months and much success, you may shop alone.
- As necessary, graze (nibble healthy treats, grapes, apples slices etc) throughout the day, never eating any one big meal. Keep fresh fruit handy for the quick nibble or for momentary grazing.
- Use a very small plate (if necessary) to control portions until you can naturally do it.
- If eating in a restaurant, get out of the habit of cleaning your plate. Restaurants do not understand you, your needs or your urges.
- Eat slowly. Eating is not a race. Savor every bite, as this is the last time you will ever taste it. In macrobiotics it is encouraged to chew food 100 times before swallowing.
- Always try to eat with a friend (not in isolation).
- Avoid fast food, (due to sugars, sodium, grease, etc.), as it would even make a non-bulimic vomit. So-called "fast foods," un-balance the body and ultimately leave the body open to infection and sickness.
- Avoid buffets as this encourages over eating.
- Keep remaking the choice to not be bulimic until it is no longer an issue.
- Own a scale and use it first the thing every morning to insure you are meeting your targets and goals for your body.
- Start and maintain an exercise program that contributes to your targets and goals.
- Make friends with a former bulimic and support each other.
- If so needed, get roommates who support you and your quest.
- Do a detox, using formulas or perhaps a sweat or sauna program to get your body free of the waste that it has been craving.
- Be good to yourself. No one can put you through the kind of hell that you can. No one will ever feel as ashamed as you will about your weakness. Know that your weaknesses are just this side of your strengths. You can get there. You just have to decide to do it.

Defeating urges is not a psychiatric problem, yet psychiatrists insist that it is. They assume that your moods and habits are due to a lack of medication. It is just the opposite. The amount of toxicity (from junk food) has overwhelmed your liver and made it very difficult to think straight. Anything you do to help yourself should involve reactivating your liver and kidneys.

When they are working at their maximum, your urges are controllable. Have you noticed that your urges come almost the same time every day? This illustrates that your liver and kidneys need support at that moment and doing anything worthwhile to help them, will help you.

Do not let anyone tell you that to beat your condition you have to be hospitalized or drugged.

There is another well known eating / starving habit.

71 What is Anorexia?

Definition: Anorexia (pronounced—AN-UH-REX-E-UH) is the practice of not eating or starving oneself in an attempt to control our body image and weight. A person who is anorexic may be remarkably lean or skinny yet sees himself or herself a very rotund or overweight. The anorexic may be taking vitamins or supplements (tablets or capsules) for metabolism at a remarkable rate (8 to 12 times a day or more).

Note: Any one or two of these signs does not guarantee that anorexia is present. But when a number of these symptoms are present, then it is time to be interested.

Up to 95% of those pronounced to have anorexia are women. But do not neglect the slow rise in men obsessed with their weight. It was believed the off spring (baby boomers) of the depression of 1929 and WWII families (who had to conserve food, etc.) were the most likely candidates for eating issues. Because parents enforced deviant eating habits on their children, a case can be made for manic control of food as the result.

It is even a joke to kid someone who leaves food on their plate, that "You should be ashamed of yourself not cleaning your plate; there are children who are starving right now in South Africa."

Some post WWII mothers even resorted to hiding food so that the food in question would "last longer." Now that is some odd computational thinking. For the child of the 1960s, it was a crime to not clean ones plate. Somehow making the plate the determiner of how hungry the child was makes no sense.

Even today there is a push to take leftovers home from restaurants. Sure it is food that is paid for, but a certain percentage of those who use doggy bags do it compulsively.

Oddly, the term doggy bag originally meant it was for the dog. It's only been since the 1990s that that term has completely fell out of vogue for the "To-go-bag."

Rationing was common in WWII households and these two eating abnormalities may very well still have their roots in this conflict. Add to that the push pull of advertisers promoting fit bodies on one channel and a moment later another commercial is promoting the latest Pizza toppings and crust.

Regardless of the source of their motivation, an anorexic person craves control. Like the bulimic, controlling ones environment is just as paramount as controlling one's body. Interestingly, the higher the family economic stratum, the more likely an eating deviation will be present

Signs and Symptoms of Anorexia

- Perfectionism
- Constant fear of gaining weight
- Fear of food or eating
- Use of diet pills or stimulants
- Eats very little
- Exercise to extreme on stomach, hips thighs
- Reclusive
- Own more than one scale

- Always watching exercise tapes of DVDs
- Owns extreme amounts of exercise equipment
- Counting calories and weighing food before eating
- Extremely tight fitting clothes or extremely loose clothes
- Constantly weighing
- Mood swings
- Sunken eyes
- Hollow cheeks
- Colon cleansing junkie
- Detox (herbal or otherwise) junkie

Anorexia is just as devastating as Bulimia and features many of the same traits but not all. At its heart, Anorexia is a severe distortion of a person's body image. While the mirror reflects skinny the person perceives that there is fat than needs to come off.

It has been said, "You can never be too skinny or have too much money." Perhaps the money aspect of that statement is true but the rest of it is pure folly.

Imagine the people held in concentration camps. Walking bags of bones, these people did not intend to lose weight at the rate they did. An Anorexic needs to lose weight, as they are always fat. Right up until their death.

Not all Anorexics starve themselves to death but small percentages have slipped through the cracks and have. Some of you older readers will remember the "The Carpenters." They were a musical duo (Richard and Karen) that reached their pinnacle of fame in during the mid1970s.

Karen never received the diagnoses of Anorexia, as at the time it in 1975 it was unknown. When she died in 1983 she was 80 pounds. She had been 140 lbs. in 1975 and quickly (via a water diet) dropped down to 120 and then 115 pounds.

Karen Carpenter routinely used prescriptions drugs for thyroid disorders and huge amounts of vitamins to help her feel better as she slowly wasted away. She sought out medical help and received drugs, which aid in her demise.

No one ever accepts help unless they want it. Anorexia is a cry of "Help me help myself; I want to gain control of my life." The person who is starving him or her for beauty or image needs to compare black to white. Literally the anorexic person, no matter how lean, sees himself or herself as fat.

Anorexia at its base is an aversion to eating based on a distortion of personal perception. The anorexic is literally starving, as they believe they are grotesquely overweight. One of the easiest ways to help them is to via comparisons. I will explain this later.

Help them via comparison and education but not drugs or surgery. These sorts of attitudes about food and image come from very extreme points of view.

Eating aberrations are far more common than we think. One estimate indicates that 4 out of every 10 people have a distortion toward food that corresponds to a distorted view of their body.

The bulimic and anorexic use their secret habit for an emotional purpose. These emotional attachments skew the perceptions of the Bulimic and Anorexic, thus justifying their very extreme behavior.

A huge problem with anorexia and bulimia is that the participant has no real concept of how their body works. Most have no real understanding of what it takes to maintain their body via diet.

With so much misinformation on human health, the bulimic and anorexic must fully understand the complexities of <u>their own body</u>. The question that needs answering is what makes MY body tick?

Too often, the fear of gaining weight is alloyed with no real understanding of what the body needs to survive. It does not matter what works for others, it matters that the subject fully understand and appreciate their body and condition.

Beating Anorexia

Have the anorexic individual identify 3-5 celebrities who the anorexic agrees are not too fat and not too lean.

Get photos full body photos of these celebrities.

Have the anorexic compare full body photos of their body to the body of the healthy celebrity previously identified. The purpose here is to have the person see the differences between a healthy body and an anorexic body.

Next it is very important to start to educate the anorexic on what food is and how the body uses it.

Finally, the pictures of the healthy celebrity should be blown up and placed around the mirrors of the anorexic so that a comparison is always possible.

Does the anorexic need drugs or surgery? No. The anorexic needs education and the ability to see and identify similarities and differences among themselves and others. He or she also needs proper nutrition that they are themselves participating in, either by food preparation or via shopping for the ingredients.

Anorexia and Bulimia as per medical "experts" is a nervous condition than can only be treated with drugs and surgery. I refuse to use this term, as this gives license to abuse to drugs and give surgery to people who will be only be poisoned and made weak by these efforts.

All disease requires the acceptance that there is no personal responsibility for their condition. This is false and is a victim mentality.

The anorexic and the bulimic must make a moment-to-moment choice to participate in their slow demise. No one can make that choice for them. They may have lost sight of it, but it is a choice. They were not caught by a bug or attacked by something beyond their control.

Beating Any Addiction

- Deciding one can be cause over one's body and life.
- Deciding to be in charge of one's own life and body
- Admitting the problem (the larger the group the better) as a secret will remain a secret if it is not acknowledged
- Education on the subject and how it affects the body

- Education on proper nutrition
- Proper nutrition
- Continually deciding to be in charge of one's own life and body
- Use of as support group
- Avoiding isolation as isolation can lead to secrets such as bulimia or anorexia
- Continually deciding to be in charge of one's own life and body

In conclusion we chose who we are, what we do, how we live and our state of health. Anorexia, bulimia / rumination are choices that are made from moment to moment. Do not let anyone tell you otherwise. Drugs and surgery are not the answer. The answer lies within.

Each of us has the power to control what we do. Our society has taught us that this is not the case. Just because we are told that the sky is pink does not make it pink. Just because the so-called "authorities" say that this condition needs this kind of handling does not make it so.

What is true is true for you. You must be the one who decides that you want help. You do know what the truth is. You do know when you are being lied to. That is why you are reading this book.

You can identify truth and make your life healthy and happy.

Choose yourself, choose man and help me help the planet. The biggest helper you will ever have is you. I need you but the planet needs you more.

Final Notes on Addictive behavior

Who is the AMA or the APA (American Psychiatric Association)? These two organizations have a vested interest in convincing the American public that they are sick. One way or the other they want every American on one drug or another.

If you believe you are sick, you are a candidate for drugs and surgery, you immediately become a valuable resource for BIG PHARMACUITALS & INSURANCE. If you are not on the medical and insurance rolls you are useless.

72 Control = Cause

You have no doubt noticed that much of this book is taken directly from my life. This chapter is no different.

Much of my early trouble in life came from being in a hurry to do anything else other than what I supposed to be doing. In the 4th grade we were given an I.Q. test. Having zero interest in this examination, I hurried through it marking the questions randomly. All I wanted to do was play outside. As a result it was believed that I had the I.Q. of a rodent.

Rightly or wrongly, I was placed in "slow" groups for the next 5 years of my school life. The results of that I.Q. test would haunt me until I was in 10th grade in high school.

Back in the fourth grade, the first consequence of my flippant approach to evaluation was to be placed in the "slow" reading group. Every three days or so, our class divided into two groups all of those who could read and all of those who couldn't.

The good readers were given written assignments and the poor readers (five of us) were grouped together to read out loud. Ridden with stage fright, dyslexia and who knows what else, reading out loud was nearly impossible.

While reading out loud, I would stutter, stammer and improvise what I thought what was on the page. To hide my nervousness, I would go so far as to give my opinions on the book and the writer.

I was unintentionally very funny, yet I was completely out of control.

Standing up to read, it would all start again.

First Mrs. Reel (my teacher) would warn the rest of the class, "Pay no attention, Roger is going to read." She might as well have told them to take copious notes on my performance.

Bumbling and fumbling, the class laughter would swell to a crescendo and then I would finally sit down, released from my torment.

Kids laughing, Mrs. Reel laughing, Me, I was dying.

Three different times teachers from adjoining classes barged in wanting to know what was so funny. There I stood the center of attention. Mrs. Reel, doubled over howling, sponging tears from her eyes, would cackled, "Its Roger, he's reading"!

Swaying back and forth did help me read better. Yet Mrs. Reel told me to stop and just read. Reading out loud felt like my skin was being peeled away.

Jumping ahead to the 10th grade, It was about to start all over again.

I took an English "Elective" class on Greek Mythology; it sounded like a good idea. One of our first assignments was to create our own myth, and then read it out loud in front of the class. My good idea was not so good after all.

My myth was on the "God of Hamburgers."
(An interesting subject choice considering the content of the last chapter)

As I stood up to read, my entire previous trauma returned. I was in 4th grade all over again. But this was worse, these were my own words, and I still could not read them.

I was in terror as I started mumbling the "*God of Hamburgers*."

I lost my balance, stuttered, made faces; gave commentary on my reading and fell backwards over the table I was leaning on. I was Jim Carrey, Don Adams (Get Smart), Jerry Lewis and Woody Allen all wrapped up into one.

Kids were rolling on the floor with laughter. On guy told me he wet his pants he was laughing so hard.

With four lines left to go on my story, the bell rang signaling the end of class.

I was an unintentional riot.

Mrs. Thomas (my teacher) told me that I should be on stage, and refused to give me my grade until the class heard the full myth again the next day. I was going to have to do it all again the next day!!!!

I was going to die.

Something happened for the first time. Kids told me, "You are so funny" etc., I was asked, "Did you mean to do that?" I did not know what to say. I said, "Yea, I meant to do that, it is all practiced and stuff, I do that all the time."

Now I was in big trouble. Because the kid asked me that question, I was going to have to do it all again and this time mean to be funny.

I went home and rehearsed fake nervousness for hours. I perfected the art of stuttering. This was mandatory, as my "funny reputation" was on the line. I turned my affliction into an act.

When I performed the next day I was funny, yet not as funny as the first day. Because I was rehearsed I was not nervous at all.
Standing in front of a crowd did not bother me! I was under control. My stage fright was gone. I could finally read all of the words on the page.

Jimmy Stewart, an actor from the 1940s to 1980s, was a terrible stutterer. Yet, in his films he did not stutter at all. On film he was rehearsed. In life he was the victim of a mechanism out of his control.

The reason my affliction was "released" was because that kid asked me, "Did you mean to do that"? This question might as well have been, "Roger, who is the source of your stuttering"? Or, even more simply "Who did it"?

By me saying, "Yea, I meant to do that, it is all practiced and stuff, I do that all the time." I became cause over my difficulty. I might as well have said, "I did it."

Being creator of my trouble meant that I could have or not have my reading / stage fright crisis at will. When I said, "I did it" the problem VANISHED.

This story may seem like an allegory for taking responsibility for one's life and it is. But this story is 100% true.

No quandary can remain a quandary once the source of it has been correctly identified. Bombs do not detonate around people who take responsibility for their creation.

I always thought someone or something else made me the way that I was. Nervousness must have come from my shoes or the center of the Earth. Surely I had nothing to do with it. And I did not, until I correctly said, "I am the source of my nerves."

Explaining exactly what I accidentally did has caused six stutterers to become former stutterers. Taking ownership, thus naming the correct source / cause of a problem it the first step to eliminating it. Again, six out of six have had the same results.

What are the limits of this or uses of this? I have no idea. Feel free to find out.

Remember the author of the story can write his characters anyway he or she wants. You are the author of your own life. You are the author of your own story.

Do not forget, control equals cause, equals zero affect.

Keys to mastering any habitual personal problem:

- Name the problem (I stutter, etc.)
- Answer the question: who is the source of the problem? The answer is always YOU!
- Practice the affliction until you are extremely good at it and can do it anytime on cue.

Crowds of as many as 1500 people cause me no fear whatsoever. Public speaking to 15 or 15,000 is welcome and fun.

Where Do We Go Now?

Due to the controversial nature of my writings on Big Pharmaceuticals, soft drink makers, and other purveyors of death Oprah will probably not have me on her show, as she would lose advertisers. This means you have to talk this book up. Between us we can affect the lives of millions. I am speaking to everyone within earshot constantly. I am lecturing and teaching 13-20 weekends out of the year. *(continued on last page)*

15 lbs/mo lost

"By using the tools in my book, in only four months I repaired years of damage and lost 61 pounds. At 46, (2007) I have re-achieved my high school football playing weight."

About the Author

"Don't believe the lies from the AMA and FDA. You can fix any problem of the body."

— Roger Bezanis

Roger Bezanis has passionately worked in the field of health since 1991. He is an expert on detoxification of the human body, master formulator, teacher, speaker and motivator for social and health change. He is entirely self-trained and therefore not beholding to any group, social or medical dogma. Debunking the brainwashing, deceptions & lies spewing from Big Pharma, FDA, AMA and APA mega-criminals drives him.

The self-regulating question that motivates all of his labors is 'does it work'? Results are the beacon that illuminates the fog of sickness and leads the way back to rejuvenation and vigor.

Because of his miraculous vision and ability to make the complex simple, he has re-trained thousands of practitioners via his lectures and presentations. Rogers's ability to see and understand connections that heretofore have remained invisible is a marvel to medical science.

His presentations, classes, weekends and lectures are often standing room only. Seldom has a light so bright emitted from such a powerful speaker, transporting us home to health.

Find out where Roger is speaking next and bring your whole family.

How Roger has changed...

American Diet /	**Raw Food Diet**
225 LBS	*164 LBS (his high school football playing weight)*
35-inch waist	*29-30 inch waist*
26 % body fat	*13-15 % body fat*

I eat a 98% raw food diet that features little or no protein (only the trace amounts found in fruit & veggies). This is a very old, yet cutting edge approach to health. It works.

Every morning I start with 12 to 36 ounces of fresh squeezed OJ or tangerine juice. Those who have employed my diet have dropped weight (as needed) and body fat. I live for Caesar salads (with no croutons or cheese), Pico de Gallo and anything fresh out of the ground.

Remember, if the worst thing that you eat is some dressing (that is out of a bottle), so be it. It is also better to shop at farmers markets and eat locally grown organic produce. Your body will be better grounded.

The most important aspects of life are circulation / energy / oxygen. With these points "in", the body can heal anything. It is never too late, until you stop breathing.

photo by: Janet Barnett | rocknmotion.com

This book bleeds with passion and is the focal part of my life. I am here to help mankind. That is the totality of my purpose. It is my mission to leave earth in better shape than when I found it.

You now have the full weight of my knowledge / understandings and awareness. Your journey is not over; it is beginning at this very moment. You now must be responsible for your new awakenings. You are fully conscious and obligated to push these truths forward, thus reversing the brainwashing administered to mankind.

Ignoring this responsibility is tantamount to turning your back on 'who you really are'. Please don't make me do this alone. Together we can change the future of our globe. We are engaged in a battle of epic proportions, the outcome of which will determine the future of this planet. It is a huge job.

Man needs your help. I am one person against a machine of untold power. Having finished reading this book it is NOW up to you to take it forward carrying on my words and work. The chapters in this manuscript are your friends. Use them often.

Stand up straight and enlighten everyone you care about with my message. Take this book to work and leave it on your desk. Keep a copy in your car and on your living room table. Unborn generations are counting on your efforts.

The future of earth is in the hands of our children. Because of that, get this book into the eager hands of every-pre-brainwashed-under- 20- year- old you know. The world must at least become aware of the title of this book. The future of mankind is hinged on you taking responsibility for what you now know.

We all need your help. The choices you make henceforth will affect all of us.

Which side of the ledger will your name appear on? Will you sit back and do nothing? Will your name appear among the remarkable people who changed the world for the better? We must not fail or we move a little closer to the brink of oblivion for mankind. Do you want the blood of such a disaster on your hands?

What you do with this book is up to you. Perhaps you will put it down and never speak of it again. Could you forgive yourself if you did? The choice you make will shape the future of earth.

Welcome, I have been waiting for you.
Your Friend,
Roger Bezanis